The European Economic Community has recently been enlarged by the accession of the New Members — Denmark, Ireland and the United Kingdom. From the 1st January 1973 competition law of the E.E.C. applies to the New Members as well as the Original Members. Restrictive trade agreements and practices in existence on the 1st January or adopted later must be notified if exemption is sought. In some cases, application may be made for negative clearance. All parties to restrictive arrangements will have to consider their policy, whether to notify, seek negative clearance, amend or terminate.

This Practical Guide has been written to meet the needs of the businessman, and his legal adviser, who is trading with the E.E.C. The text sets out first the economic background and the general principles of Articles 85 and 86 and Regulation 17, followed by several chapters dealing with particular types of agreements likely to be encountered in practice, such as distribution agreements, intellectual property agreements, joint research, joint selling, etc. Each of the chapters dealing with individual types of agreements has its own check list — in this rather complex branch of law the check list is a valuable aid towards ensuring that nothing is overlooked. The relevant cases are reviewed in the text.

This branch of E.E.C. Law is still in the process of development. It is intended to keep the Guide up-to-date by means of Supplements.

The Author, James P Cunningham, qualified first in economics, and was later called to the English Bar. He has acted as legal adviser to a large industrial group in the City of London for many years, and has made a special study of competition law.

# The Competition Law
# of the E.E.C.

# The Competition Law of the E.E.C.

## A PRACTICAL GUIDE

**James P. Cunningham**  B. Com. (Lond.)
of the Middle Temple, Barrister-at-Law

Foreword by
DR. W. SCHLIEDER

NOYES DATA CORPORATION

Park Ridge, New Jersey          London, England

1973

# FOREWORD

From the 1st January, 1973, enterprises in the new Member States forming the enlarged Community will, to a greater degree than hitherto, be directly concerned with the Competition Rules of the Treaty establishing the European Economic Community. From that date, it will be important for enterprises to be fully aware of the scope of those Rules as indicated both by their application in practice by the Commission and also by the related body of law developed by the Court of Justice of the Communities. It is necessary, therefore, for the aims and objectives of the Community's competition policy to be set out clearly for enterprises. In my view, works such as that which Mr. Cunningham has devoted to the Community's Rules of Competition can play an essential role in this context by making available for enterprises very comprehensive information on the competition policy followed within the Common Market and the effective scope of the legal system established to implement that policy.

As the author has very rightly emphasised, the complexity of the Rules must not lead enterprises to adopt a purely formal and legalistic approach to the policy of competition. On the contrary, it is important that enterprises should conform to the fundamental objective of that policy as enshrined in the Treaties creating the European Communities, which is to permit the optimum utilisation of the factors of production within the Common Market as an essential pre-condition for a continuous improvement in the standard of living and in the level of employment within all the Member States of the Community. By conforming to the Rules of Competition, enterprises will also show that the freedom of action which the Rules are intended to guarantee within the Common Market do not operate solely to the benefit of consumers but also permit an optimum expansion over the whole range of production and distribution.

W. SCHLIEDER

# TABLE OF CONTENTS

|  |  | page |
|---|---|---|
| *Foreword* |  | 5 |
| *Preface* |  | 9 |
| *Table of Cases* |  | 13 |
| *Table of Check Lists* |  | 19 |

## PART 1 GENERAL PRINCIPLES

| | | |
|---|---|---|
| 1. | Competition and Restraints upon Competition | 23 |
| 2. | The European Economic Community — The "Common Market" | 39 |
| 3. | Cartels and Concerted Practices — Article 85 | 42 |
| 4. | Cartels and Concerted Practices (contd) — Regulation 17 | 73 |
| 5. | Monopolies and Dominant Positions — Article 86 and Regulation 17 | 100 |

## PART 2 VERTICAL AGREEMENTS

| | | |
|---|---|---|
| 6. | Distribution Agreements | 119 |
| 7. | Resale Price Maintenance | 138 |
| 8. | Intellectual Property | 145 |

## PART 3   HORIZONTAL AGREEMENTS                                  *page*

9.   Joint Research Agreements                                      177

10.  Joint Production, Selling and Purchasing                       184

11.  Standardization Agreements                                     191

12.  Specialization Agreements                                      196

13.  Exchange of Information Agreements                             203

14.  Other Forms of Co-operation                                   211

## PART 4   MERGERS AND ABUSES OF DOMINANT POSITIONS

15.  Mergers                                                        219

16.  Other Abuses of a Dominant Position                           227

## APPENDICES

A.   Extracts from the Rome Treaty                                  233
B.   Council Regulation No.17/62                                    240
C.   Commission Notice, December, 1962, relating to Sole
     Agency Contracts.                                              253
D.   Commission Notice, December, 1962, relating to Patent
     Licence Agreements                                            256
E.   Commission Regulation No. 99/63                                259
F.   Council Regulation No. 19/65                                   264
G.   Commission Regulation No. 67/67                                268
H.   Commission Notice, July, 1968, concerning Co-operation
     between Enterprises.                                           274
I.   Commission Regulation No. 1133/68.                             281
J.   Commission Notice, May, 1970, concerning Minor
     Agreements.                                                    288
K.   Council Regulation No. 2821/71                                 291
L.   Council Regulation No. 2822/71                                 295
M.   Aide Memoire submitted by the United Kingdom
     Government to the E.E.C. Commission                            297
N.   Draft Council Regulation laying down limitation periods.      301
O.   Draft Commission Regulation concerning the application of
     Article 85.3 to categories of specialization agreements.      305

*Index*                                                            309

# PREFACE

This is a book for the businessman and his advisers. As from the 1st January, 1973, the law of the European Economic Community will be directly enforceable within each of the three New Members — in Denmark as part of Danish law, in Ireland as part of Irish law, and in the United Kingdom as part of U.K. law.

The Community is based upon the principle that all the Member States together constitute one united market within which goods and services are to be produced and circulate freely without artificial restraints. To this end, Community competition law prohibits arrangements between competitive business concerns which restrict competition in the trade between Member States, although exemptions are allowed in certain cases. Community law also prohibits abuse of market power by any business concern which has a dominant share of the market in any particular goods or services in any substantial part of the Community.

Consequently, Community competition law is an important factor for any businessman who is carrying on business within or exporting to one or more of the Member States. He must know what arrangements with his competitors are forbidden under pain of substantial fines, and what are permitted. If he has any arrangements falling within Community competition law, the businessman in the New Members, for example the United Kingdom or Ireland, has until the 30th June, 1973, to decide whether to terminate those arrangements or to send them to the Commission in Brussels with a view to obtaining exemption or clearance. It is an important factor also for the businessman who controls a significant part of the market for some particular goods or services in a substantial part of the Community. He is not free to decide and pursue whatever policies may seem to him to be best. He must avoid whatever Community law regards as abuse of his market-dominating position, or else run the risk of substantial fines.

The form of this book has been designed to meet the needs of the businessman and his advisers. Competition law in essence seeks to achieve economic objectives by legal enforcement. To understand competition law, one must understand those objectives. This is the aim of Chapter 1, to explain the economic background. The United States and the United Kingdom have been active in this field, and I have drawn mainly on their experience for this chapter. Chapter 2 gives a brief outline of the European Economic Community. Chapters 3 and 4 deal with the general principles of E.E.C. competition law as regards cartels and concerted practices, and Chapter 5 with the general principles as regards monopolies and dominant positions. Laws are laid down in general principles, but in business one is faced with specific problems, not general principles. The remaining chapters show how those general principles apply to particular situations. Chapters 6, 7, and 8 deal with "vertical" agreements, such as agreements with distributors (Chapter 6), and agreements relating to patents, trade marks, and other forms of intellectual property (Chapter 8). "Horizontal" agreements, such as joint production, joint selling, joint buying, joint research, exchange of information, etc., are covered in Chapters 9 to 14. Chapter 15 deals with mergers, and Chapter 16 with other possible abuses of dominant positions.

I have aimed at showing how the law works by referring to actual cases wherever possible. This has presented me with a dilemma. I could have described each case in one place only, and referred back to it elsewhere. This would have meant considerable cross-referencing. Alternatively, I could have described each case anew, when it is under discussion. This would have meant considerable repetition. I have tried to reach a compromise between the two extremes. If anybody should want to study any particular case in more detail, the Table of Cases will show where it can be found.

We have in English no word to cover agreements, decisions, and concerted practices. "Cartel" is apt only for the first two. I have, regretfully, been compelled to use the expression "agreements, etc." when all three are under discussion, and can only apologise for it.

This book has been written in the Summer of 1972, and presents the law as it then stood. To cover a subject such as this adequately is a difficult task, and I would hesitate to claim that this book achieves it. In the hope that subsequent editions may give an opportunity for improvement, I would welcome comments from those who have used it.

For their kindness in consenting to reproduction of their material, I would like to thank H.M. Stationery Office, in respect of Appendices A, B, E, F, G, I, J, K, L, and M, the Organisation for Economic Co-operation and Development, in respect of Appendices C, D, and H, and the Common Market Law Reports, in respect of Appendix N. The Stationery Office wish it to be made clear that their translations of the E.E.C. documents must not be treated as being necessarily the official or authentic English texts, and that H.M. Government do not accept any responsibility for the accuracy of these transactions.

I would like to record my indebtedness to Dr. W. Schlieder, the Director General for Competition in the European Commission who has kindly written the Foreword, and to Mde. F. Espion of the Commission, Keith Green, a solicitor, and Valentine Korah of University College, London, who each read typescripts of this book and raised a number of helpful and important points.

Without their help this book would have contained more flaws and faults than it does. Needless to say, responsibility for any which remain is mine, and mine alone. I must also record my debt to Delyth Hale-Stephens who achieved the difficult feat of turning my illegible manuscript into a workable typescript.

1 Temple Gardens,                                           James P. Cunningham
Temple,
London, E.C.4.

# TABLE OF CASES

(The numbers refer to paragraphs)

C.M.L.R. = Common Market Law Reports.
L.R. — R.P. = Reports of Restrictive Practices Cases

A.C.E.C./Berliet Agreement. [1968] C.M.L.R. 418.
3—61, 3—67, 12—07

Alliance de Constructeurs Francais de Machines Outils. [1968] C.M.L.R. D23.
3—31, 10—09, 10—11.

Aluminum Co. of America, U.S. v. 148 F. 2d. 416 (2d. Cir. 1945).
1—10

American Can Company, U.S. v. Federal Supplement, vol. 87.
1—10

American Tobacco Company v. U.S. Supreme Court of U.S.A. vol. 328, No. 781 (1945).
1—09

Aniline Dyes Cartel (Commission Decision). [1969] C.M.L.R. D23.
3—05, 3—11, 3—12, 3—17, 3—30, 3—91, 4—10, 4—36, 4—40, 4—91

Aniline Dyes Cartel (European Court). — not yet published.
3—17, 3—18, 4—91, 5—40

A.S.P.A. (Association Syndicate Belge de la Parfumerie). [1970] C.M.L.R. D25.
7—12, 7—13

Asphaltoid-Keller S.A. Journal Official, L.161, 19th July, 1971.
4—62

Béguelin Import Co. v. G.L. Import Export S.A. [1972] C.M.L.R. 81.
3—16, 3—49, 3—50, 3—51, 3—55, 6—12, 6—64 —6—65

13

Belgaphos (Association Belge de Superphosphate).          3—44, 10—08
Commission press release, June, 1970.
Brauerei A. Bilger Söhne GmbH v. Jehle. Recueil,          4—53, 6—21,
'Vol. XVI, 1970-72, p. 127.                                9—04
Black Bolt and Nut Association's Agreement. L.R. 2         1—16
R.P. p. 50.
Blondel's Agreement. [1965] C.M.L.R. 180                  3—63, 3—71,
                                                          3—73, 6—42

Boehringer Mannheim Sarl. Journal Officiel, C24,          4—91
11th March, 1972.
Brasserie de Haecht v. Wilkin. [1968] C.M.L.R. 26.        4—105
Breweries — Commission decisions requiring information.   4—61
Journal Officiel, L 161, 19th July, 1971.
G. M. Brinkhof N.V. v. N.V. Nederlandse Spoorwegen.       16—04, 16—05
[1970] C.M.L.R. 264.
Burroughs/Delplanque, Burroughs/Geha Agreements.          8—19 —8—21,
Journal Officiel, L13, 17th January, 1972.                8—30, 8—34,
                                                          8—35, 8—37,
                                                          8—61, 8—85


S.A.Cadillon v. Firma Höss [1971] C.M.L.R. 420.           6—25, 6—30,
                                                          6—40, 6—55

CECIMO (Comité Européen de Cooperation des                3—69, 3—82,
Industries de Machine Outil). [1969] C.M.L.R. D1.         4—46, 14—07
CEMATEX (Comité Européen des Constructeurs de             3—70, 3—78,
Matériel Textile). Journal Officiel, L.227, 8th October,  3—82, 4—33,
1971.                                                     4—46, 14—08
(Belgian) Cement Makers' Agreement. [1969] C.M.L.R.       3—35, 4—104
D15.
(British) Cement Makers' Federation Agreement. L.R. 2     1—16
R.P. p. 50.
Christiani & Nielsen N.V. [1969] C.M.L.R. D36.            3—16, 6—10
Cimfrance. Bulletin of the European Communities,          3—22, 10—07
No.1 — 1972, Chapter 1.4.
Clima Chappée's Agreement. [1970] C.M.L.R. D7.            12—09, 13—12
Cobelaz Agreement (No.1). [1968] C.M.L.R. D45.            3—06, 3—22,
                                                          3—79, 10—06

Cobelaz Agreement (No.2.). [1968] C.M.L.R. D68.           10—06
C.F.A. (Comptoir Français de l'Azote). [1968]            3—22, 3—79,
C.M.L.R. D57.                                              10—07
Continental Can Co. Inc. [1972]. C.M.L.R. D11.            3—19, 5—04,
                                                          5—08, 5—10,
                                                          5—11, 5—14,
                                                          5—16, 5—20,
                                                          5—30, 5—31,
                                                          5—37, 5—40,

| | 5—46, 5—50, |
| | 15—14 |

Davidson Rubber Company Agreements. [1972]   8—22 — 8—25,
C.M.L.R. D52.                                8—30, 8—31,
                                            8—33, 8—39,
                                            8—40, 8—42,
                                            8—43, 8—47,
                                            8—85, 8—86,
                                            8—87, 8—88

Deutsche Grammophon GmbH v. Metro-SB-Grossmärkte   5—14, 7—15,
GmbH. [1971] C.M.L.R. 631, [1972] C.M.L.R. 107.    8—02, 8—08,
                                                   8—13, 8—14,
                                                   8—56, 8—70
                                                   — 8—74, 8—76

Dunlop/Pirelli Agreements. Journal Officiel, L323.   14—09
24th December, 1969.

E.I. duPont de Nemours, U.S. v. Federal Supplement,   1—07, 1—29,
vol. 115, p. 41. (1951).                              5—34
Eurogypsum. [1968] C.M.L.R. D1.                       9—19

Fabrique Nationale/Cartoucherie Française Agreement.   3—61, 3—67,
Journal Officiel, L134, 30th June, 1971.              3—82, 4—46,
                                                      6—34, 8—85,
                                                      9—18, 11—09,
                                                      13—16

"Flat Glass". Monopolies Commission Report. 1968.   1—06, 1—07

GEMA. [1971] C.M.L.R. D35.                           5—03, 5—12,
                                                     5—16, 5—20,
                                                     5—26, 5—29,
                                                     5—36, 5—50,
                                                     8—75, 16—01

German Ceramic Tiles Discount Agreement. [1971]   3—06, 3—30
C.M.L.R. D6.
Grosfillex Sarl Agreement. [1964] C.M.L.R. 237.   6—28
Grundig/Consten Agreement. (Commission Decision).   3—52, 3—71,
[1964] C.M.L.R. 489.                               3—73, 3—76,
                                                   6—56 — 6—61,
                                                   8—53

Grundig/Consten Agreement (European Court). [1966]   3—52, 6—62,
C.M.L.R. 418.                                        8—13, 8—53,
                                                     8—56

Heidsieck Monopole v. Buxton. [1930] 1 Ch. 330 . . . .   8—09

Henkel/Colgate-Palmolive Agreement.  Journal Officiel,          4—44, 9—15
L14, 18th January, 1972.                                        — 9—17.
"Household Detergents".  Monopolies Commission                  1—26
Report. 1966.


"Industrial and Medical Gases".  Monopolies Commission         1—08, 1—10
Report. 1957.
"Infant Milk Foods '.  Monopolies Commission Report.            1—28
1967.
"Supply of Insulin".  Monopolies Commission Report.            1—16
1952.


Jallatte's Agreements.  [1966] C.M.L.R. D1.                     3—64, 6—42
Jaz/Peter Agreement.  [1970] C.M.L.R. 129.                     12—08


Kodak.  [1970] C.M.L.R. D19.                                    6—11, 6—22,
                                                               6—52


Lever's Zeep ("Omo") v. Gegro N.V.  [1970] C.M.L.R.            8—55
281.


"Man-made Cellulosic Fibres".  Monopolies Commission           1—06, 1—08,
Report. 1968.                                                  1—29
MANS/SAVIEM Agreement,  Journal Officiel, L31, 4th            3—61, 3—72,
February, 1972.                                               3—74, 3—82,
                                                             4—46, 11—09,
                                                             12—10


"Metal Containers".  Monopolies Commission Report.            1—06
1970.
Minolta Cameras.  [1972] C.M.L.R. 391.                         7—14


Nederlandse Persil v. ENVEMA.  [1972] C.M.L.R. 23.            8—55
Nicholas Frères Agreement.  [1964] C.M.L.R. 505.              3—33, 8—60


Omega Brandt.  [1970] C.M.L.R. D49.                            3—04, 6—41,
                                                               6—43


Parfums Marcel Rochas.  [1971] C.M.L.R. 104.                   4—27, 6—46
Parke, Davis & Co. v. Probel.  [1968] C.M.L.R. 47.            5—14, 5—27,
                                                               8—08, 8—12,
                                                               8—13, 8—14,
                                                               8—56, 8—73,
                                                               8—75
"Petrol to Retailers".  Monopolies Commission Report.         1—11
1965.

S.A. Portelange v. Smith Corona Marchant. Recueil,
Vol. XV, 1969, p. 309.
— 4—26, 4—32, 4—40

Quinine Cartel. [1969] C.M.L.R. D41.
— 3—05, 3—30, 4—13, 4—91, 4—100

Raymond's Agreements. [1972] C.M.L.R. D45.
— 8—26 — 8—28, 8—30, 8—31, 8—40, 8—42, 8—43, 8—65

Research and Development. [1971] C.M.L.R. D31.
— 3—10, 8—40, 9—11 — 9—14

Rieckermann/A.E.G.—Elotherm Agreement. [1968] C.M.L.R. D74.
— 3—34, 6—29

R.P.M. for Film. [1972] C.M.L.R. 62.
— 7—14

"Rubber Footwear". Monopolies Commission Report. 1956.
— 1—30, 1—31

SAFCO. Journal Officiel, L13, 17th January, 1972.
— 10—10

S.I.A.E. (Società Italiana degli Autori ed Editori). Journal Officiel, L254, 17th November, 1971.
— 5—57

Sirena S.R.L. [1971] C.M.L.R. 260.
— 5—14, 5—27, 8—08, 8—13, 8—14, 8—54, 8—56, 8—57, 8—73

SOCEMAS. [1968] C.M.L.R. D28.
— 3—23, 3—33, 10—17

Sopelem/Langen Agreement. Journal Officiel, L13, 17th January, 1972.
— 3—72, 3—73, 6—34, 6—44, 10—14

SPAR Centrale. Journal Officiel, C35, 11th April, 1972.
— 10—16

Sulphuric Acid Association's Agreement. L.R. 4 R.P. p. 169.
— 1—16

Supexie's Agreement. [1971] C.M.L.R. D1.
— 10—07

Tag Manufacturers' Institute v. Federal Trade Commissioner. (1949) 174 F. 2d. 452 (1st Circuit).
— 1—19, 13—03, 13—11

"Tea". Monopolies Commission Report. 1957.
— 1—22

Technique Minière v. Ulm. [1966] C.M.L.R. 357.
— 3—50, 6—06

Transocean Marine Paint Association. [1967] C.M.L.R. D9.
— 3—65, 8—63, 11—07

Tyre Mileage Conference Agreement. L.R. 6 R.P. p. 49.
— 1—23

Union de Remorquage v. N.V. Schelde. [1965] C.M.L.R. 251.
— 16—03, 16—05

United Shoe Machinery Corp. v. U.S.  258 U.S. 451  1—07, 1—10
(1922).

Van Katwijk's Agreement.  [1970] C.M.L.R. D43.  3—30, 3—77
Vereeniging van Cementhandelaren.  Journal Officiel,  3—80
L13, 17th January, 1972.
Völk v. Vervaecke.  [1969] C.M.L.R. 273.  3—25, 6—24,
6—30
V.V.V.F. (Vereeniging van Vernis-en Verf-fabrikanten).  8—64, 11—08,
[1970] C.M.L.R. D1.  13—18

Wild/Leitz Agreement.  [1972] C.M.L.R. D36.  10—09, 10—12
Wilhelm v. Bundeskartellamt.  [1969] C.M.L.R. 100.  4—90

"Yoga" Fruit Juices.  [1969] C.M.L.R. 123.  3—48

Z.P.U. (Zentralstelle für Privat Uberspielungsrechte).  4—60
[1971] C.M.L.R. D23.

# TABLE OF CHECK LISTS

Distribution Agreements                              6—66

Resale Price Maintenance                            7—16

Intellectual Property                               8—90

Joint Research Agreements                           9—20

Joint Production, Selling and Purchasing            10—18

Standardization Agreements                          11—10

Specialization Agreements                           12—11

Exchange of Information Agreements                  13—19

Other Forms of Co-operation                         14—10

19

# PART 1

# GENERAL PRINCIPLES

# CHAPTER 1

# Competition and Restraints
# upon Competition

## 1. Introduction

1—01     The aim of this book is to describe, for the businessman and his advisers, the competition law of the European Economic Community, i.e. that branch of Community law which relates to private restraints upon competition between business concerns, whether as sellers or as buyers. What is "competition" in this context? What are "private restraints" upon competition?

## 2. What is competition?

1—02     Mr. Smith was employed in the buying department of a large manufacturing group. He had to order further supplies of a raw material, and telephoned a number of suppliers to get their latest quotations. He had recently been left a house in his father's will into which he and his wife were about to move, and consequently he was in touch with auctioneers about selling their present house by auction. Meantime Mrs. Smith was in the furnishing fabric section of a large department store, looking for new curtain material. Not liking any of the materials the store had to offer, and thinking the prices too high, she thanked the assistant who had been attending to her, saying she would see what other stores had to offer.

1—03     In effect, both Mr. Smith and his wife were relying upon competition. Mr. Smith was working on the basis that the various suppliers he approached would quote him independent and possibly differing prices for the raw material, so that he would be able to choose the most favourable. By putting his house up for auction, he hoped to tap a wider market of potential buyers, and to get the best price as a result of the buyers competing with each other. Mrs. Smith was assuming that other stores would have different ranges of fabrics to show her, and at different prices. In so far as they were buyers, Mr. Smith and his wife each based their policy upon the assumption that there would be competing suppliers; and in so far as they were sellers, their selling policy assumed the existence of competing buyers. In each case they assumed the existence of alternative suppliers or buyers, and that those suppliers or buyers would each be acting independently, i.e. in competition with each other. These are two quite separate assumptions. The existence of alternative suppliers or buyers implies the absence of monopoly. The existence of competition between those suppliers or buyers implies the absence between them of restrictive trade practices, i.e. restraints upon competition.

### 3. Monopoly — Dominant Position

1—04    Strictly speaking, "monopoly" signifies a single seller in the market. Where there is only one buyer, the term is "monopsony". In practice, it is more convenient to use "monopoly" to cover both situations, i.e. either a sole seller in the market or a sole buyer, except where it is necessary to distinguish the one from the other.

1—05    The concept of the "market" in this context presents difficulties in practice. It is delimited in two ways, first territorially, and second by reference to the goods (or services) in question. For example, it is fairly common to grant a legal monopoly to public utility concerns, such as those supplying water, gas, or electricity. The legal monopoly will determine the area within which the gas concern, for example, has the sole right to distribute and sell gas, and will consequently determine the "market" territorially. Judged from the commodity point of view, if the "market" is "gas", then the gas concern has a monopoly. But if the "market" is fuel, then it does not have a monopoly, but may be in competition with electricity, oil, and coal. The extent to which a commodity constitutes a water-tight market depends upon the presence or absence of substitutes, and their closeness or otherwise to that commodity. Before one has bought a central-heating boiler, gas, electricity and oil are all fairly close substitutes; once a gas boiler say, has been bought and installed, electricity and oil become more remote substitutes. To some people, a monopoly of one form of breakfast cereal would not be significant, because other forms of that cereal or other cereals might be equally acceptable. But to a man to whom only porridge was acceptable, a monopoly of porridge oats, charging a higher price, would be more serious. To the former, the "market" is breakfast cereals, to the latter it is "porridge oats". Containers made of glass, plastic or tin-plate may each be treated as separate markets or as constituting part of a wider "container" market; nylon, rayon, cotton, wool, etc. may be regarded as separate individual markets, or parts of a wider fibre or textile market; similarly with metal windows and doors and wooden windows and doors; lead, copper, and plastic pipes; and so on.

1—06    Leaving aside state-controlled economies such as Russia, and legal monopolies such as those created by statute or by patents, it is comparatively rare, in the free enterprise economies of the Western world, to find a complete monopoly. Thus, although Pilkingtons were the only United Kingdom manufacturers of flat glass, they had only 91.0% of the United Kingdom sales of raw flat glass, the balance being made up of imports. Courtaulds had 98% of rayon production in the man-made cellulosic fibres industry, but there remained an independent United Kingdom producer, Lansil. Consequently, there has been developed the concept of the "dominant supplier", the firm with a "dominant position" in the market or industry. For example, the Monopolies Commission when investigating the metal containers industry found that Metal Box was the "dominant supplier" in the United Kingdom of "general line" containers, having about 56% of the market with the remaining 44% coming from 45 other manufacturers. There is no fixed level at which a firm becomes "dominant". It depends upon all the circumstances, and whether in practice the firm is able to exercise a determining influence on the market as regards price levels, etc.

1—07    Basically, there is no objection to a firm or group building up a dominant position in a market. This may be due to the firm's competitive efficiency — for example, duPont's position in the U.S. cellophane industry was the "result of research, business skill and competitive activity". To use the American expression, the monopoly may have been "thrust upon" the firm in question — the firm may be able to show, in the words of one American judge in the *United Shoe Machinery* case, that " ... it owes its monopoly solely to superior skill, superior products, natural advantages (including accessibility to raw materials or markets), economic or technical efficiency, (including scientific research), low margins of profit maintained permanently and without discrimination, or licenses conferred by, and used within, the limits of the law, (including patents on one's own inventions, or franchises granted directly to the enterprise by a public authority)." The optimum size of plant may be so big that even large markets will support only one producer — in its *Flat Glass* report, the Monopolies Commission accepted " ... that the tendency towards national monopolies in flat glass is due mainly to the large capital investment required to lay down the most efficient and economical plant and to the fact that the maximum efficiency and savings of such a plant can only be realised if it is producing for a very large market."

1—08    What then is the vice in monopoly or a dominant position? The vice lies in abuse of the market power given by the monopoly or dominant position. The first abuse which springs to mind is charging high prices and making unjustifiably high profits. The Monopolies Commission in its report on *Certain Industrial and Medical Gases* found that British Oxygen (the group had over 98% of the United Kingdom market) had made unjustifiably high profits, and that its prices for oxygen and dissolved acetylene were too high. But charging low prices may not necessarily be regarded with favour. Low prices may be adopted as a deliberate policy to discourage competitors and so increase control of the market, as the Monopolies Commission noted in relation to Courtauld's policies in the 1930s, in the report on man-made cellulosic fibres.

1—09    Other methods of extending market control or forcing out competitors have been condemned. British Oxygen followed a consistent policy of taking over or buying out other producers primarily to preserve its market dominance with regard to oxygen and dissolved acetylene, and also used secret fighting companies (companies not known to be its subsidiaries and so under its control, but ostensibly operating in competition with it) to eliminate competition by making discriminatory price cuts. Three large American cigarette companies used to buy up large quantities of the cheaper tobacco used by their competitors in the manufacture of lower-priced cigarettes with the object of weakening their competitors' position — by depriving them of part of their raw material, and by pushing up the price of that raw material so that the price of the lower-priced cigarettes was forced up and so made less competitive (*American Tobacco* case).

1—10    Firms in dominant positions have adopted a variety of policies to prevent competitors establishing themselves or extending their activities. In the *Aluminium Company of America* case, Alcoa was held to have "anticipated and forestalled all competition", to have kept "doubling and redoubling its capacity before others entered the field". A common practice is to insist upon "exclusivity contracts", in which the supplier requires the buyer to take all his requirements from the supplier, or not to buy from other sources without the supplier's consent. If most or all of the major buyers in the market are tied in this way, a new entrant cannot break into the market. The Monopolies Commission criticized a term in British Oxygen's standard form of contract with large buyers under which the buyer had to take all his requirements of certain specified industrial gases from British Oxygen. The American Can Company used to lease to canners machines for closing the cans after filling, and to insist upon five-year "requirements" contracts, i.e. the canner had to undertake to buy all his can requirements from American Can for five years. The court condemned the five-year requirements contracts as illegal, foreclosing competitors from a substantial market, (but indicated that one-year contracts would be acceptable, bearing in mind that the buyer may wish to have an assured supply). The insistence upon leasing equipment and refusal to sell it outright, is in itself a method of maintaining market control. The United Shoe Machinery Corporation had formerly had tying clauses as part of its leasing arrangements. The tying clauses were dropped to meet criticism by the Supreme Court, but the policy of only leasing, and not selling, its more important machines was also condemned.

1—11    A comparable system, whereby suppliers sought to maintain control over their outlets, was the "solus site" arrangement adopted by United

Kingdom petrol suppliers. The Monopolies Commission found that most suppliers made agreements with petrol retailers involving exclusive dealing and the acceptance of other restrictions. The Commission recommended in its report on *The Supply of Petrol to Retailers* that the retailers should not be restricted from dealing in competing brands of such things as lubricating oils, anti-freeze, etc., that the length of any solus agreement should not exceed five years (although it may be renewable annually) or the life of any loan made to the retailer, and so on.

1—12    Ownership or control of patents can form an effective foundation upon which to build a monopoly or dominant position. In essence, a patent is a monopoly granted by the state to exercise the invention which is the subject of the patent. The owner of the patent may keep the exclusive exercise of the invention to himself for the life of the patent, or he may allow others to use the invention by granting them licences. He may seek to use the licences as a means of building up or protecting a dominant position. For example, he may insist, as part of the terms upon which a licence is granted, that the licensee buys some unpatented material (e.g. some raw materials) from him. He may also insist upon "package deals", under which the licensee has to take, and pay for, a licence in respect of a wider range than he needs. Abuses of patent monopolies may be dealt with under the relevant patent laws (this is the case in the United Kingdom) as well as by any laws relating to abuse of monopoly or dominant position.

## 4. Restrictive Trade Practices
### Cartels

1—13    In a market in which there are a number of suppliers without any having a dominant position, a dominant position may nevertheless be achieved if a sufficient number of the suppliers agree to act together — a monopoly may be achieved if they all agree to do so. They may agree as to any one or more of a number of aspects of commercial and production policy. Most such agreements have been as to selling price. But there is no point in agreeing the selling price if such things as cash discount and length of credit are left free. Any party to the agreement could extend his trade, assuming the other parties made no change, by offering his customers a cash discount, or a higher discount than the other suppliers, which would be the equivalent of a lower price. Longer credit terms would have the same effect. In the same way, if the agreement is between manufacturers who supply several grades of customer (wholesaler, retailer, etc.) the trade discounts will have to be fixed as well. In many cases a fixed price for a product can be circumvented by having a different, and lower, price for a slightly different grade of the product which is just as acceptable to the buyer as the standard product or which is made acceptable by the lower price. Consequently, attempts to fix a price by agreement may well end up with discounts, credit terms, and qualities being fixed as well. In many cases, price-fixing agreements have involved comprehensive agreement on all commercial matters, such as prices, discounts, rebates, allowances, credit terms, qualities, standard conditions of sale, etc., and extended to such things as market-sharing through quotas, joint patents and patent licensing, etc.

1—14    Because of the complexity of such agreements, and perhaps the need for control and supervision, in many cases their administration has been entrusted to trade associations with independent staffs. In such cases the "agreement" may take the form of a decision of the trade association, or perhaps of its committee of management. But it should be noted that not all trade association activities are solely for the benefit of the parties. For example, standardization of products may be beneficial, permitting interchange of parts, and may be demanded by buyers. The standards, in such cases, are frequently agreed by joint committees comprising representatives from the buyers' trade associa-. tion as well as from the sellers' association. Similarly, government departments usually prefer to deal with an association representing an industry as a whole, rather than to have to deal with each individual manufacturer which may involve deciding differences of opinion or policy between the individual manufacturers.

1—15    A useful expression to cover agreements and trade association activities which restrain competition is the word "cartel". It does not have, in English, a precise legal meaning, but is a useful generic term.

1—16    Cartels are not necessarily all bad. Some have been held to be in the public interest, and allowed to continue. Examples are the price-fixing and other arrangements between the manufacturers of black bolts and nuts in the United Kingdom; the Restrictive Practices Court held that the agreement conferred substantial benefits on buyers by, for example, saving them from having to "shop around" among suppliers. The agreement between United Kingdom cement manufacturers was also approved, because the Court considered it held prices down. In another case, the Court approved an arrangement for joint purchasing of sulphur by United Kingdom manufacturers of sulphuric acid; by acting together they were better able to negotiate fair purchase terms with the major supplier of sulphur, the American Sulphur Export Corporation (Sulexco). (This is an illustration of the growth of "countervailing power", a concept developed by Professor J. K. Galbraith who argued in his "American Capitalism" that a monopoly or dominant position on one side of the market frequently results in a monopoly or dominant position emerging on the other side.) The joint arrangements set up by the insulin manufacturers for the co-operative purchase of ox-pancreas, the principal source of insulin, was approved by the Monopolies Commission. The last two cases, sulphur and insulin, demonstrate that cartels can be found on the buying as well as on the selling side of a market.

### Information agreements

1—17    Not all agreements between independent traders on the same side of a market are restrictive of competition, or directly restrictive of it. In the same way as a military headquarters during war seeks to find out what the enemy has done or is planning to do, so a businessman needs to keep himself informed of what his competitors are doing or planning to do. Otherwise, a competitor may be stealing a march on him, without his knowing it, e.g. by lowering prices or improving a product and so taking business away from him, or he himself may be continuing an unsatisfactory policy after it is no longer necessary — if his competitors have put up their prices, he is no longer bound to keep his down if he does not want to. In other circumstances, a businessman may find his trade slackening off, and fear that he is losing out to his competitors, whereas it may be that the total demand for the product has fallen (and in fact his *share* of the market may have gone up, although the absolute level of his deliveries may have declined); conversely, he may be satisfied with his expanding sales, but if the total of all the deliveries of all the firms in the market has been expanding at a greater rate, unknown to him his share of the market has been falling and he has fallen behind his competitors. One of the requirements for "perfect competition", the classical analytical model of theoretical economics, is that all firms in the market should have complete and instantaneous knowledge of competitive prices and other factors affecting the market.

1—18    Because of the practical need for such market information, "information agreements" of various kinds have been made. An early example was the "open price" policy proposed by an American writer, A. J. Eddy, in his book "The New Competition" published in 1912. He suggested that prices should be open and available for all to see, both competitors and customers, through a system of filing with a central office.

1—19    Accurate and speedy information as to competing prices is particularly essential in those industries which supply materials used by other industries. In such cases, there are no shop windows in which current prices are shown. Each firm may issue its price list, either publicly or merely to its own customers. But if a businessman obtains a copy of a competitor's price list, he is by no means certain that his competitor's sales are all made at the list prices. Special "off list" prices may have been negotiated with individual buyers, particularly the bigger buyers who can bring more pressure to bear on a seller by threatening to buy from another supplier. The mere possibility of such special prices can be used by buyers to achieve them. A buyer may say to a supplier "Your price is £X. — I can buy at £Y below your price, so that if you do not drop your price by that amount you will lose my business." Provided he has another source of supply at £X, the buyer cannot lose if the supplier refuses to lower his price. And if the supplier does lower his price, the buyer can then use the reduced price against other suppliers. This is the phenomenon known as "buyers' tales". A genuine "open price" scheme whereby a seller knows or can find out quickly what his competitors' prices are is a way of combating such "tales". In the *Tag Manufacturers* case, the U.S. court held that a scheme for reporting and distributing information about list and off-list prices was not illegal.

1—20 Some schemes provide for manufacturers to report periodically production or deliveries, either by unit (tons, number, etc.) or by value. The figures are then totalled and the totals then communicated to the participants. Each manufacturer can then see how he is faring as compared with his competitors. In some industries, information as to costs is exchanged, as a stimulus to efficiency.

1—21 Nevertheless, it must be recognized that, while there are genuine "exchange of information" schemes, such arrangements can be a cloak for collusion. If there is a secret arrangement between A, B and C that all three will follow A's prices, an "open price plan" will enable them to put their arrangement into operation. Similarly, information as to the total market may enable A, B and C to keep within any market shares agreed between them.

### Concerted practices

1—22 It is possible for firms to adopt a course of conduct towards each other which, while falling short of positive agreement, may nevertheless achieve similar results. Where there is some positive action by the firms to "concert" their activities, they are referred to as "concerted practices". In the *Report on the Supply of Tea* issued in 1956, the Monopolies Commission explained that Brooke Bond and Lyons had each followed a practice of informing the other, some five weeks or so in advance, of intended changes in the prices of packet teas. The intention was to allow the other to change its prices at the same time, if it so wished. There was no agreement that such advance notice would be given. The Commission concluded that the firms were "keenly competitive" and that the price notification arrangement was "no more than a reasonable administrative measure" which did not limit competition nor operate against the public interest. It could be said that the practice adopted by the two companies of giving each other advance information of their intended price changes was a "concerted practice".

1—23 A comparable scheme, but with different legal consequences, was operated by eight tyre manufacturers in the United Kingdom. The manufacturers were each concerned in mileage contract business — contracts entered into between the owner of a fleet of vehicles (such as a bus operator) and a tyre manufacturer under which the latter undertook to provide tyres for the vehicles in return for a "mileage rate", i.e. a payment for each mile run by the vehicles. The manufacturers had had an agreement between themselves under which they would meet to discuss mileage rates. The meeting would bring out the lowest rate insisted upon by any of the manufacturers. Thereafter, under the agreement, each manufacturer was bound not to quote to a customer a mileage rate lower than the lowest rate which had emerged at the meeting, without first notifying the other manufacturers. This agreement was condemned by the Restrictive Practices Court.

In place of the agreement, the manufacturers operated a "Rate Notification Scheme". The Scheme was partly obligatory and partly permissive. The obligatory part required each member to notify to the office any enquiry received from a fleet operator for supply of tyres on a mileage basis and also the mileage rate the member had quoted to the operator; but there was no obligation to notify until the member had submitted his quotation to the fleet operator. The office circulated the information received to the other members. Under the permissive part of the Scheme, each member was free, but not bound, to notify the mileage rate he *intended* to quote, i.e. which he had not already communicated to the operator. Again, the office circulated any information so received. A member could notify a new rate, if he had changed his mind, and the new rate would be circulated by the office. By receiving such advance information of what other members were proposing to quote, a manufacturer would be guided as to what he should quote. With some rare and concealed exceptions, each member operated the permissive part of the Scheme. The Court concluded that there was a reciprocal moral obligation upon each member, binding upon the honour of the companies concerned, not to take advantage of the advance information so supplied by his competitors without himself reciprocating fully, and that it would have been a breach of moral obligation for a member receiving information to have refrained from notifying the mileage rate he intended to quote if it was lower than the lowest rate circulated. There had been no agreement or discussion between the members as to their complying with the permissive part of the Scheme. But each did operate it, and it was clear from the reciprocal nature of the Scheme that none would have continued to operate it if the others had not done so. In other words, a practice was adopted as a result of the conduct of each member, i.e. a "concerted practice". (In fact, the Court held that the operation of the permissive part of the Scheme was a breach of an Undertaking given to the Court on behalf of the companies concerned, and imposed a fine of £10,000 upon each.)

1—24 A recommendation by a trade association to its members, or by one firm to others, would result in a concerted practice if followed. For example, the recommendation might be to "black list" a buyer. If all concerned followed the recommendation their activities would, to that extent, have been "concerted".

*Oligopoly*

1—25     Where there are only a few firms on one side of a market, the management of each quickly realises that commercial policy cannot be decided as if trade were being carried on in a vacuum. To take the simplest case, the management of one firm may decide to try to extend trade by cutting prices. This may succeed, but in so far as it does so by taking business from competitors they will quickly react. The result would be similar if a few buyers were bidding for a scarce material and one sought to extend its purchases by raising its price. Consequently, where there are only a few firms, they soon realise that when taking policy decisions they must take account of what competitors' reactions may be to any policy they adopt. Thus, if a proposal to seek to gain extra trade by cutting prices is under consideration, account will be taken of the reactions to be expected from competitors. If firm A, which is considering the price reduction, thinks it can extend its trade and keep the trade so gained — perhaps because of goodwill from having initiated the price reduction — despite similar price reductions from competitors, it may decide to go ahead. But if it is thought that such a step might induce a larger competitor, B, to become aggressive and perhaps cut prices even lower than A would willingly do, A might decide not to upset the *status quo.* In effect, such firms, where there are so few that they are in fact mutually interdependent, quickly recognise that interdependence, a situation known as "oligopoly" (a few sellers) and "oligopsony" (a few buyers) in contradistinction from monopoly and monopsony (where there is only a seller and one buyer).

1—26     An example of an oligopolistic situation is that which obtained in the supply of household detergents in the United Kingdom. In 1962 Unilever and Procter & Gamble held 46% and 45% respectively of the market by value (50% and 41% by weight) and in 1964 44% and 46% by value (45% and 43% by weight). The case put by the companies to the Monopolies Commission was that each decided its prices independently. Competition between them made it inevitable that their prices would tend to be the same; "neither would put up its prices unless it were satisfied (as is generally the case) that the other, being subject to the same cost pressures, would be likely to follow, and neither could as a rule afford not to follow if the other reduced its prices."

*Conscious parallelism*

1—27     In view of the fact that it is, in modern conditions, unlikely or very rare that one oligopolist can procure a continuing lead over its rivals by introducing some change in its prices or other aspect of its commercial policy — in other words, a change by one can be quickly followed by the others, if they so wish — recognition of their mutual interdependence means that their respective policies, although decided completely independently and without collusion or collaboration, will tend to be similar. They will, consciously, parallel each others' policies, because one will not normally introduce a change unless it is likely to be acceptable to the others. This situation is known as "conscious parallelism".

1—28 Of course, it is not surprising that firms, faced with the same problems and conditions as their rivals, will tend to adopt similar policies. There may well be "unconscious parallelism" as well as "conscious parallelism". In the supply of infant milk foods in the United Kingdom both Cow & Gate (with its subsidiary Trufood) and Glaxo — who between them had over 80% of the market — followed policies of confining retail supplies to qualified chemists, allowing grocers to handle supplies only in areas where there were no chemists shops. The Monopolies Commission found that Cow & Gate had followed this policy for at least forty years, and it had been Trufood's policy for many years before they were taken over by Cow & Gate. Similarly, most of the petrol suppliers in the United Kingdom adopted the practice of "solus sites".

1—29 *"Price Leadership"* One form of parallelism which deserves separate mention is "price leadership", which can be of the "conscious" or the "unconscious" form. Where the change is a change in price, either up or down, and the change is initiated by one firm, the others following either willingly or unwillingly, that is price leadership.

In the United Kingdom, after the price agreements between electric-cable makers were cancelled in 1959, prices fell by some 20%. After some months, British Insulated Callenders Cables, which had established itself as the leading firm in the industry, raised its prices by 7½% for one type of cable, and then by 5% for another. In both cases its rivals followed. B.I.C.C. was the "price leader".[1] In the United Kingdom rayon industry, Courtaulds in the late '20s followed a policy of low prices which yielded only a small profit margin to Courtaulds and little or no profits to its competitors. In 1933, Courtaulds made a further cut in prices. The smaller producers protested, but had to follow Courtaulds' lead.

It is difficult to know whether to call such a situation "conscious" or "unconscious" price leadership — the smaller producers had no option but to follow. Similarly in the case of cellophane in the U.S.A., where Sylvania was the small producer and duPont the dominant firm in the period between 1930 and 1947, whenever duPont made a price reduction Sylvania, after obtaining a copy of the new duPont price list from its own customers, would issue its own price list but back-dated to the date of the duPont change. Sylvania had to follow the duPont prices in order to remain competitive.

1—30 When the United Kingdom rubber footwear industry was under investigation by the Monopolies Commission, the Manufacturers'

[1] J.B. Heath. *Restrictive Trade Practices and After*. The Manchester School. 29. 1961. pp. 173—202.

Association explained that meetings were held at the beginning of each buying season at which manufacturers announced to each other the prices they proposed to charge in the coming season. The manufacturer with the biggest stake in each line would tend to be the "price leader", and for some years North British Rubber had been the leader for overshoes and Dunlops for the rest. Dunlops' prices had been the lowest suggested, and from 1953 onwards Dunlops had attended the meeting with their price list already printed or in proof. The Association argued that the manufacturers were not *obliged* to follow the "leader", but did so because the "leader's" commanding position in the market and knowledge of it made it sensible for the others to follow. In other words, this was a case of "price leadership" and not of agreement. For a variety of reasons, the Monopolies Commission concluded that the uniformity of prices charged by the manufacturers did in fact arise from agreement.

### Terms

1—31    The *Rubber Footwear* report illustrates one difficulty in using these terms. Like the elephant, "which is impossible to define but you can recognise it when you see it," the concepts to which these terms relate are difficult to define precisely so as clearly to delineate the point at which one ends and another begins. It is more a continuous spectrum than of disparate areas. At one end of the spectrum there is the "cartel" with its positive agreement or decision. In the middle of the spectrum come "concerted practices". The extent to which the parties have gone in "concerting" their activities may in some cases bring the position over the line into positive agreement and a "cartel", or the extent of the "concerting" may be so little as to make it arguable that the case is really towards the other end of the spectrum, i.e. one of "conscious parallelism". In the words of the U.S. Attorney General's Committee:

> " 'Conscious parallelism' is a phrase of uncertain meaning and legal significance. For some it is an inartful label for one type of evidence which may or may not be relevant in proof of conspiracy. In this sense, "conscious" may mean no more than knowledge that a particular course of conduct has been followed by competitors. And "parallelism" may be used as a synonym for "collusion" or only to signify uniformity of business behaviour, where "uniformity" is a neutral term."[2]

1—32    Throughout this book, the terms are used so as to be mutually exlusive and not to overlap. "Cartel" applies to the position where there is positive agreement or joint decision by the parties. "Concerted practice" is where the parties have taken some steps, falling short of agreement or joint decision, to align their activities. And "conscious

[2] Report of the U.S. Attorney General's National Committee to Study the Antitrust Laws. March, 1955. p.36.

parallelism" means that the activities of the parties are similar, not as a result of positive agreement or joint decision or of steps taken to align those activities, but because each firm has quite separately and independently decided that what its rival has done is a sensible thing for it to do. In this way, "price leadership" is used in this book to mean that one firm has taken a separate and independent decision to adopt for itself a price change adopted by one of its rivals.

1—33   *Services* It will be recognized that the term "market" may relate either to the supply of goods (textiles, motor-tyres, footwear, etc.) or to the supply of services (such as haircutting, medical and legal advice, transport, etc.). Competition and restraints upon competition can exist equally in relation to services as to goods. For example, at one time, the major United Kingdom banks had an agreement as to the rates of interest they would allow on deposit accounts. There were agreements between insurance companies as to the rates they would charge. And so on. For convenience, throughout this book the word "goods" will be used as implying both goods and services unless there is some particular reason to distinguish between them.

## 5. Control of Private Restraints upon Competition

1—34   At this point, it may be helpful to set out briefly the main principles upon which control of private restraints upon competition is based, and also — equally briefly — the methods adopted in each of the six present Members of the E.E.C. and each of the three new Members expected to join the E.E.C. on the 1st January, 1973.

### Main Principles of Control

1—35   There are three main principles. First, and most obvious, is outright prohibition by law of any private restraint upon competition. According to this principle, such restraints are bad in themselves, and therefore prohibited without any investigation to see if they do operate against the public interest. In practice, the prohibition principle is more usually found in a slightly modified form, which provides for some means of exempting restraints where they are considered to be in the public interest.

1—36   Clearly, it is difficult to enforce a legal prohibition of monopolies or dominant positions. A firm may become dominant in its industry by virtue of its competitive efficiency. To prohibit it from doing so would be, in effect, to prohibit efficiency. Hence the second main principle, the "abuse" principle. Under this principle, restraints on competition are not prohibited in themselves. What is forbidden is the abuse of the economic power which they give. On this principle, monopolies, dominant positions, cartels, and concerted practices are all quite legal and will not be interfered with unless and until the firms concerned abuse the power so obtained.

What is "abuse" will vary from situation to situation, but is essentially action which is considered to be against the public interest. Clearly charging unjustifiably high prices and making unjustifiably high profits is an abuse. But charging unnecessarily low prices may also be an abuse, if the object is to drive out independent competitors.

1—37     Finally, there is what might be called the "expediency principle", under which nothing is done because nothing can be done. For example, nothing can be done against genuine price leadership, because the law cannot reasonably forbid a firm from meeting its rival's price. In the words of the U.S. Attorney General's Committee's Report:

> "It is the essence of effective competition that competitors should try to meet, or offer an equivalent for, any superior inducement which one of them offers. Meeting a rival's inducements is the means whereby competition diffuses the gains of productive efficiency. To forbid a seller to meet his rival's price would involve a *reductio ad absurdum*, so long as the market structure itself is untouched. For example, in the case of homogeneous products, if A only part-way meets B's price, it does A no good — he still cannot sell his goods — and if A more than meets B's price, then B cannot sell his goods, or not until he in turn has more than met A's price. Under these circumstances, in the absence of a change in demand, there is no place where competitive price can level off, and no adjustment permitting a number of competitors to remain in the market in question, unless a seller is permitted to meet his competitor's price. This is the error in holding that a firm is not competing unless it is exceeding its rival's prices."

## Forms of Control in the Six E.E.C. Member States

1—38     The forms of control in the six present E.E.C. Member States can be summarised briefly as follows:

*Italy*               Persons having a "legal monopoly" must not refuse to supply, and the terms on which supplies are made must be non-discriminatory.

Cartels are permitted, but must be in writing. If they have "external activities" such as joint buying or selling, they must be registered. There is provision for compulsory cartels.

*Holland*           Dominant positions are not forbidden, but the Minister of Economic Affairs can take steps to deal with abuses.

Cartels are not forbidden, but must be notified to the Minister. The Minister has power to proceed against abuses, and also to impose cartels compulsorily on non-members.

*Belgium*          Dominant positions are permitted, but there is power to take proceedings in the event of abuse.

Cartels also are permitted, and again there is power to take proceedings in the event of abuse.

*France*    The law prohibits activities of dominant firms which interfere with the normal operation of the market. But there is exemption for anything done under a legislative power, or where the activities further economic progress.

Cartels and concerted practices which restrain competition are forbidden, but subject to exemption in cases where there is legislative approval or the activities further economic progress. The exempting provisions have been extensively used.

*Luxembourg*    Abuse of a dominant position is forbidden.

Cartels and concerted practices are forbidden if they restrain competition and conflict with the public interest. Exemption may be granted if the activities in question result from legislation, or improve production or distribution, or promote technical or economic progress.

*Germany*    The Cartel Authority has power to forbid abuses of dominant position.

Cartels are forbidden, but the law has exemption provisions covering some thirteen classes of cartel.

Normally, activities which relate exclusively to exports are either not covered by the law or are exempt.

### Forms of Control in the Three New Member States

1—39    There are at present three countries expected to join the E.E.C. on the 1st January, 1973 i.e. United Kingdom, Denmark and Ireland. Their systems for controlling restraints upon competition may be summarized as follows:

*United Kingdom*    Dominant positions are not forbidden, but may be investigated by the Monopolies Commission, and action taken against any activities found to be against the public interest.

As regards cartels, there is no law against those relating to the supply of services. Cartels relating to the supply of goods must generally be registered and investigated by the Restrictive Practices Court. The Court must condemn each cartel unless it is satisfied that the cartel comes within one of eight narrow exemptions and is also not unreasonable.

*Denmark*    There is power to take action against abuse of dominant position.

Cartels must be notified if they exert a substantial influence on price and other matters. Action can be

37

*Ireland*

taken to deal with abuse.

There is no law against dominant positions or cartels as such. Investigations can be made by the Fair Trade Commission into the supply and distribution of any kind of goods (including ancillary services). If the Commission finds any conditions which restrain trade and are unfair or against the public interest, the Minister for Commerce and Industry may take steps to deal with such conditions. He can prohibit agreements, and also refusals to supply, discrimination in supply, etc. Consequently, there is power to deal with abuse by a dominant firm or by a cartel.

Again, export cartels are usually outside the legislation.

(Norway originally applied to join the E.E.C., but decided not to pursue its application after a referendum which gave a majority against joining).

## CHAPTER 2

# The European Economic Community — The "Common Market"

## 1. Introduction

2—01    On the 25th March, 1957 in Rome six countries — Belgium, France, Germany, Holland, Italy, and Luxembourg — signed the "Rome Treaty". The first Article of the Treaty — the Treaty is divided into two hundred and forty-eight Articles, many of which are subdivided again into paragraphs — established the "European Economic Community". The task of the Community is to promote the development and expansion of economic activities, to increase stability, to accelerate the rise in the standard of living, and to bring about closer relations between the Member States.

These aims were to be achieved by establishing a "Common Market" and by progressively harmonising the economic policies of the Member States (Article 2 — 17-02).

## 2. The Common Market

2—02    The "Common Market" is the central feature of the Community. In place of the four separate economic groups — France, Germany, Italy, and Benelux (the economic union already formed by Belgium, Holland, and Luxembourg) — there was to be one unified market in which all four would be merged, comprising over 170 million people. This common, unified, market was to be achieved by eliminating customs duties and other barriers affecting the import and export of goods between Member States, and by setting up a "common external tariff" ("C.E.T.") around the Six (Article 3 — 17-03). Once goods had passed through the C.E.T., they were free to circulate within the whole of the common market.

The dismantling of inter-Member tariffs and the creation of the C.E.T. could not take place at a stroke. The Rome Treaty, which came into force on the 1st January, 1958, provided a transitional period of twelve years at the end of which inter-Member tariffs were to have disappeared and the C.E.T. to have been established.

Quantitative restrictions upon imports and exports between Member States were also prohibited (Articles 30 and 34 — 17-06 and 17-07), but restrictions arising from such considerations as public morality, public security, protection of health, and protection of industrial and commercial property (patents, trade marks, copyright, etc.) were permitted (Article 36 — 17-08).

2—03    *Freedom of Movement* The freedom of movement for goods across inter-Member boundaries was not enough. To achieve one unified economy, there would have to be freedom for workers to move from one Member State to another seeking work or better pay and conditions, also freedom for businessmen to set up establishments in other Members and to transfer capital. Various Articles of the Treaty provide for freedom of movement for workers (Article 48), the freedom of establishment in other Member States (Article 52), and the freedom to transfer capital (Article 67).

## 3. Common Policies

2—04    Provision was made in the Treaty for special treatment of certain important economic sectors, particularly the Common Agricultural Policy and the Common Transport Policy. The coal and steel industries were already the subject of joint supervision by the six Member States under the "Paris Treaty" signed in April, 1951 setting up the European Coal and Steel Community — E.C.S.C. The atomic energy industries were covered by the Euratom — European Atomic Energy Community — Treaty signed in Rome on the 25th March, 1957, the same day as the E.E.C. Treaty.

The Social Policy was adopted to improve working conditions and the standard of living, and includes the European Social Fund aimed at improving employment opportunities. As part of its social provisions, the Rome Treaty specifically provides for equal pay as between men and women for equal work (Article 119).

## 4. The Institutions

2—05    To carry out the tasks entrusted to the Community, the Rome Treaty set up four Institutions — the Council, the Commission, the Assembly, and the Court of Justice (Article 4 — 17-04). The Council consists of one representative from each Member State, the office of President being held by each member of the Council for six months in turn according to the alphabetical order of the Member States. The Council is the principal decision-taking and legislative body. The Commission consists of nine members chosen for their independence and general competence; not more than two may be from one Member State. The Commission is the chief executive body, and has a large staff. The Assembly consists of delegates from the Parliaments of the respective Members, and has only advisory and supervisory powers. The Court of Justice consists of eleven judges, and is the tribunal for deciding disputes between Members and interpreting the Treaty. It also has jurisdiction to rule upon the validity of acts of the various Institutions, and can be appointed the body to interpret regulations issued by any bodies set up by the Council. There is also an Economic and Social Committee, which has only advisory status. It has some one hundred and one members representative of various categories of economic and social activity, representing the farmers, professions, workers, producers, etc.

## 5. Competition Rules

2—06     The elaborate provisions in the Treaty for removing inter-Member tariffs and restrictions upon trade, and also those ensuring freedom of movement for workers, businesses and capital could have been rendered wholly or partly nugatory if firms were free to adopt private restraints upon competition between themselves, such as price-fixing, dividing up markets, and so on, or if firms holding a dominant position were free to use their economic power as they thought fit. Consequently, the Rome Treaty states as early as Article 3(f) that the activities of the Community include:

> "(f)    the institution of a system ensuring that competition in the common market is not distorted;"

This is implemented by a series of provisions under the general title "Rules of Competition" comprising Articles 85 — 90. Article 85 (17-09) deals with cartels and concerted practices, and Article 86 (17-10) with dominant positions. Articles 87 — 89 are mainly of a procedural nature. It is the purpose of the following chapters to outline the provisions of these Articles, particularly Articles 85 and 86, and the subordinate legislation and decisions issued under them.

Because of their special characteristics, agriculture and transport will not be dealt with.

# CHAPTER 3

# Cartels and Concerted Practices
# — Article 85

## 1. Introduction

3—01 The general principles laid down by the Treaty with regard to cartels, i.e. agreements between undertakings and decisions of associations of undertakings, and to concerted practices, are contained in Article 85. The detailed application of those principles is dealt with in Regulation 17. The purpose of this Chapter is to give an account of Article 85, and of its interpretation in practice. Regulation 17, so far as it applies to cartels and concerted practices, is dealt with in Chapter 4.

3—02 Article 85 is sub-divided into three paragraphs. Paragraph 1 contains the prohibition on cartels and concerted practices. Paragraph 2 deals with certain legal consequences. And paragraph 3 sets out the conditions for exemption.

## 2. Article 85. Paragraph 1

3—03 The prohibition in 85.1 is simple and direct:

"The following shall be prohibited as incompatible with the common market: all agreements between undertakings, decisions by associations of undertakings and concerted practices which may affect trade between Member States and which have as their object or effect the prevention, restriction or distortion of competition within the common market . . ." (17-09)

Thus, for the prohibition to apply, four requirements must be satisfied:

(i)     There must be either an agreement, or a decision of an association, or a concerted practice.

(ii)    There must be more than one "undertaking" involved.

(iii)   The agreement, etc., must be one which has an effect upon inter-Member trade.

(iv)    The agreement, etc., must have the object or effect of preventing, restricting, or distorting competition within the Common Market.

**Agreements, decisions by associations and concerted practices**

### *"Agreements"*

3—04    There are no formal requirements as to what constitutes an "agreement". If the parties have agreed between themselves, that is an agreement. An agreement may be in writing, but need not be. It can be oral. The agreements between Omega Brandt and its general agents were oral only.

3—05    In the *Quinine Cartel* case, the quinine manufacturers had two export agreements, which were in writing and signed, under which export prices and quotas were fixed and certain markets reserved to certain manufacturers. In addition, there were two "gentlemen's agreements" which were in writing but not signed, under which each national market was protected in favour of the national producer, and the price-fixing and quota provisions of the export agreements extended to cover the national markets. In its decision on the case, the Commission held that the "gentlemen's agreements" were "agreements" within Article 85.1 even though they had not been signed. Fines ranging from $1,000 to $29,000 were imposed.

Admittedly, in that case, the texts of the agreements were in writing. In practice, it is difficult to obtain direct evidence of an oral agreement except from the parties themselves, so that, more usually, the existence of an oral agreement has to be established, not from direct evidence but by indirect evidence from the conduct of the persons concerned. In so far as that conduct constitutes a concerted practice, it is unnecessary to prove the existence of an agreement, as the *Aniline Dyes* case shows (3-11).

### *"Decisions by associations"*

3—06    The expression "decisions by associations" of undertakings covers the situation which results, not from direct agreement between the undertakings concerned, but out of some other legal relationship between them. For example, they may have set up a trade association with a constitution providing for a small committee elected by the members and giving the committee power to fix or vary prices. The individual member of the trade association would not then be a direct party to the price fixing (except for committee members) but would be bound by the decision. It is not unknown for a senior official of a trade association (such as the director or the secretary) to be given authority to fix or change prices, for example, in accordance with pre-determined rules. This would be a decision of an association.

In one case, twelve German manufacturers of ceramic tiles, representing some 99% of the German production, had taken a decision at a general meeting of their "Interessengemeinschaft" laying down the discounts to be given to purchasers of tiles. The discounts varied with the quantity purchased during the period, increasing as the quantity purchased increased, and all purchases by each buyer from the German manufacturers could be added together to arrive at the discount quantity, but not purchases from non-Germans. Consequently, there was a positive incentive for buyers to take as much as they could from the German manufacturers, and a positive dis-incentive not to buy from non-German manufacturers — it had the same effect as a "loyalty rebate", in which the buyers get a higher discount by buying all their requirements from the cartel members. The Commission held that the case came within Article 85.1, and condemned it.

In another case, the *Comptoir Belge de l'Azote* ("Cobelaz"), the Belgian manufacturers of certain nitrogenous fertilisers had agreed to sell through a joint sales office (Cobelaz) their supplies in the Belgian home market and also in export markets outside the E.E.C. The agreement gave Cobelaz power to decide the prices and conditions of sale upon which the supplies would be sold.

3—07 The expression "association" suggests a trade association or something similar to the English reader. It must be remembered that other legal systems, particularly some in Europe, have forms of collaboration not known in Common Law systems. For example, there are the German "interessengemeinschaft", the Italian "consorzio", the French "groupement d'interêt economique", and so on. The expression "decisions of associations" should probably be interpreted widely, to cover any legal relationship between undertakings in which decisions can be taken which are binding upon the participant undertakings (but excluding situations which come within the term "agreements").

### "Concerted practices"

3—08 As already explained (1-22 — 1-24), the expression "concerted practice" relates to the situation where positive steps, falling short of an agreement, have been taken to align the undertakings' activities, for instance where they follow a recommendation by one of their number or by a trade association, where they exchange advance information of intended prices in a scheme which necessarily involves mutual reciprocity, and so on.

3—09 The Commission has reported upon a number of cases of concerted practices. German and Italian manufacturers of flat glass had concerted practices aimed at preventing direct exports between their two countries.[1] In the field of cables and insulated power lines, the firms belonging to the International Cable Development Corporation adopted various practices for mutual protection of their home markets, including bans on investment or acquiring holdings in other producing countries, a ban on advertising in such countries, and a refusal to supply customers in other producing countries either at all or on terms more

[1] Commission of the European Communities. *Premier Rapport sur la Politique de Concurrence.* Brussels, 1972. p.27.

favourable than the local terms.[2]

3—10    In its *Decision re Research and Development* the Commission drew attention to the possibility of concerted practices where two or more undertakings set up a joint company. In that case, two undertakings proposed to set up a joint company to carry out joint research and development, the capital and management being shared equally between the two "parents". The Commission pointed out that, if the joint company took out patents in Member States and the question of instituting proceedings for infringement arose, in so far as such proceedings were taken as a result of a decision of, or with the approval of, the two parents, there would be either an agreement or concerted practice between them. If the proceedings were to stop parallel imports, there could be an agreement or concerted practice with the object or effect of restricting competition within the Common Market, and also affecting inter-Member trade.

3—11    The *Aniline Dyes Cartel* case is of particular interest. The Commission carried out an investigation following information supplied by the representative trade bodies in the leather, textile, dyeing, and printing industries in several Member States. Price increases in the six Member States were introduced in 1964, 1965 and 1967 by ten dyestuffs manufacturers, four German (B.A.S.F., Cassella, Bayer, and Hoechst), one French (Société des Matières Colorantes — Francolor), one Italian (Aziende Colori Nazionali), three Swiss (Ciba, Geigy, and Sandoz), and one English (I.C.I.). Between the 7th and 20th January, 1964, a uniform increase of 15% was made in the prices of certain dyestuffs in Italy, Holland, Belgium and Luxembourg. On 1st January, 1965, the same 15% increase was extended to Germany, and nearly all the manufacturers made a uniform 10% increase in the prices of the remaining dyestuffs and pigments in all five countries. On the 16th October, 1967, an increase of 8% was made by nearly all the producers in Germany, Holland, Belgium and Luxembourg; the increase in France was 12%; there was no increase in Italy.

    The parties concerned argued that their actions resulted from "parallel behaviour" in an oligopolistic market, each following the firm which had introduced the increase, i.e. price leadership. The Commission rejected this argument, concluding that there had been a concerted practice, for a number of reasons. There was the closeness of the dates on which the increases had been applied. For example, the January, 1964, increase was announced (coming into effect immediately) in Italy on the 7th by Ciba, in Holland on the 9th by I.C.I., and in Belgium on the 10th by Bayer, the other producers following suit in each instance within two or three days. As regards the increase in Italy, messages by Telex or telegram were sent to their respective Italian representatives on the evening of the 9th January at the following times — by Sandoz at

---

[2]  Commission of the European Communities Press Release. 3rd March, 1969.

5.05 p.m., by Hoechst at 5.09 p.m., by Bayer at 5.38 p.m., by Francolor at 5.57 p.m., by B.A.S.F. at 6.55 p.m., and by Geigy at 7.45 p.m. The Commission noted a similarity of content in the various messages sent, especially in the January, 1964, increases, even to the extent of exactly identical phrases. There was also the identity of the increases applied and, with some exceptions, the identity of the materials to which the increases related.

Because it had concluded that, at the very least, there had been concerted practices within the meaning of Article 85.1, the Commission took the view that there was ". . . no need to examine whether the increases are the result of an agreement." Fines of $50,000 were imposed upon each of the undertakings concerned, except Aziende Colori whose fine was $40,000.

3—12 The Commission rejected the manufacturers' argument that there had only been parallel behaviour, holding that the increases and the way they were carried out could not be explained by the oligopolistic structure of the market. The actions in question went further than parallel behaviour, and resulted from a concerted practice. It is interesting to note that the Commission did not reject the implied argument that parallel behaviour itself does not constitute a concerted practice. The issue cannot be regarded as finally settled until there has been a reasoned judgment on the point by the European Court, but in the meantime it would seem safe to work on the basis that mere "conscious parallelism" without anything further does not constitute a "concerted practice".

3—13 "Agreements", "decisions of associations" and "concerted practices" are not mutually exclusive, distinct, concepts. They can overlap. A unanimous decision taken at a trade association meeting at which all member firms are represented would probably also constitute an agreement between those firms. A decision by a trade association to recommend a price change, followed by adoption of the recommendation by the members, would be part and parcel of a concerted practice. So long as the factual situation falls within one category, it does not matter if it could also fall within either or both of the other categories.

3—14 It must be remembered that the parties concerned cannot change the character of their activities merely by applying a particular description to them. For example, if a number of manufacturers discussed together the possibility of introducing "conscious parallelism" between them — perhaps all following the lead given by one of their number as regards prices — the resulting situation would not be "conscious parallelism" or "price leadership" because it would have been introduced by deliberate arrangement. In fact, in those circumstances, there would be either an agreement or a concerted practice. It may be worth repeating that "conscious parallelism" is a situation which develops by completely separate and independent decisions of the undertakings concerned, and without any arrangement between the concerns to bring about the situation.

### "Undertaking"

3—15 The word "undertaking" is not defined in the Treaty. It is wide enough to cover all legally recognised types of economic unit, including those adopted in countries whose legal system is based on Common Law, such as an individual carrying on a business, partnerships, companies, corporations established by charter, statutory bodies, local authorities carrying on a business, charities which are trading, co-operative societies, and so on. That public undertakings are included is made clear by their special mention in Article 90 (17-11).

### "Enterprise entity"

3—16 In some situations, two separate legal entities may be regarded as forming one undertaking. In law, normally, a company is treated as a quite separate legal person, completely distinct from its shareholders. If all the shares in one company are owned by another company, both companies are normally regarded as separate and distinct legal persons. However, where a parent company decides the policy of and controls the subsidiary, so that the subsidiary has no autonomy, the two may be treated as forming one enterprise, i.e. one undertaking. There is no competition between them. This is the doctrine of "enterprise entity". It was applied by the Commission in the *Christiani & Nielsen* and *Béguelin* cases. The Commission in each case treated distributorship agreements between the parent and its wholly-owned subsidiary, restricting the right of the subsidiary to export, as falling outside 85.1 because they were not agreements *between undertakings* — because of the doctrine of enterprise entity, there was deemed to be only one undertaking involved, in each case.

3—17 The Commission sought to apply the doctrine in the *Aniline Dyes* case, where there was a procedural difficulty facing it. Article 191 of the Rome Treaty provides that decisions, in the case of the Commission, shall be "notified to those to whom they are addressed and shall take effect upon such notification" (17-19). As four of the companies in question were established and located outside the Common Market, the Commission had to find some means of actually serving its decision upon them so as to make the decision effective. Each of the four had subsidiaries within the Common Market. The Commission held that proof of the alleged concerted practices had been established against the parent companies, but not against the subsidiaries. Nevertheless, the Commission took the view that the decision could be served upon each of the four companies by service upon their respective subsidiaries:

> "Such notification is carried out when the decision enters into the 'internal sphere' of the addressee. The subsidiaries of the undertakings Ciba, Geigy, Sandoz and I.C.I. in the Common

Market which are wholly controlled by their parent companies are part of the 'internal sphere' of these four undertakings. Therefore, notification to those undertakings may validly be made at the seat of one of their subsidiaries."

The doctrine is not accepted in the United Kingdom, and the United Kingdom Government rejected the doctrine in the Aide Mémoire it submitted to the Commission in connection with the *Aniline Dyes* decision (Appendix M). The companies appealed to the European Court against the decision. In deciding upon I.C.I.,'s argument that notification *via* its German subsidiary was not valid notification, the Court side-stepped the "enterprise entity" issue by ruling that as I.C.I. appeared to have complete knowledge of the contents of the decision and to have acted upon that knowledge, any irregularities there may have been in the method of notification were immaterial.

3—18 However, the Court appeared to give some approval to the doctrine in another aspect of the appeal. I.C.I. had argued that none of its relevant actions had taken place within the Common Market and therefore, upon the "territorial" jurisdiction principle, the Commission would not exercise jurisdiction over I.C.I. The Commission, in its decision, had taken the view that if the *effects* of the actions were felt within the Common Market, it did have jurisdiction (the "territorial" jurisdiction and "effects" principles are discussed in section 5 below). The Court held that the actions of a wholly-owned subsidiary controlled by the parent company could be imputed to the parent, and on that basis I.C.I. must be deemed to have committed acts within the Common Market and therefore came within the Commission's jurisdiction. By this means, the Court avoided giving a ruling upon the "territorial" v. "effects" issue, but has given some confirmation to the doctrine of "enterprise entity".

3—19 The doctrine has also been applied by the Commission in the *Continental Can* case, where the Commission has held that the actions of Europemballage, Continental Can's wholly-owned subsidiary, can be imputed to Continental Can. That decision is the subject of an appeal to the Court.

### "Affect trade between Member States"

3—20 The mere fact that something constitutes an agreement between undertakings, or a decision of an association of undertakings, or a concerted practice, does not mean that it is *ipso facto* within Article 85.1. The agreement, decision or practice must be one which "may affect trade between Member States".

3—21 There are a wide variety of circumstances in which an agreement, etc., may have no effect upon trade between Member States. In the first place, it may be one which does not have an impact upon trade at all. An agreement between manufacturers to exchange information about hygiene problems within their works, or about treatment of effluent, is not likely to affect trade. Nor is one by which they agree upon a suitable warning label on toxic materials, or suitable packaging. Nor would an agreement to set up a joint office to advise on taxation or accountancy matters, etc.

3—22 Even if an agreement, etc., does affect trade, it may not affect trade between Member States. Its impact may be only upon internal trade within one Member State, or only upon trade to countries outside the Common Market, outside the E.E.C., i.e. trade with non-Member States. In the *Cobelaz* case, the sphere of the joint sales office set up by the Belgian fertiliser manufacturers was strictly limited to sales within the Belgian home market and to export sales to countries outside the E.E.C. As regards sales within other Member States, each manufacturer acted separately and independently. Each was free to decide what quantity of his production he would offer for sale through Cobelaz and what quantity he would retain for his own direct sale in other Member States. In fact, the Commission found that the manufacturers had developed increasingly important sales efforts in other Member countries. The Commission therefore concluded that the Cobelaz arrangement did not restrict the parties' freedom to import into Belgium from other Member States or to export from Belgium to other Member States. Consequently, there was no ground under Article 85.1 upon which the Commission could intervene in the case, i.e. Cobelaz did not affect trade between Member States and negative clearance was granted. The Commission reached the same conclusion in connection with the corresponding joint sales office set up by the French manufacturers, the Comptoir Française de l'Azote, which dealt with sales in France and non-Member countries, leaving each manufacturer to handle his own sales in other Member States. In its first report on competition policy, the Commission points out that as early as 1964 it had taken a similar decision in relation to the Dutch Engineers and Contractors Association, comprising four Dutch firms collaborating in connection with civil engineering work outside the E.E.C.; and also in relation to "Cimfrance", a joint selling organization outside the E.E.C. set up by French cement producers.

*"Appreciable effect"*

3—23 Even if an agreement, etc., does affect trade between Member States, it does not necessarily follow that Article 85.1 applies. The Commission has, very reasonably, developed the doctrine of *"effet sensible"* (i.e. an "effect which can be felt"). This doctrine was first applied in the *Grasfillex* case (6-28) and is illustrated by the *SOCEMAS* case. SOCEMAS was a co-operative import agency set up by some French chain stores selling food and provisions, representing about 20,000 shops scattered throughout the whole of France. In 1965, the imports organized by SOCEMAS amounted to only 0.1% of the turnover of the stores, and in no case did the SOCEMAS imports from other Members (e.g. tinned fish from Germany) exceed 1% of the production in that Member. Consequently, the Commission concluded that SOCEMAS did not have any "noticeable effects" upon the position of the suppliers in the markets for the products in question, and therefore the SOCEMAS agreement did not have the effect of preventing or restricting competition within the Common Market.

3—24   In practice, as will be seen from paragraph 3-36 below, the Commission has usually expressed its conclusion in the form that there is no appreciable effect upon competition. This is usually because there is no appreciable effect upon inter-Member trade — if trade is not affected appreciably, competition will not usually be affected appreciably. Theoretically, there could be a situation in which there is an appreciable effect upon trade, but no appreciable effect upon competition, but that does not appear to have arisen in practice so far.

3—25   The Court has confirmed the doctrine in a ruling based upon the insignificant market share of the parties to an agreement. In *Völk v. Vervaecke*, the plaintiff, a German manufacturer of washing machines, sued the Belgian defendants for breach of the contract under which the Belgian firm was to act as the plaintiff's distributor and to buy a number of his machines. The defendant argued that the contract was invalid as infringing Article 85.1, because it provided for the defendants to have the exclusive right to sell the plaintiff's machines in Belgium and Luxembourg and for the plaintiff to "protect" their market. The plaintiff's production of washing machines was very small in relation to the market. The European Court ruled that an agreement may escape the prohibition in Article 85.1 if "it only affects the market insignificantly, account being taken of the weak position held by the parties on the market in the products in question".

3—26   The doctrine of "appreciable effect" has been taken further by the Commission "Notice Concerning Minor Agreements" issued in May, 1970, (Appendix J), and by Council Regulation 2822/71 made in December, 1971, (Appendix L). In the Notice, the Commission expressed the view that Article 85.1 does not apply to agreements which "do not affect to a significant degree competition and trade between Member States" (25-02). To fall within the prohibition in 85.1, the agreement must have an appreciable effect upon market conditions, i.e. it must "appreciably modify the market position of non-participating undertakings and of consumers, that is, their outlets and sources of supply". The Notice gives a quantitative meaning to the word "appreciable". If the products to which the agreement relates do not exceed 5% of the market and if the total annual turnover of the undertakings concerned does not exceed 15 million "units of account" (or 20 million in the case of commercial undertakings, i.e. non-manufacturing) the agreement does not fall within Article 85.1 (25-06) — the "unit of account" is equivalent to 0.88867088 grams of gold (4-93). In calculating the turnover of the undertakings concerned, account is taken of the turnover of certain associated undertakings but inter-party business is ignored (25-08). The market shares and turnover can exceed these limits by 10% in two consecutive years without bringing the agreement within 85.1. Agreements between undertakings which exceed these limits may still fall outside Article 85.1, but have to be investigated individually by the Commission (25-03).

3—27    Regulation 2822/71 related to "specialization" agreements where the products concerned do not exceed 15% of the market for those products or substitutes in a substantial part of the Common Market *and* the turnover of the parties does not exceed 200 million units of account (27-02 — v, 4-51).

### Restraint upon competition

3—28    Even if there is an agreement between undertakings, or a decision of an association of undertakings, or a concerted practice, and even if it affects trade between Member States to an appreciable degree, it still does not fall within Article 85.1 unless it also has as its "object or effect the prevention, restriction, or distortion of competition within the common market".

3—29    It will be noted that this requirement distinguishes between "object" and "effect". For an agreement, etc., to come within 85.1 only one is needed, not both. An agreement which in effect restrains competition, even if that is not its object, is as much within the prohibition of 85.1 as one which has the purpose of restraining competition. In principle, if an agreement has the object of restraining competition but does not have that effect (i.e. it fails to achieve its purpose) it is still banned by 85.1. In practice, however, this situation is likely seldom to arise — an ineffective agreement is not likely to continue for long. Nor is a concerted practice which is intended to restrict competition, but which fails in its object. However, it must be remembered that an ineffective agreement, etc., is as much within Article 85.1 as an effective one, and can expose the parties concerned to the relevant fines. Before embarking upon a course of action which is or might be within the prohibition of 85.1, those concerned would be well advised to consider their position carefully, because a plea that the course of action failed in its purpose will not relieve the parties of liability for having infringed the Article.

3—30    In practice, however, most cases which have arisen have concerned agreements, etc., which had the effect of restraining or distorting competition within the Common Market. For example, there were the "gentlemen's agreements" in the *Quinine* case, the trade association decision in the *Ceramic Tiles* case, and the concerted practice in the *Aniline Dyes* case. Many other agreements, etc., have been condemned as being prohibited by Article 85.1, i.e. as restraining competition. In the *Van Katwijk* case, between a Dutch firm and a Belgian firm, both making specialised cardboard tubes for the textile industry, Van

Katwijks were forbidden by the agreement to sell in Belgium, and the Belgian firm was forbidden to sell in Holland in excess of a certain quantity. The agreement was condemned by the Commission, and the firms required to put an end to their restrictions. Other agreements to be condemned have included:[3] a building materials cartel between a considerable number of Belgian, Dutch, and German firms, providing for reciprocal exclusive dealing and market sharing; a market-sharing agreement between Dutch and Belgian detergent manufacturers; a cartel with exclusive reciprocal dealing between a number of Belgian manufacturers, importers and wholesalers of sanitary ware; and so on.

3—31  Of course, not all agreements, etc., between undertakings restrain competition. If the parties are not competitors, because they are not dealing in the same goods, an agreement between them is not likely to restrain competition. This was the position in the *Alliance Machines Outils* case. Eight small to medium manufacturers of machine tools in France were members of the Alliance, and had granted to it the exclusive right to promote and negotiate sales on their behalf in all countries except France. Each member fixed the price at which his goods would be sold, the Alliance receiving only reimbursement of its expenses. As part of the arrangement, each member firm undertook not to make or sell machine tools of the type made by any other member. When the Alliance was formed the members were specialising in different machines and were not in competition with one another. The Alliance represented only a small part of the total production and sales of machine tools in the Common Market, including imports. In these circumstances, the Commission accepted that there was no restraint upon competition and granted negative clearance.

3—32  There are many other types of inter-firm agreements which do not restrain competition. In July, 1968, the Commission published its "Notice Concerning Co-operation between Enterprises." An English translation is at Appendix N. Some seventeen different types of co-operation are listed, all of which are considered not to restrict competition. They include the exchange of information and experience (but *not* exchange of information as to prices or turnover — 23-14), co-operation on accountancy, financial and fiscal matters, collaboration on research and development, etc.

### "Appreciable effect"

3—33  The doctrine of *"effet sensible"* or "appreciable effect" applies in determining whether or not the agreement, etc., has as its "effect the prevention, restriction or distortion of competition within the common market". Although the doctrine was first developed in the *SOCEMAS* case, the reasoning underlying it can be discerned in an earlier case,

[3] Commission of the European Communities. Eighth General Report. Brussels, 1965. pp.70—72.

*Nicholas Frères.* Nicholas had taken over another manufacturer of cosmetic products, Vitapointe. Vitapointe held in a number of countries various patents and trade marks relating to hairdressing products, and had given an English company, Vitapro, an exclusive concession to market the products in the United Kingdom and Commonwealth countries. After Nicholas had taken over Vitapointe, Nicholas and Vitapro entered into an agreement whereby the former sold to the latter the Vitapointe business in the United Kingdom and Commonwealth together with the right to use the patents and trade marks registered in those countries, including the trade name "Vitapointe". Vitapro undertook not to use the trade names outside the United Kingdom and Commonwealth. In addition, each party agreed not to manufacture or sell hairdressing products in the other's territory, whether with the trade marks in question or not, for a period of five years. In effect, therefore, Nicholas was protected from competition from Vitapro within the Common Market both as regards goods carrying the "Vitapointe" and other trade names and other goods. However, Nicholas was not one of the largest undertakings in the field and was in lively competition in the products in question with numerous other firms in the Common Market. In these circumstances, the Commission concluded that there was no reason for it to interfere with the Nicholas/Vitapro agreement under Article 85.1, i.e. negative clearance was given.

3—34 A more recent case concerned the agreement between Rieckermann and A.E.G.-Elotherm, by which the latter appointed the former its exclusive distributor in Japan. The Commission concluded that there was and would continue to be no noticeable effect on competition within the Common Market as a result of the agreement, and gave negative clearance.

3—35 Another case, of interest because of the light it throws on business practice, is the (Belgian) *Cement Makers Agreement.* In 1936, when conversion of lime-burning plant making natural cement to the production of artificial cement was still relatively easy, the Belgian Association of Portland Cement Manufacturers made an agreement with thirteen lime-burners under which the latter undertook to make only natural cement and to limit their sales of natural cement to a maximum of 2.75% of the sales of artificial Portland cement by the Association's members. In return, the Association agreed to pay the lime-burners a quarterly sum based upon the total cement sales of its members. The Association was wound up in 1947, and the cement makers sought to stop their payments to the lime-burners, but the Belgian courts held that the 1936 agreement had been continued. In 1962, the cement makers again sought relief from the obligation to continue paying the burners, on the ground that the agreement infringed Article 85.1. In 1965, ten of the thirteen burners came to an arrangement with the cement makers, but the other three sought to continue with the agreement. When the Commission took its decision, there was only one producer of natural·cement still in production in Belgium, with an annual output of about 1,000 tons, as compared with an output of some 5,000,000 tons of Portland cement. Because of technical and economic factors, it was no longer profitable to set up a new cement factory with a capacity of less than 200,000 tons a year, involving a capital expenditure of 400 — 500 million Belgian francs. A considerable area of land would also be necessary. The three lime-burners who had continued the agreement did not have enough land or quarries to set up a new installation. The Commission came to the conclusion that, because of the economic and technical factors, the lime-burners were in fact excluded from the production of artificial cement, and could no longer be regarded as even potential competitors of the manufacturers of artificial cement. The production ban preventing the lime-burners from making artificial cement did not "restrict competition noticeably", and would not be liable to influence the supply of Portland cement in Belgium, let alone the Common Market. Consequently, the agreement did not infringe Article 85.1 (and the cement makers would have to continue the payments to the lime-burners!).

3—36  From the information given in the decisions, it could be argued that in the *Rieckermann* and *Cement Makers* cases there was in the first place, no appreciable effect upon inter-Member trade, and therefore, in the second place, no appreciable effect upon competition, but the Commission has expressed its conclusions in the latter form, i.e. no appreciable effect upon competition. For all practical purposes the distinction is irrelevant, because on either basis Article 85.1 does not apply, i.e. if there is no appreciable effect upon competition, it does not matter in the last resort whether that is because there is no appreciable effect upon inter-Member trade and so indirectly upon competition, or because there is no appreciable direct effect upon competition.

3—37  As already noted in dealing with the application of the doctrine of "appreciable effect" to effect upon trade between Member States (3-26), the May, 1970, Notice (Appendix J) gives some indication of what is an "appreciable effect" and a quantitative level up to which the effect can be deemed to be not "appreciable". Regulation 2822/71 (Appendix L) prescribes rather higher limits for "specialization agreements".

## Particular types of agreements, etc., prohibited by Article 85.1

3—38  Having noted which kinds of agreement, etc., do not restrict competition or do not do so to a material extent, i.e. do not have an "appreciable effect", this is the stage at which to ask which types of agreement, etc., are regarded as preventing, restricting, or distorting competition. Article 85.1 gives an indication of the types at which it is aimed in specifying:

> ". . . in particular those [agreements, decisions, and concerted practices] which:
> (a)  directly or indirectly fix purchase or selling prices or any other trading conditions;
> (b)  limit or control production, markets, technical development, or investment;
> (c)  share markets or sources of supply;
> (d)  apply dissimilar conditions to equivalent transactions with other trading parties, thereby placing them at a competitive disadvantage;
> (e)  make the conclusion of contracts subject to acceptance by the other parties of supplementary obligations which, by their nature or according to commercial usage, have no connection with the subject of such contracts." (17-09)

In view of the absence of any requirement as to size or territorial extent, it is clear that these are examples of agreements, etc., which are considered to have the "object or effect" of preventing, restricting or distorting competition.

The wording used is simple, and avoids legal technicalities. There is no attempt to describe by precise legal formulae the particular instances of prohibited activity. On the contrary, they are identified by their economic character, described in broad non-technical language. The simplicity of the language used should not obscure the fact that these five particular categories are very wide in scope.

3—39  *Category (a)* As regards (a), fixing buying or selling prices or other trading conditions, it will be noticed that this category alone employs the expression "directly or indirectly". Thus an agreement between manufacturers of items made specially, to specification, not to quote a price without first taking out costs might — even though it did not bind the parties as to what price should be quoted (whether above or below costs) — be considered to be within 85.1, on the ground that it fixed prices "indirectly".

Category (a) is concerned with all the terms on which transactions are carried out in the supply of goods and services, not merely with buying and selling prices. It covers agreements, etc., which fix such terms as discounts for cash payment, credit terms, discounts for quantity (either per load, per order, or offtake over a period), status discounts (to wholesalers, retailers, etc.), extras for packaging or special qualities, etc. Agreements, etc., as to standard conditions of sale or purchase are also covered. In short, (a) covers any agreement, decision or concerted practice between undertakings by which they restrict themselves as to the terms on which they will do business.

3—40  *Category (b)* Category (b) is concerned with the control or limitation of markets or production both in the short and long term, i.e. production itself and also research and development and investment (which determine future production). Production can be controlled by such things as quotas, perhaps with penalties for excess or compensation for under-production, agreements for specialization or rationalization (one party concentrates on one item, another party on a different item), patent licences limiting the licensee as to what he may produce (either by quantity or type), etc.

Markets can be limited or controlled in a variety of ways. There may be protection for home markets — the parties do not export to the country of another party. There can be exclusive dealing — manufacturers may agree to supply only certain wholesalers, who may agree to buy only from the manufacturers in question, and the wholesalers may agree to supply only certain retailers, so that the whole distribution system is stratified. Markets can be divided up by patent licences determining in which areas the licensee may sell, or by trade mark licences determining the goods upon which the licensee may use the mark or the areas in which he can sell goods bearing the mark.

Research and development can be controlled by various means. The parties may agree to pool their research and development activities in a joint organization, undertaking to carry out none individually. As part of a pooling operation, there might be agreement as to which party will be entitled to the benefit of the results obtained in particular lines — perhaps one party may be entitled to free use of some patents while another has to pay a royalty. Or the parties may have an agreement to specialize their research programmes, one taking one field, the other another field.

Investment can be controlled by similar types of arrangement.

3—41   *Category (c)* Categories (b) and (c) overlap. Methods of controlling production or markets may also involve sharing the markets or available supplies. But markets and supplies can be shared in ways which do not necessarily involve their control. If the parties set up a joint sales office, agreeing the proportions in which the sales will be split between them, they may not control or limit the market although they are sharing it between them. Similarly, if they have a specialization agreement, under which one manufactures one quality of the product and supplies the other party, while the latter concentrates on another quality and supplies the former with it, they are dividing between themselves that part of the market which they supply.

3—42   *Category (d)* Category (d) is concerned, not with agreements, etc., which fix trading terms, but with those which fix discriminatory terms, e.g. where the terms to one buyer are different from the terms to another buyer for equivalent transactions. For example, manufacturers who wish to retain the small shop-keepers as their outlets may refuse to grant lower prices for larger quantities to super-markets or discount stores so that these cannot undercut the small shop-keeper. Or manufacturers whose policy is to operate resale price maintenance may agree not to supply, or only to supply at a higher price, traders who undersell the fixed price.

Category (d) is not concerned with discriminatory terms operated by one individual trader but with those applied in agreement or collaboration with his competitors. The individual trader can determine his own terms as he wishes, although if he has a dominant position in the market and his discriminatory terms constitute an abuse of that position, Article 86 may apply (v. Chapter 5).

3—43   *Category (e)* Finally, category (e) deals with agreements, etc., by which the parties agree to impose "tying" clauses, such as a requirement that somebody seeking to buy one product must also buy another not connected with the first either by its character or by usual commercial custom. Thus, the manufacturers of a particular type of machine might agree between themselves that each will not supply the machine unless the buyer undertakes to buy from the machine manufacturer all the raw material which the machine will consume.

Again, as with category (d), (e) is not concerned with the individual trader who decides that he will impose a "tying" provision, but with tying clauses imposed by traders as a result of an agreement, etc., with other traders. The individual trader's trading terms are a matter for him to decide. (But if he holds a dominant position in the market, Article 86 may apply in the event of his terms being considered an abuse of that position — v. Chapter 5.)

3—44   Although the particular categories of agreements, etc., specified in Article 85.1 are broad in scope and comprehensive, they are not exhaustive. They do not represent the full extent of the prohibition in the first part of 85.1. If an agreement, decision, or concerted practice affects trade between Member States and has the object or effect of preventing, restricting, or distorting competition within the Common Market, in both cases to an appreciable extent, then it is within Article 85.1 even though it does not fall within any of the categories (a) to (e).

For example, an agreement between traders to pool their profits may not be within the five categories. But if the agreement provides that the profits are to be shared between them in some pre-determined proportions, the effect may be to restrict competition between them and the agreement may be within 85.1 if the other requirements are met. In the *Belgaphos* case, an arrangement to equalise the prices received on all transactions by working out average prices at the end of the period and suppliers who received higher than average prices making corresponding payments to those who received less than the average, was condemned as falling within 85.1. (This is not to say that *all* profit pools are necessarily within the prohibition of 85.1 — it may be possible to devise a profit-pooling scheme which does not have the object or effect of restricting competition.)

Similarly, an agreement between manufacturers not to advertise in each other's countries may restrict competition without being within (b) or (c), (but equally a code of professional conduct which forbids *all* advertising may not be restrictive of competition).

## 3. Article 85 Paragraph 2

3—45    Paragraph 2 of Article 85 is admirably terse:

"2. Any agreements or decisions prohibited pursuant to this Article shall be automatically void." (17-09)

It will be observed that the paragraph does not include concerted practices — it refers only to agreements and decisions. From its very nature, a practice is something which cannot be made void. It consists in doing something. Once that thing has been done, it is done. An agreement or decision, by contrast, is an agreement or decision to do something. An agreement or decision can, therefore, be declared void for the future.

3—46    For an agreement or decision to be void under Article 85.2, it must first be within the prohibition in 85.1. This depends upon the facts of the individual case. Thus, if it is a question of an agreement, before the agreement is void under 85.2, the agreement must have an appreciable effect upon trade between Member States, and it must also prevent, restrict or distort competition within the Common Market to an appreciable extent. If these criteria are satisfied, the agreement is void.

3—47    Who decides whether the criteria are satisfied? This depends upon the circumstances. If two parties to an agreement concur in the view that their agreement meets those criteria, then they decide that it is void. If the agreement has been sent to the Commission for negative clearance, the Commission will decide whether it falls within 85.1 or not, subject to the parties' right of appeal to the European Court. If the parties are involved in litigation over the agreement before their own national courts, the latter will decide whether 85.1 applies to the agreement.

3—48    For example, in the *"Yoga"* case, an Italian company making fruit juices had entered into an exclusive distribution agreement with a German company. The Italian manufacturer undertook to supply its "Yoga" juices exclusively to the German distributor for marketing in West Germany and not to sell or allow others to sell the juices in that territory in competition with the distributor. The distributor undertook to sell in the territory only juices supplied by the Italian manufacturer. Differences arose between the parties, and the German distributor started proceedings for damages for breach of the agreement. The German appeal court held that the agreement fell within the prohibition in 85.1, and consequently was void under 85.2. Because the agreement was void under 85.2 it could not be enforced, and could not give rise to a right to damages.

3—49    Similarly in the *Béguelin* case, the French subsidiary of a Belgian parent company held an exclusive concession to market certain Japanese pocket lighters in France. A German company held a similar exclusive concession for Germany. The German company sold 18,000 of the lighters to G.L. Import Export in Nice. Béguelin applied to the French courts for an injunction to stop G.L. Import Export from marketing the lighters in France and for damages for "unfair competition" (laws against "unfair competition" exist in France and Germany). The French court referred the matter to the European Court, which ruled that, if the agreement satisfied the requirements of Article 85.1, the agreement would be void under 85.2 and could not be used as a basis for action against third parties.

### Severability

3—50 In the *Béguelin* case, the ruling was that the whole agreement was void. This need not always be the case. In the *Technique Minière* case, a French company was given "the exclusive sales right" in respect of certain earth-moving plant in France on behalf of the German manufacturer. The French distributor was free to export the goods to other countries, and other French concerns were free to import the goods into France, i.e. parallel imports were not forbidden. The German manufacturer delivered six of the machines, which the French distributor refused to accept as being unsuitable. The French court decided against the distributor, who appealed to a higher court on the ground that the agreement was void as being contrary to Article 85.1. The question was referred to the European Court, which ruled that contracts "granting an exclusive right of sale" are not automatically within the prohibition in 85.1. They fall within that prohibition only if the requirements of 85.1 are met. So far as Article 85.2 is concerned, the Court ruled that automatic nullity under 85.2 applies to those provisions in the agreement which are incompatible with 85.1. As regards any other provisions in the agreement, the "consequences of that nullity . . . are not the concern of Community law".

3—51 This suggests that the provisions of an agreement will be void under 85.2 if they are prohibited by 85.1, but any which are not prohibited by 85.1 will not be void. Where, however, the void provisions are the essence of the contract, and cannot be severed from the remainder, the whole agreement may be void (as in the *Béguelin* case). In most cases it is likely that the agreement will stand or fall as a whole, as an agreement usually consists of one organic whole not of several disparate parts. But it is not impossible to have an agreement which can be severed into distinct parts, each standing on its own.

For example, a manufacturer in one Member State might grant an exclusive distributorship, with absolute territorial protection, to an independent trader in another Member, the agreement requiring the distributor to order a certain quantity of the goods each year. Such an agreement, given the other requirements, is likely to fall within the 85.1 prohibition, and be void and unenforceable, but it is doubtful if that nullity would apply to an order for a supply of the goods — the order would probably be enforceable as a separate transaction, and if payment had not been made for the goods the manufacturer could obtain redress in the courts. Similarly, one might imagine a button manufacturer in one Member, who also owned a clothing factory in another Member State, contracting to sell the factory and to grant the buyer an exclusive distributorship, with absolute territorial protection, in his buttons. If the button manufacturer refused to go through with the deal because he had received a better offer for the factory, arguing that the contract was prohibited by Article 85.1 and void and unenforceable under 85.2, it is likely that the courts would say that the sale of the factory was a separate transaction which could be severed from the exclusive distributorship and enforced in the courts.

3—52    In one very important case, the European Court actually over-ruled the Commission on this point. In the *Grundig/Consten* case, the German manufacturer of tape-recorders, radios, etc., Grundig, had given an exclusive concession to a French concern, Consten, to distribute Grundig products in France. Consten undertook not to sell competing products, and not to export, directly or indirectly, to other countries. Grundig had imposed a similar ban on exports upon its distributors in other countries. Grundig undertook not to deliver, either directly or indirectly, to other persons in Consten's area. And finally, Consten as part of the overall arrangement registered in its own name in France the Grundig trade mark "GINT" (Grundig INTernational) which all Grundig products carried. The Commission condemned the whole arrangement between Grundig and Consten as being contrary to Article 85.1. On appeal, the European Court pointed out that the Commission's decision did not hold that the Grundig undertaking not to make direct deliveries to France except to Consten infringed 85.1. The Court added:

> "The automatic annulment decreed by Article 85 (2) applies only to those elements of the agreement which are hit by the prohibition, or to the agreement as a whole if those elements do not appear severable from the agreement itself."

Consequently, the Commission's decision was annulled in so far as it extended the nullity of 85.2 to clauses of the agreement which the Commission had not shown to be contrary to 85.1.

### Meaning of "void"

3—53    As has been seen from the *"Yoga"* case, an agreement, or a provision in an agreement, which is void under Article 85.2 is not enforceable in the courts. It might be though that an agreement which is "void" would be one which had no effect. Thus, if money had been paid over under a "void" agreement, it might be thought that, as the agreement was a nullity, the recipient would have no title to the money and that the money could be recovered from him, by action in the courts. It is unlikely that this is so. For example, the legal systems based upon Common Law have long recognised the doctrine of "restraint of trade" — a covenant in restraint of trade is void. Thus, if an employee agrees not to compete with his employer after the end of his employment and the restraint imposed upon the ex-employee is wider than is reasonable in the circumstances, the covenant will not be enforceable against him, but any money paid to him in respect of the covenant will not be recoverable. Similarly, under English law, gaming and wagering contracts were made void by statute. This would suggest that, if A and B made a wager under which A undertook to pay B £1,000 if a certain horse won the Derby, and the horse won and A paid the money, then A would be able to recover the money because the wager was "void". But in such circumstances the law did not allow the money to be recovered once it had been paid over, although equally the law would not allow A to be sued for the money if he did not pay.

3—54 It would seem prudent to regard the word "void" in Article 85.2 as meaning "unenforceable at law". This has important consequences. If money is paid over under a void agreement, the money cannot be recovered if the agreement cannot be enforced. Thus if a manufacturer, A, in one Member State has developed a substantial trade for his goods both in his own country and also in another Member State, and approaches a trader, B, in the latter, offering to grant B an exclusive distributorship for the goods in the second Member State, with absolute territorial protection, in return for a substantial capital payment, B would be well advised to proceed warily. If he concluded the transaction and handed over the capital payment, he might find that the distributorship was declared void and unenforceable under Article 85.2. He would not be able to get his money back, he would not be able to stop imports of the goods, and he might not be able to force A to continue to supply him. The moral is — do not part with your money if there is any possibility of the agreement infringing 85.1 and being void under 85.2, without first obtaining negative clearance or exemption.

### Private suit

3—55 The *Béguelin* and similar cases illustrate the value of Article 85, paragraphs 1 and 2, as a defence, as a shield. Someone is sued for breach of an agreement, or for infringing a right conferred by an agreement. He replies that the agreement is prohibited by 85.1 and therefore void under 85.2, so that the agreement is unenforceable or confers no rights.

3—56 This prompts the question — can Article 85, paragraphs 1 and 2, be used as a sword, as well? If somebody has suffered loss as the result of the operations of a cartel, can he sue for damages where the cartel infringes 85.1? In other words, does the prohibition in 85.1 allow a private person, as well as the relevant cartel authority, to bring an action, a private suit against the cartel members for damages caused to that person by the cartel? This question was studied by a group of European professors, at the request of the Commission, and their report was published in 1966.[4] They came to the conclusion that whether or not private suit would be possible depended upon the national law in the particular Member State. Broadly speaking, private suits would be possible in Belgium, Luxembourg, France, and Italy. As regards Germany and Holland, it was thought that private individuals might be able to recover damages. A definitive answer cannot be given for any country until the issue has been settled by the courts.

3—57 The position in the United Kingdom seems quite clear. Private suit was not possible under the Common Law in respect of a registrable agreement which had not been registered under the Restrictive Trade Practices Act, 1956. The right to sue in respect of such agreements had to be given by statute, and was introduced by section 7 of the 1968 Act. That section made it unlawful for any person carrying on business in the United Kingdom to enforce a registrable agreement which had not been registered, and gave a right of action to any other person suffering loss as a result of enforcement of such an unlawful agreement. As no right to sue has been given in respect of infringement of Article 85.1, it seems clear that private suit is not possible in the United Kingdom for such infringements.

## 4. Article 85 Paragraph 3

3—58 The power to grant exemption from the prohibition in 85.1 is contained in paragraph 3 of Article 85:

"3. The provisions of paragraph 1 may, however, be declared inapplicable in the case of:

—any agreement or category of agreements between undertakings;

—any decision or category of decisions by associations of undertakings;

—any concerted practice or category of concerted practices;

which contributes to improving the production or distribution of goods or to promoting technical or economic progress, while allowing consumers a fair share of the resulting benefit, and which does not:

(a) impose on the undertakings concerned restrictions which are not indispensable to the attainment of these objectives;

(b) afford such undertakings the possibility of eliminating competition in respect of a substantial part of the products in question." (17-09)

This power can now be exercised only by the Commission, subject to appeal to the European Court — Regulation 17, Article 9 (17-10).

3—59 Four requirements must be satisfied for paragraph 3 to apply:

(i) The agreement, etc., must contribute:

either (a) to the improvement of *production* of goods;

[4] European Economic Community. Série Concurrence 1. *La Réparation des Conséquences Dommageables d'une Violation des Articles 85 et 86 du Traité Instituant la C.E.F.* Brussels, 1966.

or (b) to the improvement of *distribution* of goods;

or (c) to the promotion of *technical* progress;

or (d) to the promotion of *economic* progress.

(ii) Consumers must be allowed a fair share of the resulting benefit.

(iii) The restrictions imposed on the parties must not exceed whatever is necessary to achieve (i) and (ii) above.

(iv) The parties must not be able to eliminate competition in respect of a substantial part of the products.

It will be more convenient to deal separately with each of these requirements, and also to discuss separately each of the four possible grounds into which requirement (i) subdivides.

### Improving the Production or Distribution of Goods or Promoting Technical or Economic Progress
*Improving the production of goods*

3–60    The first possible ground under requirement (i) is "contribution to improving the production of goods". Because it is restricted to goods, this would seem to discriminate against service industries. It may be that the draftsmen of the Treaty did not consider that services are "produced". In any event, the phrase "promoting technical or economic progress" is sufficiently wide to include anything which might improve the production (or distribution) of services.

3–61    Contribution to improving the production of goods has been a ground for exemption in a number of cases. For example, in the A.C.E.C./ Berliet agreement, A.C.E.C. had developed an electrical transmission system for buses and commercial vehicles; the engine was used to generate electricity which in turn drove electric motors incorporated in the wheels. Under the agreement, A.C.E.C. (a Belgian concern) was to concentrate upon development of the transmission system, and Berliet (a French concern) would develop the rest of the vehicle. If the development collaboration led to commercial production, A.C.E.C. would supply the transmissions only to Berliet in France, and only to one manufacturer in each of the other Member States (except Belgium, where A.C.E.C. would be under no restriction). Berliet would buy transmissions only from A.C.E.C. Each partner would hold any patent rights, etc., in its own particular field of development. Clearly, the agreement would limit competition between bus manufacturers, but the Commission was satisfied that it would contribute to improving production (and also technical progress). The other requirements were also satisfied, and exemption was granted until July, 1973. Other agreements in which improving the production of goods was a ground for exemption were those in the *Fabrique Nationale* and *MAN/SAVIEM* cases.

63

### Improving the distribution of goods

3—62    The second possible ground under requirement (i) is also restricted to goods, "contribution to improving the distribution of goods". Again, it is unlikely that this restriction will operate to the disadvantage of service industries because of the width of the remaining grounds under requirement (i), "promoting technical or economic progress".

3—63    In the *Blondel* case, a Dutch manufacturer of enamelled household articles had given Blondel the exclusive right to distribute the goods in France, undertaking to forward to Blondel any orders from France which it received direct. Blondel bought and sold the goods on its own account, and fixed its own prices. Blondel was not forbidden to export the goods. Blondel serviced the guarantee on the goods, and in some cases the goods were made specially to meet French habits, at Blondel's request. The Commission concluded that the agreement enabled the manufacturer to adapt more easily to the French market, and obviated the need for a more complex distribution system with contacts with a large number of traders. It therefore resulted in improvements in distribution, and exemption was granted.

3—64    A similar situation obtained in the *Jallatte* case, in which Jallatte, a French manufacturer of safety shoes, gave exclusive distribution rights for Germany to a German firm, and for Belgium to a Belgian firm. The Commission held that the agreements resulted in improvements in distribution, and granted exemption.

3—65    A different situation obtained in the *Transocean* case. Eighteen medium-sized paint manufacturers in eighteen different countries were grouped in the Association to manufacture certain marine paints (i.e. paints for ships' hulls, superstructures and interiors) to identical formulations, to distribute them under the same trade mark, and to provide a world-wide sales network. There was a complicated agreement, according to each member a "granted territory" (i.e. its own country). If a member received an order for Transocean paint from another member's territory, he could fulfil the order, but had to pay a commission to the other member; if the order were for other paints, he could fulfil the order only if the other member agreed (agreement would normally be given) and paid a commission. The members could not market a paint similar to a Transocean paint under their own trade marks, but could market paints of a higher or lower quality. The members had to accept quality controls, to exchange and keep secret technical and commercial information, and to give preference to other members in granting patent licences. The Commission granted exemption until December, 1972, after the agreement had been amended to exclude certain objectionable features, on the ground that the agreement contributed to the distribution of the Transocean types of paint.

*Promoting technical progress*

3—66    The third possible ground of exemption under requirement (i) is not restricted to goods. It is contribution "to the promotion of technical progress".

3—67    This was one of the grounds accepted by the Commission in the *A.C.E.C./Berliet* case. It was one of the grounds in the *Fabrique Nationale* case, relating to an agreement between a Belgian company, Fabrique Nationale d'Armes de Guerre and a French company, Cartoucherie Francaise. The agreement concerned sporting and industrial ammunition and cartridges. The agreement provided for each party to concentrate upon certain types of cartridge or component, and not to make any other without the agreement of the other party. Each party distributed its products in the country of the other party exclusively through the latter. In third countries, the party best known there would handle the joint business. Advertising for the joint range of products was to be controlled and paid for jointly. Each party fixed freely its selling prices for its own productions and its sales of the other party's products. In addition to contributing to improvements in production and distribution, the Commission pointed to a number of factors flowing from the agreement which contributed towards the promotion of technical progress, including the standardization of dimensions and ballistic characteristics, the extension of automation following the installation of new and improved machines, and the creation of a more specialised labour force. Exemption was granted until March, 1978.

*Promoting economic progress*

3—68    The fourth and last possible ground under requirement (i) also relates to services as well as goods — contribution to "the promotion of economic progress".

3—69    This ground is illustrated by two cases which were concerned with services, i.e. with the organization of exhibitions. In the *CECIMO* case, an organization of European national associations of machine-tool manufacturers held a trade fair every other year. Each manufacturer member was free to decide whether to take part or not in one of the organization's trade fairs, but if he did not he was forbidden to take part in any other trade fair during that year in any country which was a member of CECIMO. In intermediate years, manufacturers could exhibit wherever they wished. The Commission held that the agreement involved a restriction upon competition in the supply of services (organising trade fairs). However, the agreement rationalized participation in fairs and exhibitions, and therefore promoted economic progress. Exemption was granted until December, 1978, one of the conditions being that CECIMO would report to the Commission any cases where admission to one of its fairs was refused.

3—70    A similar situation obtained in the *CEMATEX* case, an international organization of national associations of textile machinery manufacturers. Exhibitions of textile machinery were held every four years, exhibitors being prohibited from taking part in other exhibitions in the year in which a CEMATEX exhibition was held and in the preceding and succeeding years. In addition, there was a recommendation, which was generally followed, that exhibitors should not participate in other exhibitions in the fourth year. These arrangements were altered to apply only to the exhibition year itself and the preceding year. The CEMATEX arrangements brought almost the entire supply of textile machinery together for comparison, and reduced expenses by reducing in two years out of four the costs borne by exhibitors and visitors. They, therefore, contributed to the promotion of economic progress (and to the improvement of the distribution of goods), and exemption was granted until November, 1982, subject to CEMATEX informing the Commission immediately of any refusal of admission to an exhibition.

### Fair Share for Consumers

3—71    The second requirement for the application of paragraph 3 of Article 85 is that consumers must be allowed "a fair share of the resulting benefit". In the *Blondel* case, the Commission found this requirement had been satisfied in that Blondel had lowered prices. By contrast, in the *Grundig/Consten* case, the Commission found that the price of Grundig products in France was higher than in Germany, even allowing for tax differences, showing that there was no benefit to consumers.

3—72    In English, the word "consumers" may have an implication of the user in the sense of the "ultimate consumer". This cannot be the meaning here, because otherwise, in the case of one group of manufacturers supplying other manufacturers further down the economic chain, it would be necessary to trace the product down through the varying stages to see what effect, if any, was to be found upon the eventual and final user. Such considerations, and the interpretation given to the requirement in practice, point to the word "consumers" as meaning those persons to whom the goods or services in question are supplied, being persons who are not party to the relevant agreement, decision or concerted practice. This, in the *Sopelem/Langen* case, the words used in the French texts are "acheteurs" (buyers) and "utilisateurs" (users) — "utilisateurs" is used also in the *MAN/SAVIEM* text.

3—73    In the *Blondel* and *Grundig/Consten* cases, the Commission was able to adopt a *quantitative* approach. In the *Blondel* case, prices had been lowered. In the *Grundig/Consten* case, prices were at least 23% higher in France than in Germany.

This is not always possible, and the Commission seems to be prepared to adopt a *qualitative* approach where necessary. In the *Sopelem/Langen* case, the agreement provided for one French and one German concern engaged in the manufacture of automation equipment each to specialise on complementary parts of the range, and for each to supply the other in what was in fact reciprocal exclusive supply. So far as concerned the question of allowing a fair share to the consumers, the Commission argued that the pressure of competition from other Common Market manufacturers and from imports would prevent Sopelem and Langen from keeping to themselves the cost economies resulting from the agreement; the economies would reach buyers. In addition, the agreement had produced an increase in the parties' sales, and an improvement in the quality of the products and services offered. On this basis, the Commission was satisfied that the requirement was met.

3—74    The MAN/SAVIEM agreement was also concerned with specialization and mutual supply, between one German and one French manufacturer of commercial vehicles. The Commission held that the agreement would improve production and distribution of the goods in question. In addition, there would be sufficient pressure from competitors to ensure to users a share in any benefits, and the users would be able to draw on a complete common range of vehicles from both parties together with a sales and after-sales service in the whole of the Common Market and interchangeable spare parts.

## No Indispensable Restrictions

3—75    Requirement (iii) for the application of paragraph 3 of Article 85 is that the restrictions imposed upon the parties to the agreement, decision, or concerted practice should not exceed the minimum necessary to secure the achievement of requirements (i) and (ii). It is impossible to discuss this in general, but only in connection with particular situations — the restrictions permissible must depend upon what the agreement, etc., is designed to achieve.

3—76    In the *Grundig/Consten* case, the Commission's main reason for rejecting the request for exemption was that the restrictions exceeded what was necessary to achieve an improvement in production and distribution. The main restriction lay in the absolute territorial protection given to Consten in France. The agreement and arrangements between Grundig and Consten sought to prevent "parallel imports" from other countries into France — "parallel imports" are those made by other traders independently of the concessionaire, so that the imports by the concessionaire and independent traders go on side by side with each other, i.e. they "parallel" each other. The Commission pointed out that absolute territorial protection would not be necessary for Consten to develop the French market if Consten worked to the same profit margins as distributors in other countries — there would then be no scope for parallel imports. To meet arguments for the protection based upon Consten's need to forecast the market for the goods, and upon the guarantee and after-sales service obligations, the Commission pointed to Germany where Grundig's distributors did not have territorial protection but seemed to be able to make reliable forecasts — the continuity of business relations between the parallel importers and their suppliers would permit the latter to make reasonably accurate forecasts. As to the guarantee service, the purchaser can normally only enforce the guarantee against his supplier. And as to after-sales service, this is usually charged for, so that no problem would arise.

### No Elimination of Competition

3—77    Finally, the fourth requirement for exemption under Article 85.3 is that the agreement, etc., should not permit to the parties the possibility of eliminating competition in respect of a substantial part of the products in question. In the *Van Katwijk* case, the main Dutch producer of cardboard tubes for the textile industry was forbidden by the agreement to export to Belgium, and the main Belgian producer could not export to Holland more than 20% of the Dutch requirements. The Commission rejected the application for exemption upon the ground, *inter alia*, of the complete elimination of Van Katwijk from the Belgian market.

3—78    In the *CEMATEX* case, exhibitors at the four-yearly exhibitions were required not to exhibit at other fairs or exhibitions in CEMATEX countries during the year of the exhibition and also during the preceding and succeeding years — in addition there was the recommendation to CEMATEX exhibitors not to take part in such other exhibitions during 1969, which should have been a "free" year between the CEMATEX exhibitions in 1967 and 1971. Because the CEMATEX members and exhibitors included the major textile-machinery manufacturers, and because the obligation and the recommendation not to take part in other exhibitions were complied with by practically all concerned, the Commission felt that there was too great a restriction of competition between the organizers of fairs and exhibitions. At the Commission's instigation, CEMATEX amended its rules to make the prohibition on participation in other exhibitions apply only during the CEMATEX exhibition year and the preceding year (so leaving two "free" years in each four), and also abandoned as regards the future the recommendation made in 1968. These changes meant that competition was no longer eliminated, and exemption could be given.

### Individual Exemptions

3—79    The Commission has granted exemption in a variety of individual cases, in some instances after the parties have amended their arrangements to meet criticisms, as in the *CEMATEX* case. The parties were allowed to make amendments in many other cases, such as *Cobelaz* and *C.F.A.* in which the arrangements were altered so that the joint selling offices covered only the home market and exports outside the E.E.C., and not trade with Member States.

3—80    In no case, however, has exemption been granted to arrangements for market sharing or for fixing prices or quotas. The Commission has expressed the view, in its first report on competition policy, that market sharing is unlikely to be granted exemption, nor is protection accorded to home markets. The Commission also indicated that there is little chance of exemption for collective action by firms in one Member State which establishes uniform selling conditions and prices for goods of which a substantial amount is drawn from other Member States.

This comment arose out of the *V.C.H.* case, an association of Dutch cement distributors and manufacturers. There was a reciprocal exclusive dealing arrangement between V.C.H. members and a cartel of Dutch, Belgian and German cement manufacturers. V.C.H. fixed the prices and selling terms for deliveries below 100 tons and recommended prices for larger deliveries. The members largely followed the recommended prices. The agreement was condemned under Article 85.1 and exemption refused. The parties were required to terminate immediately the forbidden activities. This is the usual practice where an agreement, etc., has been held to come within Article 85.1 and exemption has been refused.

3—81    Where exemption is granted, the Commission is required by Article 6 of Regulation 17 (18-07) to specify the date from which the exemption takes effect, and by Article 8 the period for which it is to run. In practice, the Commission specifies the date up to which the exemption runs. Extension can be obtained on application if the requirements of Article 85.3 continue to be satisfied (Regulation 17, Article 8).

3—82    The exemption can be made subject to conditions or obligations (Regulation 17, Article 8). For example, in the *CECIMO* and *CEMATEX* cases, a condition of the exemption was that the Commission should be informed immediately if an applicant were refused permission to participate in an exhibition. In the *Fabrique Nationale* case, the parties were required to submit reports every two years of their specialization measures, the development of their selling prices and discounts, and their market shares in each Member State. The parties in the *MAN/SAVIEM* case were required to make regular reports every three years, and also to advise the Commission of any agreements between them and other vehicle manufacturers affecting competition.

3—83    An exemption may be revoked or amended in the event of breach of a condition or obligation attached to it, and also if there is a fundamental change in the situation, if the exemption was obtained wrongfully, or if it is abused (Regulation 17, Article 8 — 18-09).

### "Bloc" Exemptions

3—84    Paragraph 3 of Article 85 spells out very clearly and unambiguously that exemption is available not only for *individual* agreements, decisions and concerted practices, but also for any "category of agreements", any "category of decisions" and any "category of concerted practices". This power to grant exemption to categories of agreements, etc., has led to what are known as "bloc" exemptions.

3—85    The Council has so far made two Regulations dealing with "bloc" exemption, Regulation 19/65 (Appendix F) and Regulation 2821/71 (Appendix K). These do not grant "bloc" exemptions themselves. They confer on the Commission power to make exempting regulations in respect of five categories of agreements, etc.:

*Regulation 19/65*

(i)     two-party exclusive-distributor agreements and concerted practices;

(ii)    two-party agreements and concerted practices relating to intellectual property rights;

*Regulation 2821/71*

(iii)   agreements, etc., to apply standards and patterns;

(iv)    agreements, etc., for research and development;

(v)     agreements, etc., for specialization.

Each of these categories is discussed in more detail later, in the Chapter dealing with the particular type of agreement.

3—86    The need for action in respect of exclusive-distributor agreements is shown by the fact that by March, 1965, when Regulation 19/65 was made, over 37,000 agreements had been notified to the Commission, of which about one-third related to this type of agreement. Consequently, the first, and so far the only, "bloc" exemption to be granted is in respect of two-party exclusive-distributor agreements and concerted practices, granted by Regulation 67/67 (Appendix G). This Regulation is dealt with in Chapter 6, Distribution Agreements.

3—87    It is believed that the Commission will make towards the end of 1972 or in early 1973 a further regulation granting "bloc" exemption in respect of the second category of agreements and concerted practices covered by Regulation 19/65, i.e. intellectual property agreements.

## 5. Conflict of laws

3—88    This is a convenient stage at which to deal with an important point — conflict of laws — although its full significance will not appear until later (4-35 — 4-40).

3—89    If A fires a gun and kills B, provided they are both in the same country, i.e. within the same jurisdiction, the law of that country will decide whether A has committed murder, or manslaughter, or has been innocent of any crime. But if A happens to be in country X and B happens to be in country Y, i.e. the bullet from A's gun has crossed the national frontiers of X and Y, what then? The finger which pulled the trigger is subject to the laws of country X, but the bullet hits its target, and causes its fatal consequences, within the jurisdiction of country Y and subject to Y's laws. In the case of murder, the legal systems of most countries will be reasonably similar. But what if B happened to be Public Enemy No.1 in country X, where all loyal subjects were in duty bound to achieve his destruction by any means, whereas in country Y he was a normal law-abiding person, entitled to the full protection of that country's laws? It would then be an instance of "conflict of laws" — where a particular action or actions fall to be judged by two different legal systems with different, and conflicting, results.

3—90 In the field of competition law, there are two broad, distinct, principles. On the one hand, there is the "territorial" principle, which is the one applied in the United Kingdom — the penal laws of a country do not extend beyond its own boundaries (except as regards its own subjects). On this principle, the legality or otherwise of, say, an agreement between enterprises which restricts competition is to be judged either by the law of the place where the agreement was made or by the law of the country to which the parties belong. For example, assume four companies all registered and carrying on business in, say, Italy (which has no national competition law at present) make an agreement as to the prices they will charge for their goods in the United Kingdom. And assume that none of the four carries on business in the United Kingdom, except that each has a representative who merely acts as a post office between his Italian principal and the customer. In such circumstances, the agreement between the four Italian companies would not, in the eyes of United Kingdom law, be subject to United Kingdom law, i.e. to registration and investigation under the Restrictive Trade Practices Acts, because the actions in question would not have taken place in the United Kingdom and the companies would not be United Kingdom subjects.

3—91 The second principle is the "effects" principle. According to this principle, the law of the country in which the effects of an action are felt can apply to decide the legality or otherwise of that action. The Commission sought to apply this principle in its decision in the *Aniline Dyes* case in which four of the alleged parties belonged to non-Member States (I.C.I. in the United Kingdom, and Ciba, Geigy, and Sandoz in Switzerland). The Commission said:

> "This decision is applicable to all the undertakings which took part in the concerted practices, whether they are established within or outside the Common Market. ... The competition rules of the Treaty are, consequently, applicable to all restrictions of competition which produce within the Common Market effects set out in Article 85(1). There is therefore no need to examine whether the undertakings which are the cause of these restrictions of competition have their seat within or outside the Community."

and sought to impose fines of 50,000 units of account on each of the four non-E.E.C companies.

3—92 Thus, the Commission's view is quite clear. If the effects of an agreement, decision, or concerted practice satisfy the requirements of Article 85.1, (and therefore restrict competition within the Common Market and affect inter-Member trade, both to an appreciable extent),

71

that agreement, etc., is governed by 85.1 even though the parties are resident in non-E.E.C. countries. In the Commission's view, an agreement between a Danish, an Irish, and a British company, fixing the prices at which they would sell within the E.E.C., would be subject to Article 85.1 if the effect upon competition and inter-Member trade were appreciable.

3—93   The United Kingdom does not accept the "effects" principle, as made clear in the Aide Mémoire submitted to the Commission by the United Kingdom Government in connection with the *Aniline Dyes* case (Appendix M).

3—94   The companies in that case appealed against the Commission's decision. I.C.I. argued that the Commission had no jurisdiction over it, as it was not established within the Common Market and had committed no acts there. If the Court had upheld I.C.I.'s argument, it would have ruled against the "effects" doctrine. However, the Court took a different route. It held that the actions of subsidiaries controlled by a parent, and so lacking autonomy, could be imputed to the parent. On that basis, the acts of I.C.I.'s subsidiaries in the Common Market could be imputed to I.C.I., so that that company could be deemed to have committed acts within the E.E.C. and so came within the Commission's jurisdiction. In effect, therefore, the Court has left undecided the question whether the "effects" principle or the "territorial" principle is the law of the E.E.C.

# CHAPTER 4

# Cartels and Concerted Practices (contd) — Regulation 17

## 1. Introduction

4—01 Article 87 of the Treaty required the Council to introduce the necessary regulations to give effect to the principles set out in Article 85. If the Council could not achieve a unanimous decision within three years of the Rome Treaty coming into, force, Article 87 allowed the regulations to be adopted by a qualified majority, i.e. unanimity was no longer required. The three years expired on the 31st December, 1961. Regulation 17 of 1962, the first regulation implementing Article 85, was made on the 6th February, 1962, and came into force on 13th March, 1962.

4—02 Unlike Article 85, which is short and simple, Regulation 17 is a long, complicated, document. Its logic does not flow from one provision to the next. On the contrary, considerable back-tracking — and forward-tracking — is necessary to unravel its contents. For these reasons, Regulation 17 does not lend itself to straightforward explanation, taking the provisions in order as they appear. The best approach is to take first the main subjects with which it deals — termination of infringements of 85.1, negative clearance, and exemptions — and to trace them each through their various stages. And then to deal with subsidiary aspects of general application.

4—03 Before doing so, it will help to dispose of three verbal points. Regulation 17 uses certain words in reference to particular situations.

The word "application" is used in two senses. First, it is used in relation to a request for "negative clearance" — Article 2 (18-03). Its second use is in relation to approaches by Member States or interested persons to the Commission asking it to investigate infringements of Article 85.1 — Article 3 (18-04).

Where exemption is sought under Article 85.3, the procedure is by "notification". An agreement which has been "notified" is one which has been submitted formally to the Commission for exemption.

The technical use of these two expressions is brought out in Article

24 which refers to "applications pursuant to Articles 2 and 3, and . . . notification pursuant to Articles 4 and 5" (18-25).

The third word with a technical meaning in the Regulation is "decision". It is not a synonym for a mental process, a resolution, a determination. It is a formal step necessary to achieve certain results and demanding certain specific procedural requirements. A "decision" is necessary to require undertakings to terminate infringements of Article 85.1, to grant an exemption, to impose fines, etc. Certain prerequisites are essential before certain "decisions" can be made. For example, the Advisory Committee must be consulted before a decision is taken as to an infringement, a negative clearance, an exemption, or the imposition of fines, and the parties concerned must be heard; and decisions relating to a negative clearance, termination of infringements, and exemptions must be published.

4−04    The basic provision of Regulation 17 is Article 1. Subject to certain exceptions, all agreements, decisions, and concerted practices which infringe Article 85.1 are automatically prohibited. Nothing further is required − no investigation of the case, no declaration by an authority. Since the 13th March, 1962, when Regulation 17 came into force in the present six Member States, the provisions of any agreement, etc., falling within Article 85.1 and not coming within one of the exceptions to Article 1 of the Regulation or within the bloc exemption granted by Regulation 67/67, have been prohibited under 85.1 and null and void under 85.2. If the void provisions form the essence of the agreement or cannot be severed from the remainder of it, the whole agreement is null and void. The courts of the Member States have to give effect to that nullity. They cannot enforce the void provisions or a void agreement.

4−05    The four applicant countries, Denmark, Ireland, Norway, and the United Kingdom, signed the Treaty of Accession in Brussels on the 22nd January, 1972. The Treaty will come into force on the 1st January, 1973, in respect of each of the parties who has ratified it by 31st December, 1972. Norway is not proceeding with its application to join the E.E.C. so that Denmark, Ireland, and the United Kingdom will constitute the "new Member States" and will become members of the E.E.C. (and also of the Coal and Steel Community and of Euratom) as from the 1st January, 1973. By virtue of the Act annexed to the Treaty:

> *"Article 2*
>
> From the date of accession, the provisions of the original Treaties and the acts adopted by the institutions of the Communities shall be binding on the new Member States and shall apply in those States under the conditions laid down in those Treaties and in this Act."

The Act includes a number of amendments to Regulations 17/62, 19/65, and 67/67, which have been incorporated in the texts in Appendices B, F, and G. Consequently, and assuming ratification by them by the 31st December, 1972, Article 85 and Regulation 17, together with the other relevant Regulations and Notices, will apply in Denmark, Ireland and the United Kingdom as from 1st January, 1973. Agreements, decisions, and concerted practices in those countries which infringe Article 85.1 will be null and void from that date, unless they come within any of the exceptions referred to in Article 1 of Regulation 17 or within the bloc exemption in Regulation 67/67.

4—06    With that introduction, it is now possible to turn to the four main facets of Regulation 17 — termination of infringements of Article 85.1, negative clearance, notification for exemption, and relief from the obligation to notify — and then to deal with its ancillary provisions.

## 2. Termination of Infringements

4—07    The Commission is the main instrument for ensuring that Article 85.1 is complied with. Article 89 of the Treaty (17-13), lays on the Commission the duty of enforcing Article 85 (and Article 86), and requires it to investigate suspected infringements, either on its own initiative or upon application by a Member State. The relevant authorities in Member States are also empowered to apply Article 85.1, but only so long as the Commission has not initiated action (Article 9.3 — 18-10). Once the Commission has started action, it takes over responsibility (although action by the national authority can continue if there is an infringement of national law as well — the two proceedings can continue side by side, as decided in the *Wilhelm* case, i.e. there can be "double jeopardy").

4—08    When instituting an investigation into suspected infringements of Article 85.1, the Commission can act upon its own initiative (Article 3.1 — 18-04). For example, the investigations into the flat glass and quinine cases were undertaken on the Commission's initiative.

4—09    To help it, the Commission has power to carry out "sector inquiries". Under Article 12, the Commission can carry out an inquiry into a particular sector of the economy if it appears that competition is being restricted or distorted within that sector in the Common Market, in the light of such factors as price movements or the inflexibility of prices, the trend of trade between Member States, and so on. Article 12 gives the Commission power to utilise in its sector inquiries its powers to request information from the undertakings concerned (under Article 11), to enter their premises and carry out investigations on the spot (under Article 14), and to seek the assistance of the competent national authorities (under Article 13), with the possibility of substantial fines upon the undertakings for failure to comply. The Advisory Committee set up under Article 10 (18-11) must also be consulted (Article 12.4 — 18-13). The Commission started its first sector inquiry, after consulting the Advisory Committee, in June, 1965, into the margarine industry — despite differences of prices in the various Member States, the inter-Member trade in margarine did not seem to be expanding as fast as inter-Member trade in other sectors. The inquiry was completed in 1970. It showed that differences in legislation between the Members had had an adverse effect on Community trade. The Commission has also instituted a sector inquiry into the brewery trade.

4—10    The Commission can also act upon application received from a Member State or persons (including companies and corporations) who can show a legitimate interest in the case (Article 3.2). The investigation into the Aniline Dyes cartel followed information supplied to the Commission by trade bodies in the leather, textile, and other industries.

In cases where the Commission has received an application from a Member State or an interested person to investigate a suspected infringement of Article 85.1, the Commission must send copies to the relevant authority in each Member State (Article 10.1 — 18-11).

4—11    Having initiated the investigation into a suspected infringement, the Commission has extensive powers to enable it to pursue its inquiries. Under Article 11, it can seek information from the governments of Member States and their authorities, and also from undertakings and associations of undertakings. If any undertaking or association fails to supply the information, the Commission can require the information by decision, with penalties for failure to comply — the procedure is discussed more fully in paragraphs 4-58 — 4-66 below. Under Article 14, the Commission can send its authorised officials to enter the premises of an undertaking, examine its books and business records, take copies, and ask for oral explanations, again with the possibility of penalties for failure to comply (4-67 — 4-71) below. If it wishes, the Commission can ask the competent authorities in the Member State to carry out these investigations on its behalf, under Article 13 (4-72 below).

4—12    Having carried out its inquiry and established the facts, the Commission is not bound to take formal steps to close the case. It can, if it considers that to be the most appropriate course, make recommendations to the undertakings or associations involved, with a view to bringing the infringement to an end (Article 3.3). Such a course would seem appropriate where the infringement is of a technical nature, or there is genuine room for doubt as to whether there is an infringement or not, or where the infringement is innocent. It would seem that a considerable number of cases have been disposed of informally in this way.

There are many advantages, from the point of view of the undertakings concerned, in this informal procedure. For example, there is no question of a fine (unless the parties fail to comply with the recommendation). There is no publicity, whereas if the Commission takes a formal decision on an infringement, the decision must be published (Article 21 — 18-22).

4—13    In some cases, the Commission may not consider the informal procedure appropriate. The parties may have committed the breaches of Article 85.1 quite deliberately, in the full knowledge of what they were doing. This was the situation found by the Commission in the *Quinine* case — in the words of the decision, "From 1961 the members of the cartel were aware of the fact that the whole of the agreements were as illegal as it was possible to be." Or the parties might not be prepared to follow recommendations given by the Commission.

Whatever the reason, the Commission is empowered by Article 3.1 to take a decision requiring the parties to terminate the infringement. Before taking such a step, the Commission must, under Article 19 (18-20), hear the parties and also, if necessary, any third parties with a legitimate interest — see paragraph 4-81 below. The Advisory Committee must be consulted before the decision is taken (Article 10.3 — see 4-98 below). And when the decision has been taken, the names of the parties and the main contents must be published, but safeguarding the legitimate business secrets of the parties. The Commission's practice seems to be to publish the decision in full, leaving blanks where confidential business information is suppressed.

A decision may impose upon the parties the fines provided for in Article 15.2 (18-16). These can go up to a maximum of one million units of account or 10% of the undertaking's turnover in the preceding financial year, whichever is the higher — see paragraphs 4-83 – 4-92 below.

### 3. Negative Clearance

4—14 Bearing in mind the serious consequences which can flow from infringement of Article 85.1, Regulation 17 provides a most useful procedure whereby the parties to an agreement, etc., can seek "negative clearance" for it, i.e. a declaration that it does not come within the scope of, and consequently does not infringe, Article 85.1. It might be thought that the parties would always know whether their activities were in breach of 85.1 or not, but this is not necessarily so. To constitute a breach of 85.1 there must be an appreciable effect upon competition and an appreciable effect upon trade between Member States. Except in the clearest possible case, within the limits set out in the Commission's "Notice Concerning Minor Agreements" (Appendix J) or in Regulation 2822/71 (Appendix L), it would be unwise for the parties themselves to decide that any effect was not appreciable — they would be acting as judge in their own cause. Wherever there is any doubt whatsoever, those concerned would be well advised to seek negative clearance.

### *"Bloc" Negative Clearance*

4—15 To provide some guidance to businessmen and their advisers, the Commission has issued four very helpful Notices describing types of agreements, etc., which in the Commission's view do not infringe Article 85.1. On analogy with the category exemption under Article

85.3, it is convenient to refer to the types of agreements covered by the Notices as "bloc" negative clearances. (This term is not strictly correct. The Notices merely set out the Commission's views and do not bind other bodies, such as the courts or competent authorities in Member States — see, for example, 18-08 and 23-10.)

The four Notices deal with:

(i) *Sole Agency Contracts with Trade Representatives (Appendix C)*

This Notice was published on the 24th December, 1962, and distinguishes between the "trade representative" who transacts business on behalf of his principal, and the "independent trader" who buys and sells on his own behalf. Sole agency contracts with trade representatives do not fall within 85.1 — those with independent traders may do so. The Notice is discussed more fully in Chapter 5, Distribution Agreements.

(ii) *Patent Licences (Appendix D)*

This Notice was also published on the 24th December, 1962. It specifies nine types of clauses in patent licence agreements which the Commission considers do not come within 85.1. It is discussed in Chapter 7, Intellectual Property.

(iii) *Co-operation between Enterprises (Appendix H)*

This, perhaps the most extensive of the Notices, was published on the 23rd July, 1968. It describes some seventeen types of agreements which the Commission considers do not restrict competition. The various agreements are considered in detail in Chapters 8 to 13, and cover:—

Joint procurement or exchange of information.

Co-operation on financial and fiscal matters.

Joint research and development.

Joint use of production, storage and transport.

Joint execution of orders.

Joint selling and after-sales service.

Joint advertising.

Joint quality marks.

(iv) *Minor Agreements (Appendix J)*

This Notice, dated 27th May, 1970, as described in paragraph 3-26, gives quantitative limits below which there is deemed to be no "appreciable effect" on competition and trade, i.e. 5% of the volume of business in the part of the Common Market where the agreement operates, and an annual turnover of the parties not exceeding fifteen million units of account (twenty million in the case of commercial undertakings).

Agreements coming within any of the categories described in the Notices need not be made the subject of an application for negative clearance.

### Individual Negative Clearance

4—16    If an agreement, etc., does not fall within any of the "bloc" negative clearances, and there is doubt as to whether it infringes Article 85.1 or not, the parties should apply for individual negative clearance. In theory, the relevant authorities in each Member State are competent to pronounce upon the application or not of 85.1 to an agreement, etc., so long as the Commission is not seized of the issue (Article 9.3 — 18-10). In practice, however, applications for negative clearance will be made to the Commission, under Article 2.

4—17    In litigation over an agreement, the national courts are competent to declare whether or not the agreement is within 85.1 and void under 85.2.

4—18    Originally, an application for negative clearance had to be on Form A, Form B being for notifications for exemption. In practice, the parties preferred to put in a compound request — an application for negative clearance and a notification for exemption — in the event of negative clearance being refused, the notification for exemption would procure temporary validity even if exemption were eventually refused as well. By Regulation 1133/68, the Commission introduced a joint form, Form A/B — see Appendix I.

     Fines can be imposed under Article 15.1 (a) if incorrect or misleading information is given in an application.

4—19    Copies of applications for negative clearance must be sent by the Commission to the competent authorities of Member States — Article 10.1.

4—20    The Commission is able to exercise, in relation to such applications, its right to obtain information from governments and authorities in Member States and from undertakings, under Article 11 (see 4-56 — 4-66 below), and its powers of investigation at business premises either directly through its own officials under Article 14 (see 4-67 — 4-80 below) or indirectly through the competent authorities of Member States, Article 13 (4-72 below).

4—21    Before taking a decision on an application, the Commission is required by Article 19 to give the parties and third parties an opportunity to be heard, and to publish a summary of the application (4-81 below). The Advisory Committee must also be consulted, as required by Article 10 (4-98 below).

4—22    Finally, the decision when taken must be published, suppressing any legitimate business secrets — Article 21.

## 4. Notification for individual exemption

4—23    If an agreement, etc., does not qualify for negative clearance, it must be within Article 85.1. In that event, the prohibition in 85.1 will apply to it, unless it qualifies for some form of exemption.

To obtain exemption, an agreement, etc., must have been notified to the Commission, unless it comes within a "bloc" exemption or within one of the categories relieved from the obligation to notify. "Bloc" exemption has already been discussed in paragraphs 3-84 — 3-87, and relief from the obligation to notify is dealt with in the following section of this Chapter. This section deals with notification to obtain individual exemption.

4—24     Prior to Regulation 17, the competent national authorities in Member States could grant exemptions, but any so granted expired at the latest on 12th March, 1965, by virtue of Article 23. As from the 13th March, 1962, the Commission has been, and remains, the only body competent to grant individual exemption under Article 85.3, by virtue of Article 9.1 (18-10).

4—25     In order to obtain individual exemption, the agreement, etc., must have been notified to the Commission. Notification used to be on Form B, but is now made on the combined form A/B which covers both notification for exemption and application for negative clearance (Appendix I). Fines can be imposed under Article 15.1 (a) for supplying incorrect or misleading information in a notification.

### Status of notified agreements, etc.

4—26     Once an agreement, etc., has been duly notified to the Commission, it is deemed to be fully valid unless and until the Commission has issued a decision to the contrary. This was decided by the European Court in the *Portelange v. Smith Corona Marchant* case. Smith Corona Marchant had made an agreement in July, 1961, with Portelange granting the latter the exclusive right to sell and distribute in Belgium and Luxembourg, Smith Corona office typewriters and Marchant calculators. The agreement was notified within the time limits specified in Regulation 17. Later, electric copying machines were added to the distributorship tacitly, without any amendment to the agreement. Smith Corona cancelled the distributorship with regard to the copying machines. Portelange sued for damages in the Belgian courts, on the ground that the cancellation infringed Belgian law. Smith Corona argued that the agreement, although notified, was invalid under Article 85.1. The Belgian courts referred the case to the European Court for a ruling upon the status of notified agreements. The European Court held that a properly notified agreement is fully valid so long as the Commission has not issued a decision to the contrary. (The Court considered that the arrangement as to the copying machines constituted a separate agreement which stood by itself, and had not been notified.)

4—27     In the case of standard-form agreements, i.e. where the same form of agreement is used by one party in its dealings with numerous others (for example, a standard agreement used by a manufacturer with his distributors), only the standard text need be notified with Form A/B. Once the standard form has been notified, the temporary validity so obtained applies to all agreements made in that form, both before notification (in the case of "existing" agreements notified in due time) and after notification. This was decided by the European Court in the *Parfums Marcel Rochas* case. The Company had a standard form of agreement with its distributors, forbidding exports and also forbidding sales to other dealers (sales could be made only to consumers). As an "existing" agreement the standard form was notified before 1st February, 1963. The Court held that agreements in the standard form but made after notification were within the temporary validity procured by notification of the standard form.

4—28 Notification confers immunity from fines in respect of anything done after notification, provided it falls within the notified activities — Article 15.5 (a). This immunity ceases if the Commission, after a preliminary examination, indicates that Article 85.1 applies and that exemption under 85.3 is not justified.

As regards pre-notification activities, Article 15.5 grants immunity from fines to "existing" agreements, etc., notified in due time. Otherwise there is no immunity from fines for pre-notification infringements of Article 85.1.

4—29 As regards immunity from private suit, the extent to which this is available depends upon whether the agreement, etc., is "existing" or "new", and is dealt with in paragraphs 4-32 and 4-43/4-44 below.

4—30 Regulation 17 distinguishes between "existing" and "new" agreements, etc., with special rules relating to the former. "Existing" agreements, etc., sub-divide into those in relation to the original six Members, and those in relation to the new Members. As regards firms in the new Members, there is one aspect of the distinction between "existing" and "new" which might be the source of some considerable difficulties. (See 4-35 — 4-40).

## "Existing" agreements, etc.
### In relation to the original Members

4—31 In relation to the original Members, "existing" agreements, etc., were those in existence when Regulation 17 came into force, i.e. on the 13th March, 1962. They had to be notified, if the parties wished to seek exemption, before the 1st November, 1962, or the 1st February, 1963, if there were only two parties (Article 5).

4—32 By notifying "existing" agreements, etc., in due time, the parties qualified for special treatment under Article 7.1. As recognized by the *Portelange* judgment, notification brings temporary validity until the Commission gives a decision that Article 85.1 applies but that exemption cannot be granted. Such a decision establishes that the particular agreement, etc., infringes 85.1 and on that basis, as the temporary validity has expired with the Commission's decision, the parties may be at risk of private suit. Article 7.1 provides a procedure for dealing with that situation in respect of "existing" agreements, etc. Provided notification was made in due time, the parties may terminate the agreement, etc., or modify it so as to make it eligible for negative clearance or exemption. In that event, the Commission has power to declare that the prohibition in 85.1 shall not apply to the agreement for such period as the Commission may specify.

4—33 The operation of Article 7.1 is illustrated by the *CEMATEX* case. CEMATEX had been notified in due time, but exemption could not be granted so long as the restrictions on CEMATEX exhibitors using other exhibitions applied not only in the CEMATEX year but also in each of the three intervening years. By the 30th November, 1970, the restrictions had been reduced so as to apply only in the CEMATEX exhibition year and the preceding year. Exemption was granted from the 30th November, 1970, onwards. And the Commission declared that the prohibition in Article 85.1 did not apply to CEMATEX in respect of the period 13th March, 1962, to 30th November, 1970.

### In relation to new Members

4—34 The Treaty of Accession added a new Article 25 to Regulation 17 (18-26). As regards "agreements, decisions and concerted practices to which Article 85 of the [Rome] Treaty applies by virtue of accession", Article 25 substitutes the date of accession, expected to be the 1st January, 1973, for the date Regulation 17 came into force, i.e. the 13th March, 1962. Consequently, for the new Members, "existing" agreements means those existing on the 1st January, 1973. To procure temporary validity, these must be notified within six months, i.e. by the 30th June, 1973. And if the parties wish to have the benefit of Article 7.1, the necessary modifications or terminations must be effected by the same date, i.e. 30th June, 1973.

### "By virtue of accession"

4—35 It is imperative to note that the new Article 25 of Regulation 17 applies only to agreements, etc., "to which Article 85 of the Treaty applies *by virtue of accession*". Those words may be of vital significance.

4—36 As already explained, in paragraph 3-92, the Commission is seeking to adopt the "effects" principle in situations where there is conflict of laws. Application of the "effects" principle would mean that agreements, decisions, and concerted practices between enterprises resident outside the E.E.C. but which have effects within the Common Market, and restrict competition there and affect inter-Member trade — in both cases to an appreciable extent — come within the prohibition of Article 85.1. Such agreements, etc., are, on the view taken by the Commission in the *Aniline Dyes* case, already forbidden by 85.1 and expose the parties to fines, even though they may be perfectly legal in the parties' own country.

Thus, if two companies registered in the United Kingdom had made an agreement in 1960 as to the prices they would charge for their exports to the six Member States, that agreement, assuming the other conditions of 85.1 were met, should — on the "effects" principle — have been notified before 1st February, 1963, if the parties had desired exemption, and otherwise should have been terminated by the 13th March, 1962, even though such an agreement would have been perfectly lawful in the United Kingdom, requiring only transmission of a copy to the Board of Trade (now Department of Trade and Industry). Failing such notification, the parties cannot now seek exemption, nor seek to escape fines imposed by the Commission by altering the agreement so as to bring it outside 85.1 or within 85.3.

Consequently, it will be seen that, on this basis, such an agreement is *not* one "to which Article 85 of the Treaty applies by virtue of accession". On the contrary, Article 85.1 is considered already to apply to it.

4—37 On this reasoning, an agreement "to which Article 85 of the Treaty applies by virtue of accession" is, for example, one between two United Kingdom companies fixing the prices at which they sell in, say, Ireland. Article 85 would then apply "by virtue of accession" because it would be the accession of Ireland to the Common Market which would make the effects of the agreement felt within the Common Market.

4—38 To sum up. On the Commission's approach, any agreement between undertakings resident in the new Member States which already, before the 1st January, 1973, affected trade between any of the six original Members and restricted competition within the Common Market — in both cases to an appreciable extent — is *not* an "existing" agreement for the purpose of Article 25 of Regulation 17, and would not qualify for the special treatment the Regulation envisages. On the contrary, it should have been notified or terminated already.

4—39 In contrast, the United Kingdom Government has rejected the "effects" principle, and adheres to the "territorial" principle (3-90) — see the Aide Mémoire submitted by the United Kingdom Government to the Commission reproduced at Appendix M. On the United Kingdom approach, an agreement between enterprises in any of the three new Member States restricting competition within the Six and affecting inter-Member trade, to an appreciable extent, is not, prior to the 1st January, 1973, subject to Article 85. Such an agreement will become subject to Article 85 "by virtue of accession", and will — on this view — be an "existing" agreement for the purposes of Article 25. The parties will *not* be liable to fines by the Commission in respect of anything done before the 1st January, 1973, and provided they notify by the 30th June, 1973, they should have all the rights to terminate or modify the agreement accorded by Article 7, without risk of fines.

4—40 This is an important issue, and could have serious consequences for enterprises involved in what may at present be perfectly lawful activities in their own countries, if the European Court upholds the Commission's view. It is regrettable that those concerned with negotiating the Treaty of Accession did not resolve the problem. There was some hope that the European Court would settle the issue in its judgment on the I.C.I. appeal in the *Aniline Dyes* case, but the Court was able to settle the questions at issue without deciding upon the "effects" doctrine. It is to be hoped that the problem is resolved before 1st January, 1973, and any enterprises faced with the issue should bring the matter to the attention of their government and be ready to terminate the agreement, etc., before the date of accession — this, in theory, does not necessarily free them from the risk of fines but would show some willingness to comply with Community law as soon as it becomes the law in their own country.

### New agreements, etc.

4—41     So far as the original six Members are concerned, "new" agreements, etc., are those made after the 13th March, 1962.

In the case of the new Members, any agreement, etc., coming into existence after the 1st January, 1973, (if that is the date of accession) will be a "new" one.

4—42     Notification of a "new" agreement, etc., brings immunity from fines for post-notification activities, by virtue of Article 15.5, until such time as the Commission indicates that exemption is not justified. There is no immunity as regards pre-notification activities, so that notification should always precede or co-incide with the coming into operation of the agreement or of its restrictive terms.

4—43     As regards private suit, there is no immunity for pre-notification infringements of Article 85.1, which is another reason for ensuring that notification has been completed before the agreement or any restrictive terms begin to operate.

4—44     As regards post-notification infringements, the temporary validity established by the *Portelange* judgment gives temporary immunity from private suit, but only so long as the Commission has not taken an unfavourable decision. If the Commission decides that Article 85.1 applies but that exemption cannot be granted, there is no equivalent of Article 7.1 enabling the Commission to declare that 85.1 does not apply.

This consideration points to the advisability not only of delaying the commencement of operation until after notification, but of including a term such as appeared in the Henkel/Colgate agreement. That term postponed the coming into effect of the agreement until the Commission had arrived at a favourable decision in respect of the agreement. Such a term precludes the possibility of anything being done until the Commission has granted negative clearance or exemption, so that the risk of private suit is avoided.

**Procedure**

4—45 Once notification has been effected, what happens?

Copies of notifications must be sent by the Commission to the competent authorities in Member States as required by Article 10 (see below). The Commission may obtain information from such authorities, and also from undertakings and associations under threat of fines if necessary, by virtue of Article 11 (see 4-56 — 4-66 below). And the Commission can use its extensive powers of investigation (4-67 — 4-80 below) if necessary. In most cases, however, as the parties concerned are seeking exemption for the agreement, etc., which they have notified, it is unlikely that the latter powers would be needed, as the parties will usually be happy to co-operate with the Commission in providing information.

4—46 In deciding whether to grant exemption or not, the Commission must be satisfied that the case meets the criteria laid down in Article 85.3. Under Article 10, it must consult the Advisory Committee before making its decision (4-98 below), and is required by Article 19 to hear the parties and third parties if necessary and to publish a summary of the case (4-81 below).

If it considers it necessary, the Commission may attach obligations or conditions when granting exemption (Article 8.1), as in the *CECIMO* and *CEMATEX* cases, where an immediate report has to be made to the Commission if an application to participate in an exhibition is refused, and in the *Fabrique Nationale* and *MAN/SAVIEM* cases, where regular periodical reports are required.

4—47 The Commission must specify the date from which the exemption runs. Normally, this cannot be earlier than the date of notification (Article 6), except for "existing" agreements notified in due time — when the exemption can run back to the date the prohibition in Article 85.1 came into force, i.e. the 13th March, 1962, for the original Community and the 1st January, 1973, for the extended Community including the new Members — and for agreements relieved from the obligation to notify. The exemption must be for a specified period, but may be renewed if the requirements of Article 85.3 continue to be satisfied (Article 8).

4—48 The decision has to be published, although confidential business information can be excluded (Article 21).

4—49 Finally, even when exemption has been granted, the Commission may revoke or amend it if it was obtained on the basis of false or incorrect information, if the fundamental circumstances have changed, if there is breach of a condition or obligation attached to the exemption, or if the parties abuse it (Article 8). Except in the case of revocation following fundamental change in the circumstances, the revocation may be made retroactive (so that the parties become exposed to the possibility of fines and private suit). The Advisory Committee must be consulted before revocation or amendment of an exemption (Article 10.3), and the decision effecting the revocation or amendment must be published (Article 21) again having regard to legitimate business secrets.

## 5. Relief from the obligation to notify

4—50    In view of the large number of agreements, etc., to be dealt with, and of the fact that some of them would be less prejudicial than others and consequently could be left for later consideration, Regulation 17 specifies six categories of agreements, etc., which do not need to be notified, but which can be notified if the parties so wish.

4—51    The categories are set out in Article 4.2, as amended by Regulation 2822/71, and are:

(i)    Where the parties all belong to one Member State and the agreement, etc., relates neither to imports nor exports between Member States — Article 4.2 (1).

A variety of agreements, etc., are relieved from the obligation to notify in this category. They include exclusive-dealing agreements between all the manufacturers in one Member and all the distributors in that Member, loyalty rebates allowed to buyers in one Member by the manufacturers in that Member (the rebate being based upon the total of all purchases from all the participating manufacturers), and agreements between importers in one Member as to the prices at which they sell the imported goods — but the comments in paragraph 4-54 should be noted.

(ii)   Two-party resale-price-maintenance agreements, i.e. agreements which restrict only the prices and terms on which the buyer will dispose of goods obtained from the seller — Article 4.2 (2)(a).

Resale-price maintenance is dealt with in Chapter 7.

(iii)  Two-party agreements relating to the use of industrial-property rights, such as patents, trade marks, know-how, designs, etc. — Article 4.2 (2)(b).

Intellectual-property agreements are discussed in Chapter 8.

(iv)   Agreements, decisions, and concerted practices, irrespective of the number of parties, which are concerned exclusively with developing standards or types, or with their uniform application — Article 4.2 (3)(a).

Chapter 11 deals with standardization agreements.

(v)    Agreements, etc., irrespective of the number of parties, concerned exclusively with joint research and development — Article 4.2 (3)(b).

Joint research and development is discussed in Chapter 9.

(vi)   Agreements, etc., irrespective of the number of parties, concerned solely with specialization where certain size criteria are satisfied, i.e. the agreement, etc., affects not more than 15% of the market and the parties' turnover does not exceed 200 million units of account — Article 4.2 (3)(c).

4—52
Specialization agreements are the subject of Chapter 12. The fact that an agreement, for example, falls within one of the categories in Article 4.2 does not necessarily mean that that agreement is within Article 85.1. An exclusive-dealing agreement between two small manufacturers in one Member and several small distributors in that Member would be within category (i), but if it did not affect inter-Member trade it would not be within Article 85.1, anyway. But if there were only two manufacturers in the Member and they made an exclusive dealing agreement with the only distributors in that Member, even if the agreement did not refer to imports or exports, the fact that all the manufacturers and all the distributors in that Member were parties would mean that the agreement almost certainly affected inter-Member trade, and so would come within 85.1. But Article 4.2(1) would still relieve such an agreement from the obligation to notify.

### Status of agreements, etc., within Article 4.2

4—53
The position of agreements relieved by Article 4.2 from the obligation to notify was decided in the *Bilger v. Jehle* case. Mr. and Mrs. Jehle had two establishments in Friedrichshafen, in West Germany, in which they sold beer. In 1950, they entered into an agreement with a German brewery, Bilger, under which the latter gave them financial assistance and provided them with equipment, and in return the Jehles undertook to buy their supplies of beer exclusively from Bilger; if they leased their premises to somebody else, the Jehles were to pass on to the lessee the exclusive-purchase obligation. In fact, the Jehles did lease one of the establishments but continued to run the other themselves. In both establishments special beers supplied by other breweries, not by Bilger, were sold after March, 1962. Bilger sued them in the German courts for breach of contract and the Jehles contended that the agreement, which had not been notified to the Commission, was void by virtue of Article 85, paragraphs 1 and 2. The German court asked the European Court for a ruling. The European Court decided, first, that an agreement, whereby a trader in one Member State undertook to buy exclusively from a supplier in the same State and the goods concerned did not have to cross the national frontiers, does not involve imports or exports between Member States and consequently is relieved from the obligation to notify, by virtue of Article 4.2(1) of Regulation 17.

The Court also ruled that an agreement relieved by Article 4.2 from the obligation to notify remains fully valid, even if it has not been notified, until such time as it is declared invalid (or, presumably, until Article 4.2 is varied or rescinded so as to terminate the relief from the obligation to notify).

4—54     The benefit conferred by this relief from the obligation to notify is more limited than might appear at first sight. Presumably, there can be no question of fines for infringements of Article 85.1 during the period of such relief.

But the immunity from private suit is only temporary. Presumably, as with notified agreements, etc., once there has been a declaration that the agreement, for example, infringes 85.1 and does not qualify for exemption, the temporary immunity from private suit is lost. The Commission is empowered by Article 7.2 of Regulation 17 to declare that the prohibition in 85.1 does not apply but this power is available only with regard to "existing" agreements, etc., in relation to the six original Members which were notified by the 1st January, 1967, and with regard to "existing" agreements, etc., in relation to the new Members notified by the 30th June, 1973. There is no power to make such a declaration with regard to "new" agreements, etc., or "existing" agreements, etc., not notified by those dates. In these instances, the relief from the obligation to notify can be relied upon only if the agreement, etc., would qualify for negative clearance or individual or "bloc" exemption in any event — if it were eventually notified and the Commission held that individual exemption could be given, that exemption is not limited to begin with the date of notification, but can start earlier (Article 6) and can be made to run from the date the agreement started. This brings out the true nature of the relief from the obligation to notify — it is mainly a procedural device to reduce the burden of work on the Commission.

## 6. Ancillary provisions

4—55     The remaining provisions of Regulation 17 are mainly of an ancillary nature, but no less important for that. They include such powers as the Commission's right to demand information and to carry out investigations, with penalties for non-compliance, as well as the possibility of substantial fines for infringement of Article 85.1. There are also provisions to protect the individual undertaking, such as the right to be advised of the case against it, the right to be heard, the right to have confidential business information omitted from published matter, and so on. The interests of third parties are also protected, by the obligation on the Commission to publish a summary of the agreement, etc., and to hear third parties who can establish a valid interest.

### Procurement of information

4—56     In order to enable it to perform its functions properly, the Commission must be able to obtain the relevant information. Regulation 17 provides two processes for this purpose. The first, under Article 11 (18-12), deals with the process of obtaining information from those who hold it.

4—57     Article 11 can be used where the Commission is investigating infringements of Article 85.1, applications for negative clearance, and notifications for exemption, as well as carrying out sector inquiries. Under it, the Commission can request information from the governments and competent authorities of Member States. No penalty is provided for cases where a government or authority fails to provide the information.

4—58    As regards undertakings and associations of undertakings, there is a specific procedure, involving two stages. The first stage is the informal request for the information (paragraphs 1 to 4 of Article 11). It would appear that the request must be in writing, because paragraph 2 requires a copy to be sent to the competent authority of the relevant Member. The request must set out the legal basis upon which, and the purpose for which, the information is required, and also state the penalties for supplying incorrect information. The undertakings and associations to whom the request is addressed are required to supply the information, but no penalty is prescribed for failure to comply.

4—59    However, if an undertaking or an association fails to comply with a request, the second stage can be brought into operation. Under Article 11.5 the Commission can require the information by a decision. Again, a copy of the decision must be sent to the competent authority of the relevant Member State. The decision must specify the information required and fix a time limit within which the information is to be supplied. It must also state the penalties prescribed by Articles 15 and 16 — a fine for giving incorrect information, a fine for failure to give the correct information, and a penalty for each day the failure continues after the end of the time limit. The decision must also advise the recipient of his right of appeal to the European Court. The Commission is not bound by Regulation 17 to publish decisions made under Article 11, but it has followed a practice of doing so, omitting irrelevant portions.

4—60    During 1971, the Commission apparently exercised for the first time its power to require information by formal decision. There were four instances where the power was used, and in each instance the decision was published. The first concerned the German body for collecting copyright fees on tape recorders, known by the initials Z.P.U. On the 12th March, 1970, the Commission asked Z.P.U. to supply certain information within three weeks. At Z.P.U.'s request, the time limit was extended to the 24th April. After an incomplete reply on the 10th April, the Commission wrote again on the 7th September, 1970. A reply dated 14th September was received from a related German body, GEMA, but again failing to give the required information. On the 1st February, 1971, the Commission adopted a decision formally requiring the information within one month of the decision being notified to Z.P.U., pointing out that the information was required to enable the Commission to judge of any competition-restricting effects of the agreements between Z.P.U. and the German manufacturers and importers of tape recorders. Bearing in mind that the original request was dated 12th March, 1970, and that the decision was made on the 1st February, 1971, the Commission cannot be criticized for unreasonable haste in resorting to the formal process.

4—61 A similar restraint was shown in the second case. The Commission had initiated a sector inquiry into exclusive supply contracts in the brewery industry ("tied houses"), and had sent a letter dated 14th May, 1970, to the main brewery undertakings asking them to complete a questionnaire within two months. Several concerns requested, and were granted, extensions of the time limit because the letter coincided with their busy period. However, three undertakings having failed to provide the information, the Commission took a formal decision on the 18th June, 1971, requiring the information within one month.

4—62 In the third instance, the Commission was less accommodating. Noting that the prices of bitumen in France were much lower than in Germany, but that German firms using bitumen to water-proof roofs found it impossible to procure supplies from France — which suggested that there might be some infringement of Article 85.1 — the Commission requested certain information from a French distributor of water-proofing products, Asphaltoid-Keller, by a letter dated 10th February, 1971. No reply having been received, a decision requiring the information within one month was taken on the 2nd July, 1971.

4—63 In the fourth case, the Commission acted equally speedily, and allowed only three weeks for compliance with the decision; as it is concerned with Article 86, the case is discussed in the following chapter (5-57).

4—64 From these details, it does appear that the Commission is prepared to act reasonably and to give extra time where this is needed. The Commission resorts to a formal decision only where the conduct of those concerned makes this course necessary.

4—65 It is significant that Article 11 makes no reference to "professional privilege". Professional advice received from one's legal advisers in relation to actual or anticipated legal proceedings is treated as "privileged" in some legal systems, i.e. the individual concerned cannot be compelled to disclose that advice nor any documents prepared for submission to the legal advisers on which to give the advice. Presumably, the Commission is not entitled to enforce disclosure of "privileged" information. This point is more likely to arise in connection with investigations carried out by the Commission, and is discussed more fully in that connection (4-75 — 4-80 below).

4—66 Finally, it will be noted that Article 20 imposes professional secrecy upon the Commission, competent authorities of Member States, and their officials and other employees in respect of information obtained by virtue of Article 11.

### Investigations by and on behalf of the Commission

4—67 The Commission's power to carry out investigations is conferred by

Article 14 (18-15), and applies where the Commission is dealing with suspected infringements of Article 85.1, applications for negative clearance, notifications seeking exemption, and sector inquiries.

4—68    Although it does not specifically provide for it, Article 14 seems to envisage a two-stage procedure similar to that under Article 11. Officials authorised by the Commission are empowered under Article 14.1 to enter the premises, land and vehicles of undertakings, examine and take copies or extracts of books and other business records, and ask for oral explanations on the spot. The officials must produce a written authorisation stating the subject of the investigation and its purpose, and the penalties under Article 15.1(c) for producing incomplete books and business records. In good time before the investigation is carried out, the government of the Member State concerned must be told of the investigation and given the names of the authorised officials.

4—69    No fines or penalties are provided for in the event of refusal by undertakings to allow the investigations referred to in Article 14.1 and 14.2. There are fines and penalties, however, for failure to comply with an investigation ordered under 14.3 by a decision of the Commission, which suggests that Article 14 contemplates two separate proceedings, an informal one under 14.1 and 14.2, and a formal one under 14.3.

4—70    The Commission is authorised by Article 14.3 to order by decision an investigation in respect of an undertaking or an association of undertakings, after consultation with the competent authority in the relevant Member State. The decision must state the subject and purpose of the investigation, fix the date when it is to begin, and mention the fine for refusing to submit to an investigation ordered by a decision of the Commission, and the additional penalty for each day the refusal continues. The decision must also mention the right of appeal to the European Court.

4—71    When requested by the Commission or by the competent national authority, officials from the latter may assist the Commission's officials in carrying out investigations under Article 14. If an undertaking opposes an investigation ordered by a decision, the Member State is required, by Article 11.6, to give the necessary assistance to the Commission's officials. The six original Members were obliged to introduce by 1st October, 1962, the necessary measures to enable such assistance to be given. For the new Members, the relevant date is 30th June, 1973, assuming accession on the 1st January, 1973, (Article 25.4).

4—72    If it wishes, the Commission can require the competent national authority to carry out the investigation on its behalf — Article 12. In carrying out their functions, the national officials must carry an authority in writing from the competent authority specifying the subject and purpose of the investigation. At the request of either the national authority or the Commission, officials from the latter can assist the national officials in performing their duties.

4—73    Finally, as in the case of information acquired under Article 11, documents, copies, extracts, and information acquired by the Commission, competent national authorities, and their officials by virtue of Article 14 are subjected to professional secrecy by Article 20, and not to be disclosed improperly.

4—74    *Limits of the powers of investigation* It will be noted that the power of entry into premises, etc., relates only to those belonging to an undertaking. The private residences of directors or employees of a company, for example, cannot be entered. Where an individual carries on a business himself, and runs it from his own home, it may be that in those circumstances the authorised officials might be entitled to enter his home and go into any rooms used for business purposes, but this is unlikely to happen because such enterprises are likely to be only small and consequently there would be no "appreciable effect" either upon competition or upon inter-Member trade. Moreover, only the books and records of the undertaking are liable to examination, not personal belongings of an employee which he may have in the office. "Books and other business records" probably includes all business documents, including such things as minute books, correspondence files, and even computer programmes.

*Professional privilege*

4—75    It is doubtful if the right to examine and take copies of books and documents extends to documents protected by "professional privilege". These are documents prepared for submission to or communications with legal advisers in respect of anticipated or actual legal proceedings, including copies or notes of the professional advice given.

4—76    For example, if a company expected action against it by the Commission in respect of an agreement, it might arrange for the preparation of a history of the relevant events leading up to the agreement and of the working of the agreement, with details of the policy reasons for making the agreement. Such a document would serve as a brief to submit all the facts to its legal advisers. It would not be unusual for such a brief to set out the arguments which seemed to be available against the Commission's view. Having considered the brief, and any supporting matter, and having discussed it with the officers of the company concerned, the legal adviser might then set out his views and conclusions in writing. It would be unfair if the brief and the legal adviser's advice had to be disclosed to the Commission. Although Article 14 does not specifically provide for it, it is to be presumed that the Commission's officials would not seek to examine such privileged material.

4—77    If the officials, in any particular case, insisted upon examining privileged documents, those concerned would be well advised to refuse to disclose them and should get into immediate touch with their legal advisers. For example, before entering into a particular agreement, a company might have obtained professional legal advice as to the status of the agreement under Article 85. The advice might have been that, in the adviser's opinion, the agreement was border-line — there being arguments tending to show it was within 85.1, and also arguments the other way. If the Community's officials arrived to carry out an investigation armed with authority to look at all documents "leading up to and surrounding the making of the agreement", the legal advice obtained when the agreement was made should be privileged from examination — it could damage the company's case if the Commission could say "Well, your own lawyers were not certain about it".

4—78  A similar problem might arise in connection with action by national authorities. Say the relevant authority in the State had already started its own investigation, and as a result the undertaking had prepared a comprehensive brief covering the whole of the case, and submitted it to its legal advisers. That brief, and the advice given by the advisers, should be privileged from inspection by the Commission's officers. And *vice versa*, documents prepared and advice given in relation to action by the Commission should be privileged from compulsory disclosure to the national authority.

4—79  Professional privilege should extend not only to professional advice received from outside lawyers but also from internal legal advisers.

4—80  In view of these considerations, if an undertaking finds itself the subject of an investigation by officials from the Commission it should consult immediately its own legal advisers.

## Hearings

4—81  Before taking certain decisions, the Commission must give the parties concerned, and in some cases third parties, the opportunity to be heard. A summary of the case must be published, suppressing legitimate business secrets. The decisions are those relating to termination of an infringement under Article 2, grant or refusal of negative clearance or exemption, renewal or revocation or amendment of an exemption, or the imposition of a fine or penalty. Article 19 provides that the parties concerned must be heard, and also third parties who can show that they have sufficient grounds to be heard. Other third parties must be heard if the Commission or the competent authority of the Member State considers it necessary.

4—82  The procedure for these hearings is laid down in Regulation 99/63 (Appendix E). The hearings must take place before the draft decision is submitted to the Advisory Committee. The Commission must advise the parties in writing of the objections the Commission raises against them. No fine or penalty can be imposed if the relevant objections have not been so notified in writing to the parties. And any decision made must be limited to the matters so raised by the Commission. The parties must put in their replies in writing within the time appointed by the Commission (which cannot be less than two weeks). Third parties must also be given an opportunity to submit their views in writing. Those who in their written submissions have asked for an oral hearing must be given one. They may attend in person or by legal representative; a duly authorised member of the permanent staff may appear for an undertaking or an association of undertakings. Those attending may have their legal advisers with them. The hearings are in private. Depending upon the need to safeguard legitimate business secrets, those to be heard may be heard separately or in the presence of others. The essential contents of each person's statement is taken down and recorded in minutes to be read over to and approved by him.

### Fines and penalties

4—83 Regulation 17 distinguishes between fines and penalties. The former are of fixed amount, and are imposed under Article 15. The latter are at a rate of so much per day, and are imposed under Article 16.

4—84 Article 15 provides two ranges of fines. The smaller, 100 — 5,000 units of account, can be imposed for procedural failings, i.e. giving incorrect or misleading information in an application for negative clearance or in a notification seeking exemption, failing to give information within the appropriate time limit or giving incorrect information in response to a request or decision under Article 11 or 12, and failing to produce all the relevant books and business records as required in an investigation or refusing to submit to an investigation ordered by a decision under 14.3.

4—85 The second range is much larger, from 1,000 units of account to 1,000,000 units or 10% of the undertaking's turnover in the last financial year if that is greater. Fines in the second, higher, range can be imposed only for substantive offences, i.e. for infringement of Article 85.1 (and Article 86) or breach of an obligation imposed as part of an exemption under 85.3. In fixing the size of the fine in the second range, regard must be.had to the gravity and duration of the offence. These higher fines cannot be imposed in respect of periods before notification in the case of "existing" agreements, etc., notified or modified in due time, nor as regards both "existing" and "new" agreements in respect of any period after notification unless the Commission has indicated to the parties that exemption cannot be granted. The Commission has taken this step in a number of cases.

4—86 The possibility of fines up to 10% of turnover introduces an element of discrimination between multi-product and uni-product firms. If an undertaking is supplying only one product, and making a profit of 20%, the risk of a maximum fine of 10% of one year's turnover may not be a grave deterrent if the firm has been able to continue its activities undiscovered for a number of years. But in the case of a multi-product firm, a fine of 10% of the firm's total turnover because of an infringement of Article 85.1 in relation to a product representing only 1% of that turnover, would be a very severe penalty — the fine would represent ten years turnover in the particular product (and fifty years profit if the profit level were 20%!). It is not suggested that the Commission would always impose the maximum fine calculated on the undertaking's total turnover in all products, but it would be as well for multi-product concerns to keep this possibility in mind.

4—87 Fines can be imposed only upon undertakings or associations of undertakings. Thus, fines cannot be imposed upon the directors, officers or other employees of companies. If an individual is carrying on business himself, he can be fined in his business capacity.

4—88 They can be imposed only for breaches or infringements committed "intentionally or negligently", i.e. not for innocent infringements. It may be some, but perhaps only small, comfort to know that the fines, when imposed, do not rank as criminal (Article 15.4).

4—89 Before a fine is imposed, the parties must have been given a written statement of the Commission's case against them, and have had the opportunity to present their own case in writing and orally, under Regulation 99/63 (Appendix E). And the Advisory Committee must be consulted before a fine is imposed (Article 15.3).

4—90 "Parallel" fines are possible, if the particular agreement, etc., infringes national law as well as Article 85.1. This was decided in the *Wilhelm* case. The German Cartel Office fined undertakings (and individuals) who had participated in the aniline dyes cartel, and the European Court held that parallel proceedings where the agreement, etc., infringed both national and Community law were in order — there can be "double jeopardy".

4—91 The Commission imposed the first procedural fine during 1971, "for failure to submit a complete set of business papers", amounting to 4,000 units of account.

The first fines for infringement of Article 85.1 were imposed in 1969 in the *Quinine* case, ranging from 10,000 to 210,000 units, and the *Aniline Dyes* case, ranging from 40,000 to 50,000 units, per undertaking. In the *Quinine* case, one of the firms concerned (Boehringer) asked the European Court to review the fine of 190,000 units of account, and the Court reduced the figure to 180,000. Later the firm asked the Commission to deduct from the fine of 180,000 units a fine of $80,000 imposed on it by the U.S. courts for participation in the same cartel. This the Commission refused to do, pointing out that the American fine was for restricting competition in the U.S.A., and the fine under Article 85.1 for restricting competition in the E.E.C. Boehringer has again applied to the Court on this point (on analogy with the *Wilhelm* case, presumably the Court will uphold the possibility of "double jeopardy").

4—92 Periodic penalty payments are provided for in Article 16. They range from 50 to 1,000 units per day. They can be imposed to compel undertakings to terminate an infringement of Article 85.1, to refrain from acts prohibited when an exemption has been reviewed under

Article 8.3, to supply complete and correct information ordered by a decision under Article 11.5, or to submit to an investigation ordered by a decision under Article 14.3. Once the parties have complied, the Commission is not bound to exact the full penalty calculated on a daily basis, but may fix a lower sum (Article 16.2).

A penalty can be imposed only upon an undertaking or an association of undertakings, not upon the directors, officers or employees of undertakings.

A penalty under Article 16 cannot be imposed unless the parties have been given a statement of the Commission's case and had an opportunity to present their own case and be heard, under Regulation 99/63. The Advisory Committee must also be consulted before a penalty is imposed.

4—93   *Unit of account* The unit of account is expressed, not in a particular currency or currencies, but in terms of gold. Article 18 of the Financial Regulation of the 15th November, 1960, fixed the unit of account as 0.88867088 grams of fine gold. At that time this was equivalent to one American dollar and remained so until the $ was devalued in terms of gold in 1971, when the official price of gold was raised from $35 to $38. With the present currency uncertainties, and a free market gold price about $65, it is best not to attempt to express the unit of account in terms of a currency or currencies until exchange rates have achieved a more stable basis.

## Liaison with Member States

4—94   Formal liaison with the relevant authorities in Member States is maintained at four stages.

The first stage is when a particular case is initiated. Under Article 10.1 (18-11), the Commission must send to the competent authorities in each Member copies of applications for negative clearance or for investigation of alleged infringements of Article 85.1, and of notifications to obtain exemption. When sending the copies, the Commission must also send copies of the more important supporting documents.

4—95   What each authority does, on receipt of these copies, is for it to decide. If enterprises in its own country are involved, the authority may institute investigations to see if there is any infringement of national laws, or merely to ascertain the facts so as to decide what action to take. In the case of applications under Article 3 for investigations of alleged or suspected infringements, when the undertakings concerned may not yet be aware of what is happening, some authorities may feel that they should advise the undertakings in their country of the situation.

4—96   The second stage is when the Commission is seeking information from undertakings and associations. Copies of requests for information or formal decisions requiring information under pain of a penalty (Article 11) must be sent to the competent authorities of the Member

States whose nationals are involved.

4—97    The third stage arises if and when authorised officials from the Commission are to carry out an investigation at the premises of any undertaking under Article 14. "In good time" before the investigation is carried out, the Commission must inform the competent authority in the Member concerned that the investigation is to be made and say who will be the authorised officials. If an undertaking does not comply with a request and refuses to allow the investigation, the Commission can issue a decision, carrying sanctions; the competent authority of the Member concerned must be consulted before the decision is made. Again, it is a matter for the authority to decide what action it will take, for example whether to advise the undertakings concerned.

4—98    The fourth stage comes towards the end of the case, and involves the Advisory Committee. This Committee consists of one official from each Member State, drawn from the national authority concerned with enforcing competition law (Article 11). The Committee must be consulted before the Commission takes a decision in respect of a negative clearance, a termination of an infringement of Article 85.1, an exemption under 85.3, the renewal, amendment or revocation of an exemption, or the institution of a sector inquiry under Article 12. The Committee must also be consulted before the Commission takes a decision imposing a fine (Article 15), or a periodic penalty (Article 16). In practice, the draft decision is sent to the Committee, and is considered at a meeting of the Committee. The Committee's views are set out in a report to the Commission, but the report is not published. The Commission is not bound to follow the Committee's advice, but the procedure does enable the anti-trust authorities in each Member to be aware of and to express views on the Commission's attitudes and policies.

**Limitation of actions**

4—99    In most legal systems, the attitude of the law towards litigation is somewhat like St. Paul's attitude to marriage — "it is better to marry than to burn" but no more. In the eyes of the law, it is better for people to settle their differences by litigation than by violence, but litigation is not encouraged. Many legal systems provide for "limitation" of civil actions — if one person wishes to start litigation against another claiming that the latter has injured him in some way, he must not delay too long in starting the action, but must do so with reasonable expedition, say within three or six years of the injury. Some legal systems apply the principle to criminal matters, so that the criminal cannot be proceeded against once the "limitation" period has expired — the period may vary with the type of offence.

4—100   In the *Quinine Cartel* case, the parties argued that there should be a limitation period, as all the six Members had limitation periods in their national laws, and that that period should be two years, being the shortest adopted by any of the Members. In its decision, the Commission pointed out that Regulation 17 did not provide for any limitation of action, and, even if the principle of limitation were accepted, it would not apply in that case — the infringements of Article 85.1 were not terminated until August, 1966, and the Commission had started its investigation under Article 14 of Regulation 17 in 1967 immediately upon learning of the activities of the cartel.

4—101 However, there has now been published the draft of a Council Regulation providing periods of limitation in respect of competition law — Appendix N. If the regulation is eventually adopted in its present form, the Commission will not be able to impose fines under Article 15 or penalties under Article 16 for offences in connection with the procurement of information or the carrying out of investigations, more than three years after the offence; nor will it be able to impose fines or penalties for other offences (such as an infringement of 85.1, or failure to terminate an infringement, or breach of a condition in an exemption) more than five years after the offence. But if any action is taken by or on behalf of the Commission during the limitation period in respect of the offence, the period is interrupted. Thus if some undertakings had been party to an infringement of Article 85.1 but had terminated it, the five year limitation period would start to run from the date of termination. However, if within the five years, the Commission had requested information as part of an inquiry into the infringement, the five year period would start to run again from the date of the request. If adopted, the regulation will also provide a limitation period of three years for the enforcement of fines and penalties imposed by the Commission. Again, the period can be interrupted, and starting running again, if the fine or penalty is altered or steps taken to enforce it.

4—102 While the regulation remains a draft, it is not binding on the Commission, although no doubt it can be taken as some indication of the attitude likely to be adopted by the Commission.

## 7. Conclusions

4—103 The unavoidable emphasis upon procedural detail when dealing with Regulation 17 should not be allowed to obscure the economic character of Article 85. In its conception and drafting, Article 85 is not legalistic — it does not attempt to spell out in precise legal detail what may, and what may not, be done. On the contrary, it states in broad economic terms the general principles to be applied.

The same practical, economic, approach has been evinced by the Commission in implementing those principles. There has been the doctrine of "appreciable effect", given a quantitative expression in the "Notice Concerning Minor Agreements" (Appendix J). There is the recognition that competition law should not be allowed to impede desirable inter-firm activities. In the "Notice Concerning Co-operation between Enterprises" (Appendix H) the Commission welcomed co-operation between small and medium-sized firms which would allow rationalization and help the parties to improve productivity and competitiveness. Even co-operation between large undertakings can be economically desirable without causing difficulties from the point of view of competition law.

4—104 This practical approach by the Commission is exemplified in the Belgian *Cement Makers* case. The agreement between the lime-burners and the cement makers was clearly aimed at restricting competition by the former, but as they were in fact no longer capable of competing, the agreement in its factual economic context could be allowed to continue without detrimental effect.

4—105 The European Court endorsed, in the *Brasserie de Haecht v. Wilkin* case, this policy of deciding Article 85 issues in the light of the whole economic and legal background. A café proprietor in Belgium, Wilkin, borrowed money from the Brasserie de Haecht, undertaking to buy all his supplies of beer and drinks from them until the loan was repaid and for two years thereafter. De Haecht found that the tying clauses had not been observed and brought an action in the Belgian courts. Wilkin admitted the breach of the clauses, but pleaded that the agreement infringed Article 85.1 and so was void under 85.2. Noting that there existed a large number of exclusive contracts of this type between a small number of Belgian breweries on the one hand and a large number of retailers on the other, the Belgian court asked the European Court for a ruling whether the de Haecht/Wilkin agreement had to be considered in isolation or whether it could be judged in the light of the whole economic context, including the existence of many other similar agreements. The European Court's ruling was that exclusive supply agreements were not *per se* contrary to Article 85.1, but they can be if, when taken separately or together with others "in the economic and legal context in which they are made and on the basis of a collection of legal or factual factors", the conditions of the Article are met. In short, the decision is not taken upon the narrow legal ground of the form of the agreement, but upon its object and effect viewed in relation to its whole economic and legal context.

# CHAPTER 5

# Monopolies and Dominant Positions — Article 86 and Regulation 17

## 1. Introduction

5—01    Taking competition law as comprising two broad divisions, restrictive practices law (i.e. cartels and concerted practices) on the one hand, and monopoly law on the other, Article 85 lays down the general principles of Community law as regards the former, and Article 86 serves the same function for the latter. The two Articles adopt completely different methods. Article 85 is based upon the "prohibition" principle, whereas Article 86 follows the "abuse" principle.

Regulation 17 is common to both Articles, in that it implements Article 86 as well as Article 85.

This Chapter deals with Article 86, and with Regulation 17 in so far as it applies to that Article.

## 2. Article 86

5—02    The first sentence of Article 86 reads:

"Any abuse by one or more undertakings of a dominant position within the common market or in a substantial part of it shall be prohibited as incompatible with the common market in so far as it may affect trade between Member States." (17-10)

There are, therefore, five conditions which must be met if Article 86 is to apply:

(i)     There must be one or more undertakings involved.
(ii)    There must be a "dominant position".
(iii)   That "dominant position" must be within the Common Market or a substantial part of it.
(iv)    There must be an abuse of that dominant position.
(v)     The abuse must be capable of affecting inter-Member trade.

Each of these conditions will be discussed separately in turn.

*"One or more undertakings"*

5—03    The word "undertaking" has the same, broad, meaning as in

Article 85.1 (3-15 — 3-19) and does not call for further explanation. As will be seen from the *GEMA* decision discussed below (5-12), it includes economic associations such as performing rights societies.

5—04   The doctrine of "enterprise entity" (3-16 — 3-19) also applies in considering what is an "undertaking" for the purposes of Article 86. In the *Continental Can* case, the American company, Continental Can Company Incorporated of New York, had a wholly-owned subsidiary Europemballage Corporation, of Delaware, which in turn held 85% of the share capital of a German company, Schmalbach-Lubeca-Werke, A.G. Because Continental Can controlled each of the other two companies, their actions were imputed to it, and the formal decision made by the Commission ordering the termination of an abuse under Article 86 was addressed to Continental Can only, not to the other companies.

5—05   Article 86 is not confined to cases where only one undertaking is involved. It also applies to abuse of dominant position by more than one undertaking. Assume, for example, that there were only four firms, A, B, C, and D, supplying the market, each having 25% of it. And assume that in fact none actually dominated the market. Then, if A fixed his price at an abusively high level and B, C, and D each followed that price, acting by their separate individual decision and without agreement or any "concerting" of their price changes, there could well be an infringement of Article 86. All four together would certainly hold a dominant position in the market, and the hypothetically very high price would be an abuse of that position. (Of course, if the four had acted by agreement or by concerted practice, Article 85 would have applied.) It follows that concerns in a "conscious parallelism" situation who between them hold a dominant position might find themselves the target of an action under Article 86 if their activities amounted to abuse of that position. To date there have been no decisions by the Commission or rulings by the European Court to this effect, but the wording of Article 86 appears to point clearly in this direction.

5—06   Action under Article 86 would also seem to be possible where several undertakings, between them having a dominant position in the market, are party to an agreement, say a specialization agreement, which has been granted individual exemption under Article 85.3 (or perhaps exempted under some "bloc" exemption made pursuant to Regulation 2821/71 — Appendix K). If the undertakings abused their position, Article 86 would be applicable (in addition to Article 8.3 (d) of Regulation 17 which empowers the Commission to revoke or amend a decision granting exemption — 18-09).

### "Dominant position"

5—07   Neither Article 86 nor Regulation 17 gives any definition of "dominant position". The meaning of the expression is discussed in a Study "The Problem of Concentration in the Common Market" issued by the

Commission in 1966.[1] There must be an ability to dominate the market. This cannot be expressed absolutely, in quantitative terms — it is not possible to say that a market share of so much forms the dividing line between dominance and non-dominance. A firm with, say, 40% of the market might dominate it if the other firms were all weak. Conversely an old-established, stagnating, firm with 90% of the market might not have the ability to dominate the market if faced by an aggressive new-comer with only a 10% share of the market. There must be an economic power, equated by the Study with the ability to exercise a significant influence on the market, an ability which the undertaking can foresee and exercise deliberately. That would include the ability to influence the decisions and conduct of other concerns in the market, or the ability for an undertaking to put its competitors out of the market. In general, the Study held that the price-leader in an oligopolistic situation would have a dominant position.

5—08    The Commission, in its decision in the *Continental Can* case, emphasised the ability to act independently:

"Undertakings are in a dominant position when they have the power to behave independently, which puts them in a position to act without taking into account their competitors, purchasers or suppliers. That is the position when, because of their share of the market, or of their share of the market combined with the availability of technical knowledge, raw materials or capital, they have the power to determine prices or to control production or distribution for a significant part of the products in question. This power does not necessarily have to derive from an absolute domination permitting the undertakings which hold it to eliminate all will on the part of their economic partners, but it is enough that they be strong enough as a whole to ensure to those undertakings an overall independence of behaviour, even if there are differences in intensity in their influence on the different partial markets."

5—09    Probably, the concept of "dominant position" requires the three criteria. First, the ability to influence the market significantly. But in an oligopolistic situation each firm can influence the market because all recognise their interdependence — if one lowers its price, the others must follow or go out of business — and take the likely reactions of competitors into account in deciding policy. So there must be the second criterion, the ability to act independently of the reactions of others. And the third criterion is that the dominant firm must realise that it is in a dominant position and can exercise a significant influence.

5—10    What factors can give this dominance? The Study suggested that they could lie in the field of production, of distribution, or of financial

[1] European Economic Community. Série Concurrence 3. *Le Problème de la Concentration dans le Marché Commun.* Brussels, 1966.

power. The Commission in its *Continental Can* decision pointed to market share combined with the availability of technical knowledge, raw materials, or capital.

5—11    The facts in the *Continental Can* case were complicated, but may be summarized, so far as relevant, as follows. Continental Can held all the shares in Europemballage, which in turn controlled Schmalbach-Lubeca-Werke with an 85% holding. Schmalbach had in Germany between 70% and 80% of the supply of "open top" tins used for meat and charcuterie, between 80% and 90% of the "open top" tins used for fish and shellfish, and between 50% and 55% of metal covers for glass containers. It also had a strong position in metal containers for drinks, and other types of metal containers. In addition it manufactured plastic and cardboard containers. Schmalbach had a range of some 5,000 products in all, with 15 factories and 5 sales depots throughout Germany, employing 13,000 people. Its next biggest German competitor employed 1,600. Behind Schmalbach was Continental Can itself, with its vast resources, including the manufacture of the machines for making and using cans, patents and technical know-how, licence agreements with big manufacturers of metal containers, access to international capital markets, assets amounting to some $1,200 million, and a total labour force of some 62,000. In these circumstances, the Commission concluded that Continental Can, through its subsidiary Schmalbach, had a dominant position in Germany in "open top" tins for meat and fish, and metal lids for glass containers.

5—12    The position was less complicated in the *GEMA* case. GEMA was a society consisting of composers, authors, and publishers established to protect the rights granted to them by German law. In order to belong to GEMA, each composer, author, and publisher had to enter into a contract with GEMA assigning to it all his existing and future rights for a minimum period of six years, which GEMA then had the right to exploit, by licensing in return for royalties, etc. The Commission held that GEMA was an undertaking within Article 86 because it was engaged in the supply of services, i.e. granting and managing for profit the rights assigned to it. And because GEMA had no competition in Germany, being the only body providing that service there, it held a dominant position in Germany.

5—13    In each of these two cases there was the ability to influence the market significantly, because of the market shares in the Continental Can/Schmalbach situation, and because of the absence of competition as regards GEMA. There was also the ability to act independently, because of market shares and overall economic power as regards Continental Can/Schmalbach, and again because of the absence of competition as regards GEMA. And presumably in both cases the parties were well aware of their powerful position.

5—14    The ownership of patents was one of the factors taken into account in the *Continental Can* case. The mere holding of patent rights, or other rights relating to industrial and intellectual property, does not of itself constitute a dominant position. This was first decided in the *Parke, Davis* case, in which it was held that Parke, Davis could use its Dutch patents to prevent the import of pharmaceuticals covered by the patents from Italy (where patents cannot be granted for pharmaceutical products) into Holland. In the *Sirena* case, the European Court ruled that the holder of a trade mark does not have a dominant position merely by being able to prohibit others from marketing in the territory covered by the registration of his mark goods bearing the same mark, unless in addition he is able to prevent the maintenance of effective competition in a considerable part of the market in question, taking into account the availability of similar goods and substitutes. And a similar ruling in relation to rights analogous to copyright was given in the *Deutsche Grammophon* case — there must in addition be the ability to prevent effective competition, having regard to the availability of other articles of the same kind. (These cases are discussed in more detail in Chapter 8.)

5—15 Whether or not a dominant position exists cannot be decided in the abstract. It must be decided in relation to a specific case, because one of the factors to be taken into account is the "market" in question. As explained in paragraph 1-05, the market is delimited in two ways — by commodity, and by area. To a man who will eat only porridge for breakfast, a firm with a dominant position in porridge oats able to raise the price would be a serious matter, but to a man prepared to eat other breakfast cereals it would not be. To the former the market is "porridge oats", to the latter "breakfast cereals". The area taken can be equally significant. If the "commodity" is retail food, and there is only one food shop in one particular street, if that street were taken as the relevant geographical area the single shop would be in a dominant position. That might be the case if the street were the only street in a village many miles from another village or town, but it would not be so of a street in a town with many other food shops nearby.

5—16 In the *GEMA* case there was no difficulty in determining the "commodity" and the geographical area. The former was performing rights, and the latter Germany. In the *Continental Can* case, the Commission took tins for meat, tins for fish, and metal covers for glass containers as the "commodities" and Germany as the geographical area, in deciding that Schmalbach had a dominant position. In deciding the area of "abuse", as noted below (5-20), the Commission took Benelux with North and Central Germany as the geographical extent of the market.

5—17 For completeness, it should be noted that in some circumstances the market may be delimited chronologically as well. Thus, with a "commodity" such as large nuclear power stations, there might be only three firms capable of designing and building such power stations, each firm having a capacity for only one power station at a time. If two of the firms were already engaged each in building a station, if a third one had to be built the available firm would in fact have a monopoly.

5—18 Finàlly, it should be noted that to hold a dominant position is not illegal of itself — it is only abuse of a dominant position which is contrary to Article 86. Article 86 itself accepts that dominant positions can exist, quite properly.

### *"Within the Common Market or in a substantial part of it"*

5—19 The geographical area of the "market" in question is significant not only in determining whether there is a dominant position but also in deciding whether Article 86 applies at all. Article 86 is concerned only with dominant positions within the Common Market or within a substantial part of it. There is no difficulty about the area of the Common Market itself, but what is a "substantial part" of it? How extensive must the part be to be "substantial"? Neither the Treaty nor Regulation 17 give any guidance on this point. At one time it did look as if there would be some specific authority on the point — this was in the draft issued in 1970 of what eventually became Regulation 2822/71 (Appendix L). The draft provided that the relief from the obligation to notify be extended to specialization agreements covering not more than 10% of the total turnover in similar or substitute products in the Common Market or a "substantial part of it", and added that a "substantial part" would be understood to mean, Benelux, Germany, France, or Italy. However, the text as finally adopted, which is now Regulation 2822/71, omitted that definition of "substantial".

5—20 In both the *GEMA* and *Continental Can* cases, the Commission found that the relevant dominant position was held in Germany. This does establish that Germany is a "substantial" part of the Common Market for this purpose, which would suggest that France and Italy should be considered so as well, as the draft regulation had provided. But national boundaries are not essential in delimiting a substantial part of the Common Market in this connection. As discussed below (5-29), the Commission decided that there was abuse of the dominant position in the *Continental Can* case, because the merger in that case eliminated the potential competition between Schmalbach and Thomassen in an area comprising nearly the whole of Benelux and the North and Centre of Germany — an area which the Commission regarded as a substantial part of the Common Market.

5—21 It seems clear that Germany, France, Italy, and Benelux, are each a substantial part of the Common Market for this purpose, and presumably, by analogy, the United Kingdom will be so regarded as well. Whether Denmark and Ireland will be so regarded, and whether the term "substantial" will be taken to include parts of individual Members, and if so where the minimum size limit is to be drawn, must await further decisions or legislation. For example, would London or Paris be a "substantial" part?

*"Abuse"*

5—22  The fourth condition for the application of Article 86 is that there must be abuse of the dominant position. Again, there is no definition of "abuse" either in the Treaty or in Regulation 17. Perhaps the full meaning is brought out more by the French phrase *"exploitation abusive"*, i.e. the dominant position must have been exploited (in the pejorative sense of that word). Article 86 does give some indication of what is considered "abuse", in the second sentence:

"Such abuse may, in particular, consist in:

(a)  directly or indirectly imposing unfair purchase or selling prices or other unfair trading conditions;

(b)  limiting production, markets or technical development to the prejudice of consumers;

(c)  applying dissimilar conditions to equivalent transactions with other trading parties, thereby placing them at a competitive disadvantage;

(d)  making the conclusion of contracts subject to acceptance by the other parties of supplementary obligations which, by their nature or according to commercial usage, have no connection with the subject of such contracts." (17-10)

5—23  This list does not claim to exhaust the possible types of abuse, and in fact, the Study already referred to mentioned two other possible abuses:

(i)  price cutting aimed at eliminating a competitor lacking the financial resources to support a long period of sales below cost price;

(ii)  similar price cutting to force a merger on an unwilling victim, or a merger on unfavourable terms.

The practices described in (i) and (ii) are similar to that in (c) of Article 86, in that they distort normal competition.

5—24  There is a further possible source of abuse which should be mentioned, i.e. refusal to supply. A firm may validly refuse to supply another for a variety of reasons, for example, if there are overdue debts outstanding from the latter, or if the latter is of doubtful financial standing, or if the former has a distributor already established in the area and there is not enough trade to support two distributors. But there may be situations in which refusal to supply on the part of a dominant firm constitutes abuse. For example, if company A is the dominant supplier of raw material X, and owns company B which manufactures and sells the product incorporating X, A might refuse to supply a competitor of B or a new entrant to the market for that product; if there were no adequate alternative sources of X, it might be an abuse for A to refuse to supply solely on the ground of competition with B, i.e. assuming there were no other valid grounds for refusal such as credit risk, etc. Instead of an outright refusal to supply, there may be a refusal to supply except upon terms. Where there were other purchasers taking equal quantities, on more favourable terms, insistence upon less favourable terms might amount to discrimination under (c) above, but where no other purchasers existed, it might be easier to prove refusal to supply as the abuse.

5—25 The examples cited in the preceding paragraph all have one thing in common — they envisage a situation where advantage is taken of the dominant position to cause injury to some other person, either by unfair prices or terms including irrelevant tying conditions, or by restricting production, or by discrimination — in fact, the aggressive price cutting in (i) and (ii) involves direct intentional injury.

5—26 Some of these elements were found by the Commission to exist in the *GEMA* case. By its contracts with the record manufacturers, the latter had to pay GEMA full royalty, even if the record included non-copyright work. The only exception allowed was where the protected work was less than one-third of the total running time of the side, when a royalty of one-third of the normal fee was charged. In effect, (except where the protected work was exactly one-third of the running time), GEMA exacted royalties on non-protected works.

The Commission also held that GEMA imposed unnecessary conditions on its members in three respects. First, the member had to assign to GEMA his author's rights in all respects and in all countries. Secondly, the member had to accept a "classification procedure" in relation to light music and dance music for distributing the royalties received by GEMA which excluded the author from any claim of right or appeal to the courts as regards his share, and which gave supplementary payments only to members with twenty years membership, i.e. a form of loyalty bonus. Thirdly, the rules of GEMA made it difficult for a member to transfer to another performing rights society.

Finally, the Commission decided that GEMA indulged in discrimination, against nationals of other Member States, against independent importers of gramophone records into Germany, and against importers of tape recorders into Germany. The discrimination against nationals of other Members arose from the fact that non-Germans could not be voting members, i.e. could not be ordinary or extraordinary members, and so could not eventually share in the supplementary payments under the classification procedure. As regards independent importers of records, GEMA levied the whole royalty on the record on import, even though royalty may have already been paid to it (in the case of records made in Germany and exported and now being re-imported) or to another society (GEMA had an arrangement with the corresponding French society whereby the fees paid to the latter gave the right to distribute in Germany as well as France). In the case of independent importers of tape recorders, GEMA levied royalty at the rate of 5%, as against less then 3% royalty on German recorders, on their imports (the royalty charge on tape recorders is intended to cover copyright material which will be recorded and reproduced on the recorders).

5—27    The mere charging of a higher price for a protected article does not of itself constitute an abuse. The European Court gave this ruling in the *Parke, Davis* case, in which the prices charged for the pharmaceuticals made in Italy (outside Parke, Davis's patents) and imported into Holland were sold at lower prices than the Dutch products protected by Dutch patents. A similar ruling was given in relation to trade marks in the *Sirena* case, although the Court added the rider that, while merely charging higher prices for articles marked with a trade mark was not *per se* proof of abuse, it could amount to abuse if the price difference were sufficiently large and not justifiable. The Court adopted the same view in relation to rights analogous to copyright, in the *Deutsche Grammophon* case.

5—28    A somewhat wider concept of abuse, or abusive exploitation, was put forward in the Study. According to this concept, the conduct of an undertaking constitutes abuse when it is contrary to the objectives of the Rome Treaty. Articles 85 and 86, so the argument runs, seek to establish a competitive regime within the Common Market. Consequently, it is not permissible for cartels nor for enterprises in a dominant position to eliminate competition by the creation of a monopoly situation. Thus, if a concern holding a dominant position merged with a competitor, and a monopoly resulted, that would be an abuse within Article 86. The Study argued that the merger process itself did not constitute the abuse, only the complete elimination of competition. Consequently, the more a dominant enterprise reinforced its position by mergers with other enterprises and so approached a monopoly situation, putting at risk the freedom of choice of suppliers, buyers, and users, the greater would be the probability of its coming within the scope of Article 86.

5—29    The Commission applied this concept in its *GEMA* decision. One of the abuses held against GEMA was that its system and arrangements led to the creation of national groups for publishers and prevented composers and authors freely choosing a publisher within the Community. As a result, GEMA prevented the establishment of a single market in the Community for music publishing, i.e. it eliminated competition.

5—30    This extended concept of abuse was also applied in the *Continental Can* case. The Commission there took the view that it is an abuse contrary to Article 86 for a dominant undertaking to take over a competitor thereby eliminating actual or potential competition between them. The competition eliminated in that case was potential, rather than actual. As already explained (5-11), Schmalbach was the dominant supplier in Germany of "open top" tins for meat and fish, and metal lids for glass containers. Thomassen & Drijver-Verblifa N.V. was the other party to the merger. It was the biggest manufacturer of metal containers in Benelux, having 100% of the market in "open top" tins for meat and fish in Holland, and 100% of those for meat in Belgium; as regards metal lids for glass containers its market share in Holland was 45/50%

and in Belgium 15%. Although their trading areas were adjacent, each did very little business in "open top" tins, "general line" containers, aerosol tins, and metal stoppers in the other's territory — Schmalbach exported only 0.7% of its turnover to Benelux, and Thomassen only 2.5% of its turnover to Germany. As a result of an agreed bid, Continental Can, through Europemballage, increased its share-holding in Thomassen from 10.4% to 91.07%.

Despite the relatively small trade they did in each others' areas, the Commission held that Schmalbach and Thomassen were potential competitors, because it was economic to carry empty containers distances up to 150-300 km. for the more bulky and 500-1,000 km. for the smaller containers, forming a common area available to both enterprises extending over almost the whole of Benelux as well as the North and Centre of Germany. Continental Can's acquisition of control over Thomassen eliminated the potentiality of competition between Schmalbach and Thomassen in the common area, which was a substantial part of the Common Market, and reduced the potential freedom of choice of the users of their products in that area, so constituting an abuse of the dominant position held by the former.

5—31      In the *Continental Can* case, there was no question of a take-over being forced upon an unwilling competitor. The bid for Thomassen's shares was an agreed bid. Therefore, there was no abuse of Continental Can's economic power in that direction. Neither was there any question of abuse in any of the other respects mentioned in Article 86 or the Study. The sole question was whether a take-over, not abusive in itself, could be condemned under Article 86 merely because of the consequent elimination of competition.

5—32      In considering this aspect of the case, it must be remembered that the Rome Treaty contains no provisions giving the Commission power to control mergers. In 1956 and early 1957, when the text of the Treaty was being finalised, mergers and concentration of enterprises were not seen as a problem — it was not until 1965, for example, that the United Kingdom took powers to control mergers, and legislation to that effect in Germany is only now (1972) under consideration. As will be discussed in more detail in Chapter 14, one of the purposes of the 1966 Study was to consider to what extent Article 85 or Article 86 applied to mergers, and the conclusion was that Article 86 could apply where one of the parties held a dominant position in a substantial part of the Common Market and the merger resulted in elimination of competition, actual or potential.

5—33      Continental Can has appealed to the European Court against the Commission's decision, and it will be interesting to see whether the Court upholds this attempt to widen the concept of abuse to include the mere elimination of competition — in other words, the attempt to use Article 86 as a means of controlling mergers.

5—34      To conclude this discussion of the meaning of "abuse", that abuse may either be conduct internal to the enterprise, or external. Internal abusive conduct, for example, would include a restriction of production, or a deliberate decision not to pursue a certain line of development. External conduct would include such activities as imposing unfair prices or terms, or discriminating between buyers, placing some at a competitive disadvantage.

It is foreseeable that difficulties may arise in the future in situations such as the *duPont* cellophane case (1-07). If a firm has made itself dominant in the market by its efficiency, in research and development as well as in production and marketing, will it be at risk under Article 86 if it pursues its efficiency even if that means driving the last competitor out of the market?

### Effect upon inter-Member trade

5—35   The fifth condition for the application of Article 86 is that the abuse of the dominant position must be capable of affecting inter-Member trade.

5—36   In the *GEMA* case, there was actual effect upon inter-Member trade. GEMA's practices made it more difficult for a composer or author to become a member of a corresponding society in other Member States, and formed an obstacle to the establishment of a unified market within the Community for music publishing. The double royalty payment on records imported into Germany from other Members restricted the trade in records, and the higher fee charged on imported tape recorders had the same effect.

5—37   As regards the *Continental Can* decision, the effect upon inter-Member trade was potential. Schmalbach and Thomassen could have competed with each other if Thomassen had remained independent. The take-over eliminated that possibility and was, therefore, capable of exercising a direct effect on inter-Member trade.

5—38   In theory, the doctrine of "appreciable effect" should also apply in deciding whether there is an effect upon inter-Member trade, but, given that there must first be a dominant position in a substantial part of the Common Market and that potential effect can be taken into account, it would seem that in practice there is unlikely to be any case which can be disregarded for lack of "appreciable effect".

### Conflict of laws

5—39   The conflict between the two principles — the "territorial" principle and the "effects" principle — has already been discussed (3-88 — 3-94). Although theoretically possible, it is most unlikely that in practice a situation could arise where one principle would apply but not the other in "abuse of dominant position" situations. This would require such a situation as where a firm had a dominant position in a substantial part of the Common Market without actually being physically present there and without taking any action there. To achieve this, it would have to do all its business there by post, and that is a most unlikely situation. In practice, therefore, in order to have a dominant position in a part of the Community, a firm will almost always have some establishments or be involved in some actions there so that these will be within the territorial jurisdiction of the E.E.C. just as much as the effects of those actions.

5—40 The *Continental Can* decision was, admittedly, addressed by the Commission to Continental Can itself, which is not established within the E.E.C. The Commission has done so, upon the doctrine of "enterprise entity", holding that the actions of its sub-subsidiary Schmalbach can be imputed to Continental Can *via* Europemballage. This doctrine has been approved by the European Court in its decision in the I.C.I. appeal against the *Aniline Dyes* decision (3-94).

*Miscellaneous*

5—41 To conclude, Article 86 contains nothing equivalent to paragraphs 2 and 3 of Article 85. There is no scope for a provision on the lines of paragraph 2, declaring void agreements, etc., which infringe Article 85.1, because by its nature an abuse is something done — having been done, it cannot be avoided (i.e. made void). In this respect, abuse of dominant position is comparable with a concerted practice.

5—42 In certain Members, however, it would seem that private suit is available to obtain redress for damage caused by abuse of dominant position. The Study prepared at the Commission's request (see paragraph 3-56) indicates that private suit might be possible in the six original Members. It is doubtful if such private litigation is possible in the United Kingdom.

5—43 Equally, there is no scope for an exemption provision, because an abuse is an abuse and therefore not to be exempted. Herein lies a significant difference between 85.1 and 86. Article 85.1 is based on the "prohibition" principle, i.e. it prohibits all agreements, etc., which restrict competition and affect inter-Member trade irrespective of whether they are bad or good. Consequently, there must be some procedure for allowing to continue those whose results are so desirable as to warrant exempting from the prohibition, i.e. some subsequent procedure to exempt desirable agreements, etc., from the preceding *a priori* judgment. Article 86, in contrast, is based on the "abuse" principle, i.e. it starts with no such prior condemnation. There is nothing improper in a dominant position. What is forbidden is exploiting that dominant position in an objectionable way. Consequently, for the Article to apply, there must be a preceding judgment that what has been done is wrong, and on that basis there is no place for a succeeding review to see if the wrong should be allowed to continue.

## 3. Regulation 17

5—44 Regulation 17 (Appendix B) implements Article 86. By virtue of Article 1 of the Regulation, all abuses contrary to Article 86 are forbidden. No declaration or ruling to that effect is necessary — the ban is automatic. The ban has applied within the six original Member States since the 13th March, 1962, when Regulation 17 came into force, i.e. any abuse contrary to Article 86 within the territories of the Six has been forbidden irrespective of the nationality of the enterprise concerned — Continental Can and Europemballage are both American companies but their actions took place within the E.E.C. (purchase of the shares in Thomassen) and the Commission therefore issued its decision against Continental Can, relying upon the doctrine of "enterprise entity". As regards actions amounting to abuse contrary to Article 86 in the territories of the three new Member States, anything done up to 31st December, 1972, will be outside Article 86, but actions on the 1st January, 1973, onwards will be within the Article, if the three countries accede to the Community as from that date — this is the effect of Article 2 of the Act annexed to the Treaty of Accession (4-05).

5—45   Since the 13th March, 1962, the competent authorities in the original Member States have been able to apply Article 86, and the authorities in the new Members will be able to do so from the 1st January, 1973, assuming that the Commission has not itself instituted proceedings. And from the same dates, the national courts have been and will be under an obligation to enforce the Article.

### Termination of infringements

5—46   The Commission is empowered by Article 9 of Regulation 17 (18-10) to enforce Article 86, and once it has begun proceedings it has exclusive competence. The Commission can act on its own initiative or upon applications received from Member States or interested persons (Article 3) — copies of such applications must be sent to all the Member States (Article 10). In the *Continental Can* case, on the 16th March, 1970, Thomassen published the offer by Europemballage to buy the Thomassen shares. Despite warnings as to the possible incompatibility of the take-over with Article 86, Europemballage on the 8th April, 1970, proceeded to buy the Thomassen shares, and the Commission decided on the 9th April to institute proceedings.

5—47   The Commission has power under Article 12 of Regulation 17 to carry out "sector inquiries" into whole areas of economic activity. It also has power to obtain information under Article 11 and to carry out investigations itself (Article 14) or through the competent authorities of Member States (Article 13). These powers have been discussed in paragraphs 4-56 — 4-66 (Article 11), paragraphs 4-09 and 4-72 (Article 12), and paragraphs 4-67 — 4-80 (Articles 13 and 14).

5—48   Having completed its examination of the case and concluded that there is an abuse contrary to Article 86, the Commission is not obliged to render a formal decision. Article 3.3 (18-04) allows it to make recommendations to the undertakings concerned with a view to ending the abuse informally. The performing rights societies in France, Belgium, and Holland, corresponding to GEMA in Germany, agreed to modify their arrangements after approaches by the Commission. Each had a monopoly in fact in its own country, and followed a practice of limiting its activity to that country. Coupled with the exclusive reciprocal agreements between those three societies as well as GEMA and the Italian society, this meant that a composer or author had to use the society of the country in which he lived.

5—49 Before taking a decision in an infringement case, the Commission must give the parties an opportunity to be heard, and also third parties where the Commission or the relevant competent authorities consider this necessary or the third party can establish a sufficient interest (Article 19). The Advisory Committee must also be consulted (Article 10.3).

5—50 A decision will require the party or the parties concerned to terminate the infringement. The *GEMA* decision required that body to terminate its abusive activities immediately, and to modify its constitutional arrangements within six months to remove all offensive provisions. The *Continental Can* decision gave that company just over six months in which to present proposals to the Commission to bring its violation of Article 86 to an end.

5—51 The parties have a right of appeal to the European Court under Article 173 of the Treaty (17-16). GEMA appealed to the Court against the Commission's decision, but later withdrew the appeal. Continental Can appealed against the decision, and also asked for a stay of execution pending the Court's decision on its appeal; the Court refused the stay of execution, so that Continental Can remained bound to submit its proposals to the Commission before the 1st July, 1972, although the appeal had not then been heard.

5—52 The Commission has power under Article 15.2 of Regulation 17 to impose fines for a breach of Article 86. No such fines have so far been imposed.

### Negative clearance

5—53 It is open to the parties concerned, if they wish, to seek negative clearance from the Commission if there is any likelihood of their activities being questioned under Article 86. If the Court upholds the Commission's decision in the *Continental Can* case, so that Article 86 is finally accepted as applying in merger cases involving a dominant position, the possibility of obtaining negative clearance could prove a useful safeguard for parties to a proposed merger where one of them has a dominant position within Article 86 or a dominant position is likely to result.

5—54 An application for negative clearance under Article 86 does not have to be made on any special form but must state all the relevant facts (Regulation 1133/68 — 25-02). Copies have to be sent by the

Commission to the competent authorities of the Member States (Article 10.1 — 18-11). In dealing with the application, the Commission can exercise its powers to obtain information under Article 11 and to have investigations carried out either by its own officials under Article 14 or by those of the competent authority of the relevant Member State under Article 13. As the parties are seeking negative clearance, they will be co-operating voluntarily with the Commission, and it would seem unlikely that these powers will be needed. The parties must be given an opportunity to be heard, as required by Article 19, and the Advisory Committee consulted in accordance with Article 10 before a decision is taken. The decision must be published, although legitimate business secrets may be suppressed, under Article 21.

5—55 There have to date been no published cases of negative clearance being granted in regard to Article 86.

### Procurement of information

5—56 The Commission can exercise its powers to obtain information under Article 11 of Regulation 17 in dealing with infringements of Article 86, applications for negative clearance, and sector inquiries. The procedure under Article 11 has already been discussed in paragraphs 4-56 — 4-66 above, and need not be repeated here.

5—57 The Commission has used its power to require the furnishing of information by decision, under pain of a fine and penalties for delay, in the case of S.I.A.E., the Italian counterpart of GEMA. The Commission requested the information from S.I.A.E. on the 10th June, 1971, without receiving a full reply. A reminder dated the 5th August, 1971, produced no results. A decision dated 9th November, 1971, was then addressed to S.I.A.E. requiring the desired information within three weeks of notification to S.I.A.E. of the decision.

5—58 The question of "professional privilege" can arise in connection with requests by the Commission for information, as discussed in paragraph 4-65.

5—59 Officials of the Commission and competent authorities in Member States are bound by professional secrecy, by virtue of Article 20, in respect of information obtained by exercise of the powers granted by Article 11.

### Investigations by and on behalf of the Commission

5—60 The powers of investigation accorded by Articles 13 and 14 are available to the Commission when dealing with infringements of Article 86, applications for negative clearance, and sector inquiries. These powers, and the relevant procedure, have been discussed fully in relation to Article 85 in paragraphs 4-67 — 4-80 above.

5—61 Particular note should be made of the privilege accorded to communications to and advice given by legal advisers, as discussed in paragraphs 4-75 — 4-80.

5—62 The officials of the Commission and of the competent national authorities are bound by professional secrecy in respect of documents, etc., and information acquired as a result of investigations under Articles 13 and 14 (Article 20 — 18-21).

*Hearings*

5—63 The procedure for hearing the parties and interested persons, as set out in paragraphs 4-81 — 4-82, applies also to proceedings under Article 86.

*Fines and penalties*

5—64 Article 15 of Regulation 17 empowers the Commission to impose fines of 100 to 5,000 units of account in respect of what might be termed "procedural" offences, i.e. supplying incorrect or misleading information in an application for negative clearance, or incorrect information in response to a request under Article 11 or 12, or failing to supply information within the due time under Article 11, or not producing complete books and records when required under Articles 13 and 14, or refusing to submit to an investigation under Article 14. Larger fines can be imposed for substantive offences, involving infringements of Article 86. These larger fines range from 1,000 units of account to 1,000,000, and the latter figure can be raised to 10% of the undertaking's turnover in its last financial year if that is greater. This power to base the fine on turnover can be particularly serious in relation to multi-product concerns which are fined in respect of one product only, as discussed in paragraph 4-86.

5—65 Periodic penalties of between 50 and 1,000 units of account per day can be imposed under Article 16 for failure to terminate an infringement of Article 86, or for failing to supply complete and correct information following a decision under Article 11.5, or for failing to submit to an investigation ordered by a decision under Article 14.3.

5—66 The relevant procedure is discussed in paragraphs 4-83 — 4-92. The "unit of account" is explained in paragraph 4-93.

*Liaison with Member States*

5—67 As outlined in paragraphs 4-94 — 4-98, liaison has to be maintained by the Commission with Member States. Regulation 17 provides for this liaison at four stages.

The first stage is when the case is initiated, either by an application for negative clearance under Article 2 or an application for investigation of an infringement under Article 3. Copies have to be sent by the Commission to the competent authorities in Member States.

The second stage is when information is sought from undertakings or associations of undertakings. Copies of requests or decisions under Article 11 must be sent to the competent authority in the Member

State concerned.

The third stage is when an investigation is to be carried out under Article 14. The competent authority must be advised "in good time".

The fourth stage involves the Advisory Committee which must be consulted before a negative clearance in respect of Article 86 is granted, or a decision taken requiring termination of an abuse under that Article. The Committee also has to be consulted before a fine or penalty is imposed.

## 4. Limitation of Actions

5—68    The draft regulation discussed in paragraph 3-85 will, if made, apply in relation to Article 86 as well as to Article 85. In that event, the Commission will not be able to proceed against an undertaking in respect of an abuse infringing Article 86 unless it has started proceedings within five years of the termination of the abuse. In cases of infringements relating to the procurement of information and the carrying out of investigations, the limitation period is three years. In both cases, the period could be interrupted and start running again in certain events, such as a request for information.

A limitation period of three years is also envisaged in respect of Commission decisions imposing fines or penalties.

# PART 2

# VERTICAL AGREEMENTS

# CHAPTER 6

# Distribution Agreements

## 1. Introduction

6—01    In the simplest productive enterprise there may be no distribution problem. The small horticulturalist or farmer who sells his tomatoes or flowers, eggs or milk, through a shop on his garden or farm, or the baker who bakes his bread in a kitchen behind the shop, will not be faced with the problem of how to distribute the products. But once beyond this scale, there is the need to bring the goods to the attention of potential buyers, to visit buyers to procure orders, to service the customer and maintain goodwill, to supply him with information, to deal with his complaints, and so on.

6—02    Within the same country, these needs can be met either from the main office or through branch offices throughout the country. Or if an extensive distribution network is needed, use may be made of distribution depots or independent wholesalers down to retail outlets or independent retailers. When dealing with distribution in other countries, difficulties can arise from differences of language, of habits, of standards and specifications, of legislation, and so on. There may be the simple need to have someone in the country to deal with the goods when they arrive (or fail to arrive), to clear them through customs and other formalities, and so on.

6—03    Once the level of business has passed the stage at which these functions can be served adequately from the country of origin, there are broadly four possible courses:

(1)    to set up a local branch;

(2)    to set up a local subsidiary company;

(3)    to appoint a local agent (i.e. someone who does not own the goods but handles them for the principal in return for a commission) as distributor;

(4)    to appoint a local independent trader (i.e. someone who buys the goods and re-sells on his own behalf) as distributor.

For opening up new markets, there are advantages in adopting either (3) or (4). A local firm knows the local language and conditions, has established contacts, etc.

6—04 Where a new area is to be opened up from the point of view of marketing a product, there has to be a considerable investment of time, effort, and money. Those concerned have to study and learn about the product. Potential customers have to be visited to arouse their interest. Literature must be prepared and perhaps translated. Advertising campaigns mounted, and so on. Whoever is providing all this can reasonably ask that when a market for the product is developed and established, he will reap the benefit, and that somebody else who has not borne the "heat and burden of the day" should not be allowed to come in. Equally, it is to the interest of the manufacturer to ensure that whoever is developing the market for him has an incentive, whether it is his own branch office or subsidiary or an agent or independent trader.

6—05 Consequently, particularly in the case of agreements with local distributors (i.e. agents or independent traders), it is common to specify the area to be covered and to give the distributor some exclusivity within that area, such as the sole right to buy from the principal in that area, and perhaps an obligation on the principal not to sell himself in that area and to bind his distributors in other areas not to do so. In return, the principal may require the distributor not to manufacture or handle competing products, not to sell in other distributors' areas, and so on. This "insulation" of areas or markets from each other can be very effectively reinforced by use of patents and trade marks, and other "intellectual property" rights. If the product is protected by patents, the distributor may be given an exclusive licence to sell the product in his area. If the product is identified by a well-known trade mark, the right to use that mark in the area may be transferred to the distributor. By using such an exclusive patent licence or the trade mark, the distributor would normally be in a very strong position to prevent any "parallel imports", i.e. imports of the product into his area otherwise than through him. In some countries the legal system can be used to the same effect. For example, in France the doctrine of "opposabilité aux tiers" enabled an exclusive franchise granted by a manufacturer to a distributor to be used against a third party selling the goods in the franchise area in breach of the franchise.

## 2. Application of Article 85.1

6—06 Because of terms and factors such as those just described, distribution agreements can come within the ambit of Article 85.1. But they do not necessarily do so. This was decided by the European Court in 1966, in the *Technique Minière* case. Technique Minière was appointed the French distributor for a German manufacturer of earth levellers, Ulm, with "exclusive sales right" in France. Technique Minière refused to accept and pay for some of the machines, and when ordered to do so by the French court argued that the agreement was void as being contrary to Article 85.1. The European Court ruled that a distribution agreement with an "exclusive sales right" is not automatically prohibited by Article 85.1 merely because it is an "exclusive" distribution agreement — to be prohibited, all the requirements of 85.1 must be met.

6—07 As noted in Chapter 3, those requirements are fourfold. The first is that there must be an agreement, a decision of an association, or a concerted practice. It would be unusual for a distribution arrangement with a distributor to be made by an association, and for one made by an individual principal and a distributor to be made by a concerted practice. It may be assumed, therefore, that there is an agreement. The other three requirements are that the agreement must be "between undertakings", must have an effect upon inter-Member trade, and must have the object or effect of restricting competition. Consideration of each of these in turn will show which types of distribution agreement do *not* come within Article 85.1.

### "Between undertakings"

6—08 For Article 85.1 to apply, the agreement must be "between undertakings". Consequently, if the distributor is a branch of the principal, not a separate legal entity, then the distributor and the principal are one and the same undertaking, not two undertakings. Any "agreement" there may be between them is not an agreement "between undertakings", and cannot, therefore, be within Article 85.1.

### "Enterprise entity"

6—09 Where the distributor is a subsidiary of the principal (or *vice versa*) and controlled by it, they are deemed to be one undertaking, on the basis of the doctrine of "enterprise entity". Consequently, any agreement between them cannot be an agreement "between undertakings" and cannot be within 85.1.

6—10 The Commission applied the doctrine in the *Christiani & Nielsen* case. The parent company, Christiani & Nielsen in Copenhagen engaged in civil engineering, had a wholly-owned subsidiary in Holland, and an agreement between the two companies provided that the parent would not operate in Holland and that the subsidiary would not operate outside Holland. There were other wholly-owned subsidiaries in Germany and France, with agreements restricting them from operating in countries where a subsidiary was established. The Commission held that the division of markets between the parent and subsidiary was only a distribution of functions within the same economic entity, and so could not have the object or effect of restricting competition. Negative clearance was granted.

6—11 In the *Kodak* case, the five Kodak subsidiaries in the Common Market were controlled by the American parent and were unable to act independently in the fields of activity governed by the parent. Each introduced new standard conditions of sale on the instructions of the parent. The Commission held that the identical nature of the standard conditions did not result from an agreement or concerted practice between the subsidiaries or between the parent and the subsidiaries.

6—12 This approach was approved by the European Court in the *Béguelin* case, where the Belgian parent company transferred to its French subsidiary the exclusive concession to distribute the products (Japanese pocket cigarette-lighters) in France. The Court ruled that relations between a parent and its subsidiary which did not have economic autonomy should not be taken into account in deciding the validity of an agreement under Article 85.1.

### "Trade representatives"

6—13 In describing the courses open to a principal, paragraph 6—03 distinguished between an agent and an independent trader. This distinction is important in the light of the Commission's "Notice Relating to Sole Agency Contracts with Trade Representatives" (Appendix C).

6—14 The Commission uses the expression "trade representative" to signify the "agent", i.e. someone who negotiates or concludes transactions solely on behalf of his principal, whether he does so in his principal's name or in his own name (19-01). The trade representative does not bear any financial risk (except for *"del credere"* risks, i.e. where the agent, usually for extra commission, undertakes to indemnify the principal against failure of any of the customers), but acts only as an intermediary. In effect, the principal is competing in the market through the trade representative, who acts on the principal's instructions in the same way as would a branch office or a subsidiary of the principal. The trade representative is a mere intermediary, an *alter ego* of the principal.

6—15 The "independent trader", however, is in a different position. He is trading, and competing, on his own behalf, and bears the financial risks. He buys the goods from the principal and re-sells them — if the resale price is higher than his buying price plus freight and other costs, he makes a profit, but if it is not he makes, and has to bear, a loss.

6—16 Whether a distributor is an independent trader or a trade representative is not a matter of nomenclature, of the terms used in the particular agreement. It is a question of fact, of what the distributor actually does. In the Commission's view, the distributor is an independent trader if he maintains a substantial stock of the goods in his own ownership, or if he provides at his own expense a substantial free service to customers, or decides the prices or terms on which he sells.

6—17 The Notice does not deal with a situation which may arise in practice, i.e. where the distributor acts on behalf of the principal (and to that extent is a trade representative) but has the right to buy and sell the goods on his own behalf. In such a situation, whether the distributor is a trade representative or an independent trader will be a matter of degree. If he never, or seldom, trades in the goods on his own behalf, he will probably not lose his trade representative status. But if his trading on his own behalf is substantial, he will be an independent trader.

6—18 If, as a matter of fact, the distributor in a particular agreement is a trade representative, and not an independent trader, the agreement falls outside Article 85.1. If the distributor, on the other hand, is an independent trader, the agreement may come within 85.1 if the other requirements of the Article are satisfied.

6—19 It may be objected that, even where the distributor is an independent trader, it may be that the principal is, in effect, really competing through him, and that the legal differences between the agent (i.e. trade representative) and the independent trader may not be significant in economic reality. This has, to some extent, been recognised by the "bloc" exemption granted to certain two-party exclusive-dealing agreements by Regulation 67/67 (6-33 — 6-40 below).

### "Affect trade between Member States"

6—20 Article 85.1 applies only to agreements, etc., which "may affect trade between Member States". Consequently, if the effects of an agreement can be felt only within one Member or only outside the Common Market, that agreement is not within the scope of the Article.

6—21 In theory, it would be possible for an agreement between a manufacturer and a distributor in the same Member State relating to the supply and distribution of the goods within that Member to affect inter-Member trade — for example, if the manufacturer and the distributor each had a complete monopoly in that Member, the market would be foreclosed to outside manufacturers. In practice, however, distribution agreements between parties within the same Member and relating to distribution within that Member are not normally likely to affect inter-Member trade. This was recognised in Regulation 67/67 — the Preamble (23-01) acknowledged that exclusive-dealing agreements with regard to distribution within the same Member will not normally affect inter-Member trade and Article 1.2 (23-02) excludes them from the "bloc" exemption. Moreover, where the parties to an exclusive distribution agreement are both within the same Member and the agreement does not relate to imports or exports between Members, the agreement benefits from the relief from the obligation to notify granted by Article 4.2 (1) of Regulation 17 (18-05) for new agreements and Article 5.1 (18-06) for "existing" agreements. An agreement which is not notified by reason of this relief remains valid until ruled invalid, as decided by the European Court in the *Bilger v. Jehle* case (4-53).

6—22 In the *Kodak* case, the Commission had to consider the effect of a prohibition on exports outside the Common Market. The five Kodak companies within the E.E.C. were all subsidiaries of the American parent, Eastman Kodak. The subsidiaries, acting upon instructions from the parent, had introduced common general conditions of sale which included a prohibition on export outside the E.E.C., i.e. a purchaser of goods from one of the subsidiaries was required to accept a term forbidding export of those goods outside the E.E.C. (although he could export to other Member States). Even though the adoption of the common standard conditions of sale did not arise from any agreement or concerted practice to which Article 85.1 applied (6-11), an agreement between a purchaser and one of the subsidiaries containing the term prohibiting export outside the E.E.C. could come within the Article. However, the Commission concluded that the prohibition on export outside the E.E.C. was not liable to affect trade between Member States, because re-importation of Kodak goods into the E.E.C. was unlikely bearing in mind transport costs, the accumulation of profit margins, and the customs barrier of the Common External Tariff.

### "Appreciable effect"

6—23    Even if a distribution agreement does have an effect upon inter-Member trade, the agreement will not come within Article 85.1 if that effect is not "appreciable".

6—24    This was decided by the European Court in *Völk v. Vervaecke*. Völk, a small German manufacturer of washing machines, granted a Belgian company, Vervaecke, an exclusive concession to buy and distribute his machines in Belgium and Luxembourg, with absolute territorial protection, i.e. his machines would not be sold in that area except to Vervaecke. Vervaecke was an independent trader. In litigation between the parties, Vervaecke argued that the agreement infringed 85.1 because of the absolute territorial protection granted by it. The Court ruled that for 85.1 to apply there must be a reasonably probable expectation that the agreement could influence trade between Member States (and also restrict competition); if, because of the weak position on the market, of the parties, the agreement has only an insignificant effect on the market, the agreement will fall outside 85.1, even if it does contain absolute territorial protection.

6—25    Of course, where the parties have only a weak position in the market and the agreement does not give absolute territorial protection, then there is less scope for the Article to apply. The Court gave this ruling in *Cadillon v. Höss* where the French distributor, Cadillon, had the exclusive right to buy and re-sell the German manufacturer's civil engineering plant in France but there was no ban on parallel imports, i.e. no "protection" of the market.

6—26    A quantitative indication of what is not an "appreciable effect" was given by the Commission in its "Notice Concerning Minor Agreements" (Appendix J), i.e. a market share of not more than 5% and a turnover of not more than 15 million units of account (20 million for commercial undertakings). Thus, if a manufacturer in one Member grants an exclusive distributorship to a firm in another Member and the share of the market in the latter which the agreement goods hold is not more than 5% (and the turnover of the parties is within the permitted limits) the agreement may be treated as being outside 85.1, even if the distributor is granted absolute protection by the manufacturer (and even if the distributor has exclusive patent, trade mark, or other rights).

### "Prevent, restrict or distort competition"

6—27    If a distributorship does not have the object or effect of preventing, restricting, or distorting competition within the Common Market, Article 85.1 will not apply to it. This means that an agreement which does not contain any exclusive terms is outside the scope of the Article. This would be the case with an agreement which did not put any restriction upon the principal as to the persons he could supply, nor any restrictions upon the freedom of the distributor to handle competing goods. Such situations are by no means unknown. In a densely populated area, there may be more trade than one distributor can reasonably cope with, so that the principal would be reluctant to grant exclusivity and the distributor unable to insist upon it. And if the trade is a specialist one, the distributor may wish to be in a position to offer a whole range of products from several manufacturers, as in the case of retailers of watches and clocks.

6—28    Even where the agreement does contain exclusive terms, or terms which restrict competition, Article 85.1 applies only if the object or effect of the agreement is to restrict competition within the Common Market. Thus, in the *Grosfillex* case, a French manufacturer of plastic household goods appointed a Swiss distributor, who was in fact an independent trader. Grosfillex was bound not to sell in Switzerland except through the distributor, and the latter could only sell the goods in Switzerland and could not make or sell competing goods outside that country. The Commission held that the object of the agreement was to arrange distribution of Grosfillex' goods in Switzerland, not to restrict competition within the Common Market. Nor would it have the effect of restricting competition within the Common Market to any noticeable extent, because customs duties would prevent the distributor selling the Grosfillex' goods inside the Common Market anyway, and there were a large number of other competing manufacturers of the types of goods in question within the E.E.C. Negative clearance was granted.

6—29    There was a somewhat similar situation in the *Rieckermann* case. Rieckermann undertook to promote, at its own risk and for its own account, the sale in Japan of A.E.G.-Elotherm equipment and to maintain a guarantee and after-sales service. Rieckermann was to buy goods of the type covered by the agreement solely from A.E.G.-Elotherm and could not sell the goods anywhere except in Japan, while A.E.G.-Elotherm was to sell its equipment in Japan only through Rieckermann and not to allow other purchasers to re-sell there. These restrictions meant that (a) Rieckermann could not sell the

A.E.G.-Elotherm equipment in the Common Market, nor (b) buy similar equipment for sale in Japan from other E.E.C. manufacturers. Equally, (c) A.E.G.-Elotherm could not sell to other E.E.C. merchants for re-sale in Japan, and (d) could not allow its other E.E.C. customers to sell in Japan. However, as to (a), Rieckermann did not in fact carry on business selling in the Common Market, and, as to (b), (c), and (d), there were numerous E.E.C. manufacturers and traders exporting to Japan. Consequently, the Commission held that the agreement had neither the object nor the effect of restricting competition within the Common Market, and granted negative clearance.

6—30     *"Appreciable effect"* Even if a distribution agreement between the principal and an independent trader does contain restrictive terms affecting competition within the Common Market, the agreement may still escape the prohibition in Article 85.1 if the effect upon competition is not significant. The decisions in the *Völk v. Vervaecke* and *Cadillon v. Höss* cases discussed in paragraphs 6-24 — 6-25 are relevant here, as well as the *Grosfillex* decision.

    Relevant also is the Commission's "Notice Concerning Minor Agreements" (Appendix J) discussed in paragraph 6-26.

### 3. Exemptions

6—31     In addition to the various grounds removing from the ambit of Article 85.1 different distribution agreements between a principal and an independent trader so that negative clearance can be given, temporary exemption is available to one class of agreements as a result of the relief from the obligation to notify, and "bloc" exemption has been given to another class by Regulation 67/67. Moreover, there is always the possibility of individual exemption under Article 85.3 if an agreement for some reason is not within those two classes.

**Temporary exemption — relief from obligation to notify**

6—32     The relief from the obligation to notify given by Articles 4.2 (1) and 5.2 of Regulation 17 to agreements, where the parties belong to the same Member State and the terms do not relate to imports or exports from other Members, is available to distribution agreements. This relief has already been discussed in paragraph 6-21 above.

**"Bloc exemption"**

6—33     Council Regulation 19/65 (Appendix F) gave the Commission power to grant "bloc" exemption under Article 85.3 to certain categories of distribution agreements which would otherwise have been caught by Article 85.1. The Commission exercised this power in Regulation 67/67 (Appendix G). The Regulation grants "bloc" exemption until 31st December, 1972, (the Commission has now proposed that this date be extended to 31st December, 1982) to agreements (or concerted practices — Article 8) under which the principal agrees to sell only to the distributor for re-sale within a specified area of the Common Market, or the distributor agrees to buy only from the principal, or both (Article 1 — 23-02). Apart from this exclusive purchase restriction, the only other restrictions on competition which can be imposed upon the distributor are (a) an obligation not to make or handle competing goods during the life of the agreement and one year thereafter, and (b) an obligation not to seek customers nor set up a branch or depot outside the agreement area (Article 2.1 — 23-03). The distributor can, however, be required to handle a complete range of goods or to buy a minimum quantity, or to sell in the principal's packs or under his trade mark, or to promote sales by advertising, etc., (Article 2.2).

As already noted, the exemption does not apply to agreements where the parties belong to the same Member State and the goods are to be re-sold within that State (Article 1.2). Such agreements are unlikely to affect inter-Member trade and therefore unlikely to come within 85.1, and in addition there is the relief from notification in Articles 4.2 (1) and 5.2 of Regulation 17.

6—34   The exemption cannot be used by competitors to grant exclusive rights to each other. The object of this provision is to prevent competitors from insulating their domestic markets. For example, if manufacturer A in country X and manufacturer B in country Y both made the same product, they could reduce competition between their goods, and achieve a degree of market sharing, by A granting to B the exclusive right to buy and re-sell A's goods in country Y, and B giving A an exclusive right in respect of B's goods in country X. Such cases do not come within the "bloc" exemption, by virtue of Article 3 (a).

But individual exemption may be granted to reciprocal exclusive distributor agreements between competitors if the conditions of Article 85.3 are satisfied, as in the *Sopelem* and the *Fabrique Nationale* cases.

6—35   Article 3 (b) excludes from the exemption cases where the parties use patent, trade mark, and other intellectual property rights to prevent parallel imports, or use other rights or take other steps to the same end.

6—36   The "bloc" exemption is not available where a distributor is appointed by a decision of an association of undertakings. The Regulation applies only to agreements (Article 1) and concerted practices (Article 8). However, it is only rarely that an association of undertakings will appoint a distributor, and such cases can be made the subject of an application for individual exemption under Article 85.3.

6—37   There are, in Article 6, provisions enabling the Commission to investigate cases where exempted agreements enable competition to be eliminated or are abused.

6—38   A period was allowed in which agreements could be amended to conform to the requirements of the Regulation. So far as concerns the new Member States who join the E.E.C. on the 1st January, 1973, parties to "existing" distribution agreements coming within Article 85.1 "by virtue of accession" will have up to the 30th June, 1973, to amend their agreements. For the significance of the words "by virtue of accession" reference should be made to paragraphs 4-35 — 4-40 above.

6—39 It should be noted that a distribution agreement, if it is to benefit from the "bloc" exemption, must not prohibit the distributor from *selling* outside the agreement area. Article 2.1 (b) permits a prohibition on his seeking customers (or establishing branches or depots outside the area) but does not permit a prohibition upon him actually supplying an outside customer who comes to him unsolicited.

6—40 The implications of Regulation 67/67 have been discussed in the *Cadillon v. Höss* case. A German manufacturer, Höss, gave an exclusive right to sell its products (public works plant such as cranes, cement-mixers, etc.) in France to a French distributor, Cadillon. Höss purported to terminate the agreement, and Cadillon sued for damages in the French courts. Höss claimed that the agreement was void under Article 85, relying on the fact that it had not been notified. The French court sought a decision from the European Court which ruled that notification is not necessary to obtain the benefit of the "bloc" exemption in Regulation 67/67. If an agreement complies with the conditions laid down in the Regulation, that agreement is automatically exempt, without notification.

6—41 For the sake of completeness, it should be mentioned that the fact that Regulation 67/67 gives "bloc" exemption to certain exclusive-dealing agreements, does not necessarily mean that all agreements within that category must be within the prohibition in Article 85.1. When Regulation 19/65 was made, Italy challenged its validity, and the European Court specifically ruled that the definition of a category for "bloc" exemption does not imply that all agreements, etc., within that category infringe 85.1, nor that any agreement, etc., which does not satisfy the conditions for "bloc" exemption given in the definition of the category must necessarily be prohibited — as the *Omega Brandt* case shows, an agreement which fails to qualify for "bloc" exemption can achieve individual exemption.

### Individual exemptions

6—42 Individual exemptions were granted in the *Blondel* and *Jallatte* cases prior to Regulation 67/67.

That Regulation has reduced the extent to which individual exemption must be sought for distribution agreements, but there remain some which for one reason or another do not qualify for the "bloc" exemption given by the Regulation.

6—43 This was the situation in the *Omega Brandt* case, where the Swiss company Omega Brandt, manufacturer of "Omega" watches, had a long-established distribution system comprising one "general agent" in each country and a limited number of retailers called "Omega concessionaires". The agreements with each "general agent" were oral and had been notified to the Commission. Omega Brandt were bound to sell only to the "agent" in each country and not to sell to anybody else in that country. In turn, the "agent" agreed to nominate only a limited number of concessionaires, and to sell Omega watches only to concessionaires appointed either by himself or by other Omega "general agents" and not to supply other retailers. The "agents" were free to fix the prices at which they would sell. Because of the restriction on the number of concessionaires which the "agent" could appoint, the agreements between Omega Brandt and each "agent" in Member States fell outside Regulation 67/67 and consequently could not benefit from "bloc" exemption. Nevertheless, the Commission ruled that the agreements could qualify for individual exemption under Article 85.3 if the necessary requirements were satisfied. After some modifications had been made to the agreements, the Commission held that they improved distribution and that, the other 85.3 requirements being met, individual exemption could be granted, valid until July, 1977.

6—44   In the *Sopelem* case, the parties were competitors, actual and potential. Sopelem in France and Langen in Germany were manufacturers of servo-control equipment. They entered into two agreements by which each undertook to sell in its own country the agreement products manufactured by the other, and to give up the development of new equipment which would compete with the other's production. There were provisions about training staff, publicity, etc. Although the agreements did not specify that each would supply only the other in the latter's territory, the companies recognised that there would in fact be exclusivity.

There were about 40 other manufacturers in France, about 100 in Germany, and many others in other Western European countries, and there was active competition. The Commission took the view that the agreements extended each party's range while enabling each to specialise in its production and research, so contributing to the improvement of distribution, production, and technical progress. The agreements had led to an increase of Langen's sales in France and of Sopelem's in Germany, and an improvement in the quality of the goods and of the related service; the active competition from other producers would prevent the parties keeping all the cost savings to themselves; so that consumers were obtaining a fair share of the resulting benefits. Finally, the agreements did not contain any unnecessary restrictions, and did not eliminate competition as there remained many other competing suppliers. As all the requirements of Article 85.3 were met, the Commission granted exemption for ten years up to 8th February, 1977.

**Standard-form agreements**

6—45 Where a manufacturer expects to have a large number of distributors, it is convenient to have a standard form of agreement. This avoids having to prepare a new agreement in each case, and also has the merit that all the distributors are on the same terms. Where a standard-form agreement is involved, it is not necessary to notify each individual agreement. Form A/B indicates, in Section II.1.(b) (25-07), that only the standard text itself need be notified. Once that has been done, the benefit of notification applies to all individual agreements in that form made after notification (and also to those made before notification for "existing agreements" notified in due time).

6—46 The European Court decided this in the *Parfums Marcel Rochas* case. The Company had a standard-form agreement for its distributors. This was in use before 13th March, 1962, when Regulation 17 came into force, and was notified just before the 1st February, 1963, the closing date for notification of two-party "existing agreements". Subsequently, on the 24th June, 1964, the Company entered into an agreement in the standard form with a new distributor in France. In breach of the prohibition in the agreement on sales to other dealers (the agreement allowed only sales to consumers,) and of the ban on exports to other countries, the new distributor sold to a third party in Germany who put the products on sale to the public. Proceedings were instituted under German law against the third party for "unfair competition". The third party argued that the agreement with the new distributor infringed Article 85.1 and was not valid as it had not been notified. The European Court, when the issues were referred to it, ruled that notification of the standard form constituted good notification of all individual agreements made in that form, so that agreements made after notification (but before a decision by the Commission) enjoyed the temporary validity secured by notification.

## 4. Condemned Agreements

6—47 In the treatment of distributorship agreements under Article 85, there are two concepts of cardinal importance, "market insulation" and "parallel imports". Each comprises within itself, albeit in condensed form, all the requirements of 85.1. If the agreement creates "market insulation", it affects inter-Member trade and restricts competition. But if the agreement permits "parallel imports", it does neither.

**Market insulation**

6—48 Market insulation consists in using any available means to keep out of one market goods which have been put into circulation in another market, for example, ensuring that an exclusive distributor whose exclusive territory is France does not have to suffer competition from goods sold by his principal in Germany, and bought there and imported into France by third parties. There are various ways in which this can be achieved.

6—49 The basic method is contractual. The principal and the distributor enter into mutual exclusive-dealing obligations, i.e. the principal undertakes to sell only to the distributor in the latter's territory, and the distributor to buy only from the principal. The principal undertakes to bind any other purchasers from him not to sell in the territory, and also to bind those purchasers to pass on the restriction to people buying from them in so far as legally permitted. The distributor agrees not to sell outside his territory, and to pass on that restriction to those who buy from him.

6—50 Under some legal systems, this contractual arrangement can be enforced against third parties, where the existence of the exclusive distributorship is generally known of in the trade, and to allow a third party to sell in the concession territory would be "unfair competition". Thus, under French law, an exclusive concession could be used to prevent such third party sales, on the principle of "opposabilité aux tiers", i.e. the exclusive distributorship can be set up against third parties.

6—51 In addition to enforcement through national legal systems, the contractual arrangements can also be re-inforced by using industrial property rights such as patents and trade marks and, in some cases, copyright and performing rights. If the distributor owns within his territory the trade mark under which the goods are sold, he may be able to stop sales of the goods by third parties as being an infringement of his trade mark rights.

6—52 Other ways of procuring market insulation may be available in particular situations. In the *Kodak* case, the original standard conditions of sale adopted by the Kodak subsidiaries in the E.E.C. on the instructions of the parent company included provisions which could have had the effect of isolating the market in each Member State. The conditions could be interpreted as requiring a purchaser in one Member who bought from a subsidiary in another Member to make payment to the subsidiary in his own State, and at the prices operated by that subsidiary. The effect of such a system would be to remove any price attraction in buying in another State, because the price paid would always be that applicable in the home State. The conditions were amended in response to the Commission's comments.

6—53 The result of market insulation is the artificial maintenance of separate markets, usually national markets, in place of the single unified market which is the object of the Rome Treaty. It gives those concerned greater freedom as to the prices they charge. Prices can be higher in one market and lower in another. The distributor in one market can obtain a higher margin on his sales than his counterpart in another, even adjacent, market. The distributor in each insulated market achieves absolute territorial protection. He is not exposed to competition from imports of the particular goods from other, lower price, areas. He is not exposed to competition from "parallel imports".

Where market insulation exists, in the Common Market, it must affect trade between Member States, and also must restrict or distort competition, so that if there is appreciable effect there will be breach of Article 85.1.

### Parallel imports

6—54 The concept of "parallel imports" envisages two routes for the goods. The first route is import by the distributor from his principal. The second route is import by other persons within the distributor's territory who buy from third parties in other territories. The two routes operate side by side, independently of each other — they "parallel" each other.

6—55 A distributorship arrangement which does not seek to impede parallel imports is the antithesis of market insulation. Regulation 67/67 recognised that the possibility of parallel imports ensured competition at the distribution stage, and provided in Article 3 (b) that the "bloc" exemption would not apply to agreements where the parties hinder parallel imports. The former conditions of sale imposed on the Kodak subsidiaries prevented buyers from exporting from one Member to another, and so helped to isolate each national market, but were amended so as to permit parallel imports and exports. In the *Cadillon v. Höss* case, although Cadillon was granted the exclusive sales right in France, parallel imports were not prohibited.

### Grundig/Consten case

6—56 The classic case on the application of Article 85 to exclusive distribution agreements is that concerning the agreement between the German company Grundig and its French distributor Consten. In 1957, Grundig and Consten entered into an exclusive distributorship agreement under which Grundig appointed Consten as its exclusive distributor in France for radio and television sets, tape recorders, and dictaphones. Consten undertook to buy and distribute the goods on its own behalf, to run the necessary advertising, to service the guarantees, and to provide an after-sales service. Consten was given the right to use the "Grundig" trade mark in France during the life of the agreement. The restrictions upon Consten included a prohibition on handling competing goods, and a prohibition on exporting the goods outside France either directly or indirectly. Grundig, for its part, was not to sell to other persons in France, either directly or indirectly. The prohibition on Consten exporting from France and Grundig selling into France, either directly or indirectly, were part of a contractual market insulation system applied to all Grundig distributors who were bound not to export outside their areas, either directly themselves or indirectly.

6—57 In addition to the distributorship agreement, Grundig and Consten arranged that Consten would register in France in its own name the trade mark "GINT" (*Grundig INT*ernational), and would cancel the registration or transfer it back to Grundig if Consten ceased to be the exclusive distributor. The "GINT" mark was placed on all machines made by Grundig. It originated from an attempt by Grundig to prevent parallel imports into Holland by reliance upon the "Grundig" mark. That attempt failed, and Grundig then introduced the "GINT" mark, which was registered in Germany by Grundig and in other countries by the local Grundig distributor.

6—58    A number of firms began to import Grundig machines into France, buying them from German merchants. The most important of these parallel importers was UNEF, which re-sold to retailers at prices below Consten's. Some of Consten's retailers complained and litigation ensued in the French courts.

    Consten claimed that the existence of the Grundig/Consten distributorship agreement was generally known, and that the parallel imports into France amounted to "unfair competition" and should be forbidden under French law on the principle of "opposabilité aux tiers". Consten also relied on the "GINT" trade mark, claiming that import and sale in France of goods carrying the mark infringed its right. UNEF argued that the distributor agreement was void under Article 85, and applied to the Commission for a decision to that effect. Consten notified the agreement to the Commission, seeking either negative clearance or exemption.

6—59    The Commission held that there were agreements between undertakings, so that the first two requirements for the application of Article 85.1 were met. The agreements were capable of affecting trade between Member States, in fact they were intended to reserve trade between Germany and France in the goods in question to the two parties. Only Consten could import the goods into France, and Consten could not export to other Member States. The trade mark agreement helped to isolate the French market, and so was capable of affecting inter-Member trade. Finally, the agreements were designed to restrict and distort competition. The intention was that nobody other than Consten could distribute the goods in France, thus relieving Consten of competition in the import and wholesale trade in France. The "GINT" mark was a subsidiary means to the same end. The Commission held that both agreements came within 85.1, so that negative clearance could not be granted.

6—60    As to the application for exemption, Article 85.3 requires that consumers should receive a fair share of the benefits flowing from the agreement. Consumers here included retailers. The territorial protection intended by the agreement forced retailers to buy from Consten. Consten's prices were higher than those in Germany — for one radio set the catalogue price was 44% higher after allowing for taxes and duties, and net of discounts was at least 23% higher. The differences were not justified by cost differences. Retailers' margins in France were broadly the same as in Germany, so that the higher prices must have accrued to Consten's benefit. In short, consumers were not being given a fair share of the benefits. In addition, the restrictions in the distributor agreement were not indispensable. They were necessary neither to enable Consten to forecast requirements — if parallel imports were allowed Consten could forecast its trade and the merchants involved in the parallel imports could forecast theirs — nor to enable Consten to meet the guarantee obligations, which the buyer could enforce against his supplier and which UNEF met for machines supplied by it. They were not needed to enable Consten to provide an after-sales service; the buyer had to pay for this anyway, and UNEF again provided such a service for its supplies. And they were not needed to give Consten a sufficient margin to bear the advertising costs — these amounted to only 1.9% of turnover in 1963. In short, the absolute territorial protection was not indispensable. Exemption could not, therefore, be given.

6—61    The Commission therefore held that both the distributorship and the trade mark agreement infringed Article 85.1. As the former had been notified in due time, and the latter was ancillary to it, fines could not be imposed. But the parties were required not to do anything which would impede parallel imports.

6—62    Both Grundig and Consten appealed to the European Court against the Commission's decision, and they were supported by both the German and Italian governments. The Commission opposed the appeal, being supported by UNEF (and another French importer, Leissner). The Court upheld the decision on all the points on which it was attacked, except one. The Court ruled that the agreements indisputably affected inter-Member trade — they prevented firms other than Consten importing into France, and prevented Consten exporting to other Members. They also restricted competition — they aimed at insulating the French market and maintaining artificially separate national markets. The one exception, on which the Court ruled in favour of Grundig and Consten, was that not all the terms in the agreements were void, but only those which the Commission had identified as infringing Article 85.1.

6—63    What was the ultimate result? Consten remained Grundig's sole French buyer, and was bound not to buy from anyone else and Grundig could not sell to anyone else in France. This meant that Consten could in fact be the sole distributor of Grundig machines adapted by Grundig for the French market.

But neither party could prevent other French traders from buying Grundig products in other Member States and importing them into France, or French traders from exporting from France. Parallel imports could not be stopped.

The "GINT" trade mark registered by Consten remained unaffected, but Consten could not use it to stop parallel imports. Only the exercise of the trade mark rights was restrained, not their existence (this point is discussed in Chapter 8).

It is understood that subsequently Grundig bought Consten, so that the latter is now its subsidiary.

**Béguelin case**

6—64    The second main case, illustrating agreements which infringe Article 85.1 and fall outside Regulation 67/67, is the *Béguelin* case. Béguelin, a Belgian company, entered into an agreement with the Japanese firm Oshawa, under which Béguelin was appointed exclusive distributor for Oshawa's gas pocket lighters in Belgium and France. Béguelin set up a French subsidiary, Béguelin France, to take over the French distributorship. A German company, Marbach, had the exclusive concession for Germany. The agreements between Oshawa and Béguelin Belgium and Béguelin France were not notified.

6—65    In 1969, another French company, G.L. Import/Export, bought 18,000 lighters from Marbach and imported them into France. The Béguelin companies sued Marbach and G.L. Import/Export in the French courts for unfair competition. The French court referred certain issues to the European Court. The European Court ruled that relations between a parent company and its subsidiary, when the latter does not have economic autonomy, need not be taken into account in judging the validity of a contract under Article 85.1. If an agreement between a principal and a distributor is capable of affecting inter-Member trade and has the object or effect of restricting competition, it is within 85.1 even though the principal may be established outside the E.E.C. (as Oshawa was). And a distributorship agreement is particularly capable of affecting inter-Member trade and restricting competition if the distributor can prevent parallel imports. If there is a prohibition on re-export of the goods to other Member States, the agreement cannot qualify for exemption under Regulation 67/67.

## 5. Check List for Distribution Agreements

6—66    (i)    *Note* This Check List is not intended to cover every possible aspect of every variety of case. It is intended to set out the broad general lines of approach.

(ii)    "Agreement" includes "decision" and "concerted practice".

(iii)    "Restriction" in relation to competition includes "prevention" and "distortion".

*Preliminary*

1.    Are the principal, the distributor, and the agreement territory all located outside the E.E.C.?

If so, Article 85.1 will not apply

If not, read on.

2.    Is the agreement territory outside the E.E.C.?

If so, Article 85.1 will probably not apply — see the

*Rieckermann* decision.

If not, read on.

*Where the Agreement Territory is within the E.E.C.*

3.  Is the distributor

    (a)  a branch of the principal?

or  (b)  a subsidiary of the principal without economic autonomy?

or  (c)  a trade representative (as defined in the "Notice Relating to Sole Agency Contracts with Trade Representatives" — Appendix C)?

    If so, Article 85.1 does not apply.

    If not, read on.

*Where the Distributor is an Independent Trader (as defined in the Notice — Appendix C)*

4.  Does the agreement have no effect upon inter-Member Trade?

    If so, Article 85.1 does not apply.

    If not, read on.

5.  Has the agreement neither the object nor the effect of restricting competition within the Common Market?

    If so, Article 85.1 does not apply.

    If not, read on.

6.  Are the quantitative limits in the "Notice Concerning Minor Agreements" (Appendix J) satisfied?

    If so, Article 85.1 does not apply.

    If not, read on.

7.  Is any effect upon inter-Member trade or competition within the Common Market not appreciable?

    If so, apply for negative clearance.

    If not, read on.

8.  Are the parties located in the same Member State and does the Agreement relate neither to imports nor to exports between Member States?

    If so, Article 4.2 (1) of Regulation 17 applies — the agreement need not be notified, but may be notified if the parties wish.

    If not, read on.

9.  Does the agreement comply with Regulation 67/67 (Appendix G)?

    If so, the agreement is exempt under the "bloc" exemption.

    If not, read on.

10.  Are the requirements of Article 85.3 likely to be satisfied?

    If so, notify for exemption.

    If not, read on.

*Remainder*

11.  If the agreement has already been made, it may be worth notifying it and discussing it with the Commission in case it can be modified so as to qualify for negative clearance or exemption.

Otherwise the agreement should be terminated.

If the agreement has not already been made, it may be worth discussing the proposals with the Commission.

*Timing*

(a) For "existing agreements" to which Article 85.1 applies "by virtue of accession" — notification must be made between 1st January, 1973, and 30th June, 1973, and modification needed to comply with Regulation 67/67 must be made by the 30th June, 1973.

(b) For other agreements — notification must be made before they come into operation.

# CHAPTER 7

# Resale Price Maintenance

## 1. Introduction

7—01     When the principal carries out the distribution of the goods, as through his own branches, he can control the prices, and other terms, on which the goods are sold. He can also control them where the goods are sold on his behalf by a trade representative, i.e. an agent who is not selling on his own behalf but on behalf of the principal and must, therefore, comply with the principal's instructions.

    However, where distribution is through an independent trader, someone who buys the goods and is reselling them on his own behalf, the situation is quite different. The independent trader will be able to fix his own resale prices and terms. The principal and the distributor may, if they wish, include in their agreement a term binding the distributor to sell only at, or at not less than, prices fixed by the principal (and also on other terms fixed by him — for convenience, reference will be made only to "prices" but where appropriate this should be read as including "terms").

7—02     Why should those concerned wish to have resale prices controlled in this way? There are a variety of arguments for resale price maintenance (r.p.m.). Where he is supplying branded goods, the manufacturer is particularly concerned with the condition in which they reach the ultimate consumer because they bear his brand, i.e. they are deliberately and directly connected with him. He has an interest, therefore, in ensuring proper control throughout the distribution chain. To permit such control and proper handling, the firms involved in the distribution chain will need adequate price margins on which to operate. If the manufacturer wishes to see the goods distributed through a large number of small retail outlets (as in the case of "convenience" items such as cigarettes and tobacco, confectionery, etc.), he may want to ensure that the retailer is offered a sufficient margin to attract him to handle and stock the goods on a sufficient scale. This means controlling the wholesaler's margin, and also controlling the retail selling price to ensure that large stores do not use their buying power to negotiate large margins which may be used to cut retail prices.

Where there is substantial investment in advertising to bring the branded goods to the notice of the consumer, it is essential to ensure that there are adequate retailers with stocks, so that the consumer can buy the goods if he responds to the advertising.

In the case of high-priced "prestige" goods, the high retail price is part of the sales image of the goods, as in the case of some cosmetics. If the goods are sold at a lower price, they lose their image. There may also be some element of service at the point of retail sale.

7—03 In the case of branded goods widely advertised and well established in the market, there is the risk of their being used as a "loss leader", i.e. they are sold at retail prices giving little or no margin to the retailer, who is using them as a bait to attract customers into his shop in the hope that they will buy other goods. The retailer who uses branded goods as a loss leader does not need to hold stocks of them, beyond this quantity needed for his immediate purpose. The genuine retailer then finds he can make no sales at the normal price, and is dissuaded from holding stocks. The full benefits of advertising cannot be obtained because the consumer cannot find a retailer with stocks. Cut-price selling as a loss leader may also injure the brand image.

7—04 These considerations can be seen in book selling. Without r.p.m., retail book-sellers would tend to stock only the popular, quick-selling, titles to meet whatever was the current ephemeral fashion or craze. There would be no incentive to stock the slower-moving, more serious, works. The book-shop as a place to browse in in search of something of unexpected interest would disappear, to be replaced by a shop stocking only the currently heavily-advertised books.

7—05 For whatever reason it is adopted, there are two methods of operating r.p.m., i.e. by contract and by general law. The contractual method involves contracts or agreements between all the parties concerned. The agreement between the manufacturer and the wholesaler requires the latter to sell at prices fixed by the former, and if he fails to do so the manufacturer can sue him for breach of contract. To extend the control to the retailer, the agreement between the manufacturer and wholesaler may require the latter to put a similar provision in his agreement with the retailer. If the retailer then fails to observe the provision, the wholesaler can sue him. In such a case, the manufacturer cannot sue the retailer, because there is no "privity of contract" between them. This can be overcome by having a tri-partite agreement to which all three — manufacturer, wholesaler, retailer — are all parties. The contractual method depends upon the existence of contracts which can be enforced. Consequently, it can be enforced only against those who have entered into a contract with the appropriate term, i.e. it can be enforced only against "signers" and not against "non-signers".

7—06 Some legal systems permit r.p.m. to be enforced, both against signers and non-signers, either as part of a concept of "unfair competition" or as part of a concept of r.p.m. enforceable as such. The concept of unfair competition, as it obtains in Continental countries such as Germany, France, Belgium, etc., regards it as unfair for the trader who is complying with the normal rules and standards of the trade to be prejudiced by the actions of a competitor who is taking advantage of some unlawful act. If the trader is complying with the r.p.m. obligations he has accepted, and selling at the maintained price, it is unfair for him to have to meet competition at a cut price by someone who is either selling in breach of the obligations he has accepted or who had obtained supplies free of the r.p.m. obligations directly or indirectly from someone who has broken the obligation. This is the system in Germany, and can be enforced against non-signers as well as signers. To enforce the system, however, the German manufacturer or distributor setting up r.p.m. must satisfy the court that his system is "water-tight", i.e. that the price-cutter cannot obtain supplies free of the r.p.m. obligation except by a breach of contract on somebody's part, and that there is adequate surveillance to maintain and police the system. R.p.m. agreements for branded goods in competition with others, and books, are not forbidden by the anti-cartel law.

7—07 Other legal systems may permit r.p.m. to be enforced as such. For example, the law in the United Kingdom used to allow the manufacturer to enforce his maintained prices against both signers and non-signers if he could show that the existence of the r.p.m obligation was or ought to have been known to the price-cutter.

7—08 There are arguments against permitting r.p.m. to be practised. It prevents price competition between wholesalers and between retailers. If a retailer is efficient, he is not allowed to pass on to the consumer by way of price reduction a share in that efficiency. If the margin allowed to the retailer is fixed so as to cover a service element, a lower price cannot be offered to the consumer who does not need or use the service element. Control of the wholesale and retail margins may lead to rigidity in the distribution system and inefficiency. Margins are likely to be fixed at the level necessary to allow the least efficient to operate at a profit, so that there is no overwhelming incentive to increase efficiency. And so on.

7—09 Consequently, some legal systems forbid r.p.m. The United Kingdom law was changed so that r.p.m. is generally forbidden except for particular cases which the Restrictive Practices Court is satisfied come within the permitted exemptions, (so far only pharmaceuticals and books have been exempted), although supplies of goods may be refused to retailers using the goods as loss leaders. In France, r.p.m. is similarly forbidden except for exempted cases, and luxury cosmetic and toilet goods have been granted exemption.

In Germany, r.p.m. agreements in relation to branded goods in competition with similar goods and books are exempted from the anti-cartel law, and, as explained above, r.p.m. can be enforced if the system is "water-tight", under the "unfair competition" law. In Belgium and Holland, r.p.m. may be enforced in the same way.

## 2. Application of Article 85 to r.p.m.

7—10    The effect of an r.p.m. provision in an agreement must be to restrict competition. If the agreement is between a manufacturer and a wholesaler, it restricts the extent to which the latter can compete with the former. If there are similar agreements with each of several wholesalers, price competition between them is prevented, and also price competition between the retailers if the system is extended to them. If there is a noticeable effect on inter-Member trade, the agreements will come within Article 85.1. The limits set out in the "Notice Concerning Minor Agreements" (Appendix J) are relevant in deciding if there is noticeable effect. In this context it may be proper to consider the effect of the particular r.p.m. system as a whole, not each separate agreement, because on the principle in the *Brasserie de Haecht v. Wilkin* case each agreement must be judged against the background of other related agreements.

But where all the parties belong to one Member and the goods in question are delivered only in that Member, Article 4.2 (1) of Regulation 17 gives relief from the obligation to notify. And if only two parties are involved in each agreement, that agreement will qualify for relief from the necessity for notification by Article 4.2 (2)(a), even if imports and exports between Members are involved.

7—11    Early cases which came before the national courts after Regulation 17 came into force were decided under it, i.e. the parties concerned were able to defend their r.p.m. systems by taking action against price-cutters on the basis of "unfair competition" because the agreements enjoyed temporary validity under Article 4.2 (1) or 4.2 (2)(a).

7—12    The first Commission decision came in the *ASPA* case, in 1970. ASPA was the trade association of Belgian perfumery manufacturers and distributors. Its former constitution bound its members individually to enforce r.p.m. for the goods they made or imported, and also provided for collective enforcement by all the members by boycott. The members were also bound to respect sole agencies and official channels for importing goods, and to ensure that resellers complied with those agencies and channels as well. The Commission took the view that these obligations restricted competition in the supply of branded perfumery and toiletries imported into Belgium, and also affected inter-Member trade because the official distribution channels for imports could not be by-passed. ASPA removed the offending provisions from its constitution, and negative clearance was granted.

7—13    The reasoning underlying the *ASPA* decision made clear that r.p.m. with control of or a ban on imports or exports between Member States is forbidden by Article 85.1, except for cases with no appreciable effect. Bearing in mind that r.p.m. is generally forbidden in France, this means that r.p.m. is now difficult to maintain in other Member States on both economic and legal grounds.

From the economic point of view, if distributors in one Member cannot be forbidden to import from other Members, and if prices of the same branded goods in France are sufficiently low to allow import and resale in the first Member, r.p.m. prices cannot be maintained. And if the prices in France are not lower, i.e. without r.p.m., then r.p.m. in another Member will not be necessary because ordinary market forces would seem to be keeping prices at the desired level.

7—14  From the legal point of view, if imports from another Member are possible without breach of contract, the laws against "unfair competition" cannot be used. In Germany, for example, such imports prevent the system from being "water-tight".

In the *"R.P.M. for Film"* case, decided in 1968, the defendants were "non-signers" who had quite legitimately imported from Belgium and resold in Germany branded film made by a German manufacturer and exported by him to Belgium. The German manufacturer operated an r.p.m. system in Germany, binding his distributors to sell at the fixed resale prices and not to export outside Germany. Because of the export ban, the agreements had been notified to the Commission. The German court held that the defendants could not be prevented from reselling below the fixed German prices the film imported from Belgium.

The German court came to a similar conclusion in the *Minolta Cameras* case. The German national distributor for the Japanese cameras had established an r.p.m. system in Germany, but, presumably because of Article 85.1, had not forbidden the traders he supplied to export or import from other Member States the cameras in question. The defendant, a non-signer, had sold at cut prices cameras marketed by the distributor in Germany. The court held that, because exports to and imports from other Members were permitted, the system was not "water-tight" and, therefore, could not be legally enforced.

7—15  In the *Deutsche Grammophon* case, discussed in more detail in Chapter 8, the European Court held that the rights analogous to copyright granted by German law to record manufacturers could not be used to prevent imports, i.e. to prevent records made in Germany by Deutsche Grammophon and sold in France by Deutsche Grammophon's subsidiary there (and so deemed to be sold by Deutsche Grammophon) from being imported into Germany. Because these parallel imports could not be prevented, Deutsche Grammophon's r.p.m. system in Germany was cancelled, and held by the German court to be unenforceable, as not being "water-tight".

## 3. Check List

7—16  (i)  The adoption of r.p.m. is possible only to the extent permitted by the national law in the market(s) concerned. This inevitably limits the interest in a check list on r.p.m.

(ii)    The Note in paragraph 6-31 applies to this Check List.

(iii)   By the nature of r.p.m., there will be an "agreement" rather than a "decision" or a "concerted practice".

(iv)   By its very nature, r.p.m. involves a restriction upon competition.

(v)    "Restriction" in relation to competition includes "prevention" and "distortion".

*"Between undertakings"*

1.    Are all the parties to the agreement inter-related companies (i.e. a parent and its subsidiaries, or subsidiaries of a common parent), and is the r.p.m. system imposed by the parent?
        If so, Article 85.1 does not apply.
        If not, read on.

*Inter-Member trade*

2.    Does the agreement have no effect upon inter-Member trade?
        If so, Article 85.1 does not apply.
        If not, read on.

*No appreciable effect*

3.    Are the quantitative limits in the "Notice Concerning Minor Agreements" (Appendix J) satisfied?
        If so, Article 85.1 does not apply.
        If not, read on.

4.    Is the effect upon inter-Member trade or upon competition within the Common Market not appreciable?
        If so, apply for negative clearance.
        If not, read on.

*Relief from obligation to notify*

5.    Are all the parties from one Member State, and does the agreement relate neither to imports nor exports between Members?
        If so, Article 4.2 (1) of Regulation 17 (18-05) applies – the agreement need not be notified, but may be notified if the parties so wish.
        If not, read on.

6.    Are there only two parties to the agreement, or to each agreement if more than one?
        If so, Article 4.2 (2)(a) of Regulation 17 applies – the agreement need not be notified, but may be notified if the parties so wish.
        If not, read on.

*Individual exemption*

7.    Can it be shown that the requirements of Article 85.3 are met?
        If so, notify for exemption.
        If not, read on.

*Remainder*

8.    If the agreement falls within none of the preceding categories, it

is unlikely that negative clearance or exemption will be granted. If the agreement has already been made, it would be better to terminate it unless it is an "existing agreement" to which Article 85.1 applies "by virtue of accession", when it should be notified in due time.

If the agreement has not already been entered into, there may be something to be said for discussing the proposals with the Commission.

*Timing*

(a) For "existing agreements" to which Article 85.1 applies "by virtue of accession" — notification must be made between 1st January, 1973, and 30th June, 1973.

(b) For other agreements, notification must be made before the restrictive terms become operative.

# CHAPTER 8

# Intellectual Property

## 1. Introduction

8—01    In respect of tangible things, the concept of property, of ownership, seems at first sight quite straightforward. "I own this book, it is my property, I can dispose of it as I wish". But, in many cases, ownership of some particular thing does not mean ownership of all the rights in it. Ownership of a book does not, during the period of copyright, give the right to copy and market copies of the book in a country where the copyright is owned by somebody else. Similarly, ownership of a book containing music or a play does not, during the period of the performing rights, give the right to perform the music or play in public where somebody else owns those rights. Ownership of an industrial raw material does not give the right to use it in a process which is protected by a patent, and ownership of an item of equipment protected by a patent does not give the right to copy that item and to use the copy. In all these examples, ownership of the particular thing does not confer the total right to use it in any way — the right to use something in a particular way may belong to somebody else, i.e. the copyright, the performing right, the patent right, and so on.

8—02    These rights exist independently of the material things to which they relate. They are recognised by legal systems as forms of property, intangible property albeit, but still capable of being owned. They include patents, registered designs and models, "know-how" and trade secrets, copyright, performing rights, and trade marks. Particular legal systems may create and recognise rights not necessarily recognised in other legal systems — for example, the German Copyright Statute gives to the manufacturer of a sound recording the exclusive right to reproduce and distribute that recording (this was the right at issue in the *Deutsche Grammophon* case, paragraphs 8-69 — 8-73 below). The terms "industrial property" and "commercial property" are used to signify this type of property, but they suffer from defects. They are not really apt to describe copyright or performing rights. The expression

145

"industrial property" is also used to mean industrial buildings as distinct from "residential property". The term "intellectual property" is preferable as a generic term for this kind of intangible property.

8—03    Like any other property, intellectual property can be sold and bought. It is also capable of subdivision. A patent in respect of a patented process enables the patent owner to give licences to others to use the process — one licensee may be licensed to make one product with it, another licensee a different product. A patent for a new product gives the patent owner the exclusive right to make, to use, and to sell that product. This permits him to license one person to make the product, which the patentee can then sell to another licensee to use for one purpose only and to a third licensee to use for a different purpose. In the case of a new novel, the author may keep the copyright to himself and sell the film rights, or perhaps sell the serial rights.

8—04    At present, the nature and extent of intellectual property rights are determined by the national law of each country. A European Patent Convention is in prospect which will to some extent remove jurisdiction over patents and patent rights from the national courts, but this is still in the future. While the grant of intellectual property rights is a matter for the laws of each country, the particular rights in each separate country constitute a separate piece of property. If patents in respect of a new product are held in countries A and B, the patent owner may keep country A to himself, and either assign the patent in B to somebody else or grant licences under it, or he may grant parallel licences in both countries.

8—05    The Rome Treaty does not prejudice the rules in Member States governing systems of property ownership, as is specifically stated in Article 222 (17-20). But the fundamental object of the Treaty is to create a single, unified, market. The elimination of restrictions upon the import and export of goods and the freedom of movement of services between Member States are called for in Articles 3(a), (c), (d), 30, and 34, and Article 5 requires Members to abstain from measures which could jeopardise the attainment of the Treaty's objectives. The maintenance of a competitive régime is the object of Articles 85 and 86.

8—06    There is an inherent conflict here. The very essence of intellectual property is the ability to prevent other people doing something. If A has a patent in country X in respect of a product, the patent gives him the sole right to make and sell that product in X during the life of the patent, which means that he can normally stop other people from making and selling the product there and from importing it — A has been granted a statutory monopoly. A series of national patents could, therefore, be used to insulate each national market from competition in the form of imports. If A owned patents in countries X, Y, and Z, and granted a licence to B in country X limited to making and selling the protected product in X, and similar licences to C in Y and D in Z, the result would be for B, C, and D each to have a monopoly in countries X, Y, and Z respectively, able to prevent parallel imports from the other countries.

8—07 Article 36 (17-08) goes some way towards resolving the conflict. The elimination of restrictions upon imports and exports called for by the Treaty does not preclude prohibitions or restrictions justified for the "protection of industrial and commercial property". But such prohibitions and restrictions must not "constitute a means of arbitrary discrimination or a disguised restriction on" inter-Member trade. In other words, imports and exports can be prohibited or restrained in order to protect intellectual property but not as a method of arbitrary discrimination or hidden restriction.

8—08 The European Court has interpreted these provisions as meaning that the Treaty does not affect the *existence* of intellectual property rights but does affect the *exercise* of those rights. Judgments have been given in cases relating to different forms of intellectual property (patents, trade marks, and a form of copyright). The principles of general application to all intellectual property which can be deduced from these cases may be summarized as follows:

*Abuse of dominant position*

The mere holding of intellectual property does not of itself constitute a dominant position within Article 86. There must be the ability to prevent effective competition in a substantial part of the Common Market taking into account similar goods or substitutes (*Sirena, Deutsche Grammophon* cases).

The charging of a higher price for the protected article as compared with similar non-protected goods is not of itself proof of abuse within Article 86. But it may be proof of abuse if the price difference is substantial and cannot be objectively justified (*Parke Davis, Sirena, Deutsche Grammophon* cases).

*Restriction of Competition by Agreement, etc.*

(a) Where there is an agreement, etc., such as an agreement granting a patent licence or one assigning a patent, the agreement will be judged according to Article 85. If it restricts competition and affects inter-Member trade, to a noticeable extent, it will be within 85.1 and prohibited unless exempted under 85.3 (*Sirena* case).

*Parallel imports*

(b) Where there is no agreement, decision, or concerted practice, Article 36 may apply. Intellectual property rights cannot be exercised to achieve an arbitrary discrimination or a disguised restriction in inter-Member trade. Where the owner of the intellectual property has, either directly or indirectly, marketed and put into circulation the protected goods in one Member, he cannot use his intellectual property to prevent those goods being imported into another Member (the *Deutsche Grammophon* case).

The doctrine of "exhaustion of rights" is involved, and is

discussed in paragraph 8-08 below.

(c) But the owner of intellectual property rights in one Member State can use those rights to prevent imports from another Member in which the goods are not subject to corresponding rights, i.e. a patent in one Member can be used to prevent sale in that Member of goods within the patent if they have been imported from a country where they are not patented and where they were made and marketed by somebody unconnected with the patent owner (*Parke, Davis* case).

(d) It may be deduced that intellectual property owned in one Member by one person can be used to prevent imports from another Member where the corresponding property rights are held by a different person, provided that the property of both countries has never been held, directly or indirectly, by the same person. Thus if A took out a patent in Member X for a product and B took out a patent in Member Y for the same product, and A and B are not in any way connected (i.e. they are not parent and subsidiary company, or companies in the same group, etc.), A can probably prevent imports into X from Y, and B can probably prevent imports into Y from X.

8—09   *Exhaustion of rights* To take an English case as an illustration, the champagne firm, Heidsieck Monopole, in the 1920's marketed one type of champagne for consumption in England and a different type in France, using slightly different labels. One, Buxton, bought in France supplies of the French type and sold it in England. Naturally, these supplies bore Heidsieck's trade mark, which was registered in the United Kingdom. Heidsieck sued Buxton in the English court, claimimg that selling their product under their trade mark but without their permission was an infringement of the United Kingdom trade mark registration. In effect, Heidseick were arguing that trade-mark rights give the trade-mark owner the right to control the goods carrying the mark in whoever's hands the goods come, except where the owner had released his rights in the goods. The court rejected this view. The purpose of a trade mark is to show that the goods originate from the trade-mark owner. The trade-mark cannot, therefore, be infringed by selling "genuine goods", i.e. goods which have originated from the trade-mark owner and on which he has placed the mark.

The German courts have reached the same conclusion, holding that once the trade-mark owner has put the goods into circulation he has "exhausted" his control over them, so far as trade marks rights are concerned. If his putting the goods into circulation has taken place in one country, he could not use his German trade mark registration to prevent parallel imports of those goods, i.e. "genuine goods", into Germany.

8—10   Before proceeding to discuss each type of intellectual property in turn, it may be of interest to note some figures given by Dr. W. C. Schlieder, the Commission's Director General for Competition, at the Conference of the Licensing Executive Society in Puerto Rico in October, 1971. Some 3,500 agreements in this field had been notified to the Commission, divided as follows:

| | | |
|---|---|---|
| 26.7% | referred to | patents only, |
| 5.2% | ,, ,, | know-how only, |
| 3.9% | ,, ,, | trade marks only, |
| 12.0% | ,, ,, | patents and know-how, |
| 1.9% | ,, ,, | patents and trade marks, |
| 15.2% | ,, ,, | patents, know-how and trade marks, |
| 35.0% | ,, ,, | know-how and trade marks. |

99.9%

This means that patents were concerned in 55.8% of the cases, know-how in 67.4%, and trade marks in 56%.

As regards restrictions imposed in the agreements on the licensor or the licensee, the highest number, 71.2% of the cases, were exclusive licence cases, i.e. the licensee was accorded the sole right to the property in the particular area. Next in importance were export restrictions, preventing the licensee from exporting to other Member States, in 63% of the cases.

## 2. Patents

8—11 A patent is granted in respect of an invention. The invention may relate to a new product, or a new process. In essence, the patent grants the patentee the exclusive right in the territory concerned to make, use, and sell the product, or to use the process and sell its product, during the life of the patent. The patentee may assign his rights, or share them with others by granting licences.

The potential points of contact between patents and Community competition law are threefold:

(i) the existence of patent rights;

(ii) the exercise of patent rights;

(iii) agreements relating to patent rights, particularly licence agreements.

### Existence and exercise of patent rights

8—12 The relationship between the existence and exercise of patent rights on the one hand and Community competition law on the other was considered by the European Court in the *Parke, Davis* case. The American company, Parke, Davis, held two Dutch patents relating to an antibiotic, chloramphenicol. Italian law does not allow patents for medicaments, so that chloramphenicol was manufactured and sold freely in Italy. Parke, Davis applied to the Dutch court for an injunction to stop the import of the antibiotic from Italy into Holland in breach of its patent rights. The defendants argued that to use patent rights in this way to prevent imports from another Member State infringed Articles 85 and 86. The Dutch court referred that issue to the European Court.

The European Court pointed out that Article 85.1 can apply only where there is an agreement, decision, or concerted practice, and Article 86 only where there is abuse of a dominant position which affects inter-Member trade. The grant of patent rights by a Member State involves neither an agreement, etc., nor an abuse, so that the *existence* of patent rights is not affected by Articles 85 or 86. And the *exercise* of patent rights is not affected by those Articles in the absence of an agreement, etc., or of an abuse of a dominant position. The mere fact that the patented goods were sold at a higher price than the imported goods did not necessarily constitute abuse.

8—13   *Parallel imports* Following the *Parke, Davis* decision, and taking account of the *Sirena* and *Deutsche Grammophon* decisions still to be discussed (8-54 and 8-69 — 8-73 below), the position as regards parallel imports may be stated as follows:

(a)   *Patent in importing Member, but no patent in exporting Member.*

The patent owner in the importing Member can stop imports, provided the goods were not marketed by him either directly or indirectly, in the exporting Member (*Parke, Davis* decision).

Where the goods were put into circulation by him, either directly or indirectly, in the exporting Member, he cannot stop the imports.

(b)   *Patents in both importing and exporting Member.*

Where the patents are owned, either directly or indirectly, by the same person, he cannot stop the imports (*Deutsche Grammophon* and *Grundig/Consten* decisions).

Where the patents are owned by different and unrelated persons, but had once been owned, directly or indirectly, by the same person, parallel imports cannot be stopped (*Sirena* decision).

Where the patents are owned by different and unrelated persons and have never been owned, either directly or indirectly, by the same person, it would seem that imports can be stopped.

8—14   *Abuse of dominant position* In the *Parke, Davis* case the Court ruled that a higher price for the patented as compared with the imported article is not of itself an abuse within Article 86. Combining this ruling with those in the *Sirena* and *Deutsche Grammophon* cases, it may be said that:

(a)   The holder of a patent does not have a dominant position merely because he can prevent other persons marketing the goods within the territory of the patent.

(b)  To constitute a dominant position there must be the ability to prevent effective competition in a substantial part of the Common Market in similar goods or substitutes.

(c)  A higher price for the patented article as compared with imported articles is not of itself proof of abuse, but may be if the price difference is sufficiently large and cannot be justified on objective grounds.

## Agreements relating to patent rights

8—15  Agreements assigning patents or granting licences or sub-licences under patents may fall within Article 85.1 if their terms and effect fulfil the requirements of the Article.

8—16  However, where all the parties belong to one Member and the terms do not relate to imports or exports between Members, Article 4.2 (1) of Regulation 17 applies, and the agreement need not be notified, but can be notified if the parties wish. And where there are only two parties to the agreement and the restrictions in the agreement relate only to the rights of the assignee or licensee to use the patented rights, Article 4.2 (2)(b) of Regulation 17 relieves the agreement from the obligation to notify, although again the parties may notify it if they wish. Regulation 19/65 (Appendix F) gave the Commission power to make regulations granting "bloc" exemption to two-party agreements and concerted practices relating to the use or assignment of patent rights. This power has not yet been exercised, but "bloc" exemption regulations are expected towards the end of 1972 or early in 1973.

8—17  If the agreement comes within the limits prescribed in the "Notice Concerning Minor Agreements" (Appendix J), it is deemed not to have appreciable effect, and to be outside 85.1.

Individual negative clearance is available where, even though the agreement falls outside the quantitative limits in the Notice, there is still no appreciable effect upon inter-Member trade or upon competition within the Common Market.

8—18  Finally, the "Notice on Patent Licence Agreements" of December, 1962, (Appendix D) indicated certain clauses which the Commission then felt did not fall within the prohibition in 85.1. Three recent decisions by the Commission, in the *Burroughs, Davidson,* and *Raymond* cases, have elaborated, and in some instances would appear to have modified, those views. Before dealing with the clauses concerned, it would be convenient to outline each of the three cases.

### Burroughs case

8—19  Burroughs, an American company, held patents in the E.E.C., United Kingdom, and Africa in respect of carbon paper coated with a coloured synthetic resin, and also two trade marks. There were two licensees, Delplanque in France and Geha in Germany. The Delplanque licence gave that company an exclusive manufacturing right in France under three of the patents, and a non-exclusive manufacturing right under two others in the whole of the E.E.C., the United Kingdom, and Africa. Delplanque also had a non-exclusive right to sell in the whole of the E.E.C., the United Kingdom, and Africa, with the non-exclusive right to use the two trade marks in those areas. Geha had the exclusive manufacturing rights in Germany under three of the patents and a non-exclusive right under an application for a third patent. It also had non-exclusive selling rights under the patents and non-exclusive rights to use the trade marks within the E.E.C. and six countries outside the E.E.C. There were also "know how" arrangements in both licence agreements. There had been a restriction on Geha contesting the validity of any of the patents, but this clause was cancelled. There were a number of other provisions in the agreements.

8—20     The Commission found that the carbon paper in question was relatively new, and sold at a much higher price. It represented only about 10% of the market in France and in Germany. It was made by several firms in France, Germany, and Italy, and there was no restriction upon exports to or sales in each Member State.

8—21     The Commission held that exclusive manufacturing rights can restrict competition, but in this case the relevant provisions would not do so to an appreciable extent. The shares of the markets in question were small, there was freedom to sell in the whole of the E.E.C., and the products could be transported easily and cheaply. Negative clearance was accorded to each agreement.

### Davidson Rubber case

8—22     Davidson was an American company which had invented a new and improved method of making arm-rests and cushions for cars. It held patents and patent applications in Germany, Italy, France, Belgium, and Holland, and also had extensive know-how in respect of the patented process. Davidson started to use the process in the U.S.A. in 1958, where it was an immediate success. Not being established in Europe, Davidson set up a net-work of licences with European manufacturers in 1959. It granted exclusive manufacturing and selling licences to Happich in Germany, Maglum in France, and Gallino in Italy, under the patents and also undertook to provide them with the associated know-how. There was also a "non-contesting" clause in the agreements requiring the licensees not to challenge the validity of Davidson's patents. The agreements were later amended, so that in effect the sales licences became non-exclusive and the non-contesting clause was cancelled. Happich entered into agreements with Maglum and Gallino to pass on to them the Davidson know-how in return for a royalty; there was a clause forbidding exports to the territory of other licensees but this was later cancelled. Subsequently, Davidson made another licence agreement with STAR in Italy relating to car cushions, with Gallino's consent; and Maglum granted a sub-licence, under its licence, to CIM, with Davidson's consent. Neither the STAR licence nor the CIM sub-licence contained restrictive terms. Production of the patented goods represented only a relatively small proportion of the turnover of the licensees. The licensees' production of arm-rests represented about one-third of Community production, the remaining two-thirds being manufactured by the car-makers themselves (one-third) and by other independent manufacturers (one-third).

8—23 The Commission held that the exclusive manufacturing rights given to Happich, Gallino, and Maglum could restrict competition. The licensees had a substantial share of the market. Davidson was precluded from giving licences to other licensees in Member States who might export to other Members, so that inter-Member trade was affected. Article 85.1 therefore applied to the Davidson agreements with Happich, Maglum, and Gallino, and the Happich know-how agreements with Maglum and Galino.

8—24 However, the agreements contributed to the promotion of technical progress in that they permitted the Davidson process to be exploited in Europe and enabled the process and products to be adapted to European requirements. Consumers (i.e. motor-car manufacturers) shared in the benefit in that they obtained supplies adapted to their needs from nearby suppliers. The exclusivity given to Happich, Maglum, and Gallino had been indispensable because they would not have been interested in adopting the process and investing the necessary capital without some assurance as to their markets. And the parties were not enabled to eliminate competition because they had only one-third of the market. In the circumstances, exemption could be granted to the Davidson agreements with Happich, Maglum, and Gallino, and to the two ancillary agreements between Happich and the two latter, in respect of the periods after their modification. In respect of the periods before modification, the prohibition in Article 85.1 was declared inapplicable (thereby granting protection from private suit).

8—25 As the Davidson agreement with STAR and the Maglum sub-licence to CIM contained no restriction, negative clearance was granted to them.

*Raymond case*

8—26 Raymond was a French company with a branch in Germany, engaged in the manufacture of plastic fasteners of all kinds for use in car body-work. The fasteners were protected by some thirty-five patents and registered designs in Germany, but only to a small extent in France and not at all in the other Members. The fasteners were fully protected in Japan. In addition to the patents and registered designs, Raymond had extensive know-how relating to the fasteners.

Raymond granted to Nagoya an exclusive contract to make the fasteners in Japan and sell them there and in certain neighbouring countries (but if the royalties paid by Nagoya failed to reach a minimum, the licence ceased to be exclusive and Raymond could grant other licences in the area). Nagoya was forbidden to contest the validity of the patents and designs, and also to export the fasteners outside its area. If Nagoya developed any improvements in the Raymond techniques, the agreement originally provided that these were to become Raymond's property, but on the Commission's intervention the agreement was amended so that they became Raymond's property only if they were not patentable, and if they were patentable Raymond would be entitled to a non-exclusive licence only. If the Nagoya improvements were outside the Raymond techniques, the agreement originally provided that Raymond would have an exclusive licence outside Japan, but this was amended so that Raymond would have only a non-exclusive licence.

8—27 The Commission found that Raymond was the most important supplier of these products in the Common Market and its share of the German market was more important than all the other makers combined. Nagoya was the most important supplier in Japan, and the Japanese car manufacturer Toyota had a majority holding in the Nagoya capital.

8—28 The Commission held that the fact that the licence to Nagoya was exclusive did not affect competition within the Common Market, because the other Japanese manufacturers of these fasteners, i.e. the potential licensees would have no greater interest in competing in the E.E.C. than Nagoya. The ban on Nagoya selling the fasteners outside its area meant that it could not sell in the Common Market. But the particular type of fastener to be used in a car was settled between the car manufacturer and the fastener manufacturer, and might be specially adapted to suit the particular car model. Close collaboration between the two manufacturers was necessary, involving many tests and frequent contacts. In the circumstances, Nagoya would find it difficult to do business in the Common Market, and Common Market car manufacturers were unlikely to draw supplies from Japanese makers of fasteners. The export ban would not, therefore, have an appreciable effect upon competition within the Common Market. Similarly, as regards the ban on Nagoya attacking the German patents, Nagoya was closely associated with Toyota and not likely to be interested in establishing itself in Germany. Therefore, Nagoya was unlikely to be interested in attacking the German patents, and the ban would not affect trade in the Common Market.

In short, the licence agreement as amended did not have the object or effect of restricting or distorting competition within the Common Market, and negative clearance was granted.

### Clauses in agreements relating to patent rights

8—29 The stage has now been reached at which to consider individual types of clauses which are frequently found in agreements relating to patent rights. They will be dealt with in four broad groups — terms relating to area, terms relating to the product or to the use of the process, terms affecting other relations between the grantor and licensee, and finally terms affecting relations between the parties and third parties.

The clauses will be discussed in the context of licences, but in most instances the comments are equally applicable to similar terms appearing in assignment agreements.

### Terms relating to area

8—30   *Manufacturing licence* In the "Notice on Patent Licence Agreements" (Appendix D), the Commission recognised that the grant of a licence restricted to only one aspect of patent rights, such as sale or manufacture, was really a sharing of part of the monopoly granted by the patent. On this ground, it did not fall within the prohibition in Article 85.1. On this basis a licence limited to manufacturing (or to sale) would not, of itself, infringe 85.1. Thus a non-exclusive manufacturing licence is outside 85.1.

In IE of the Notice, the Commission accepted that terms restricting the grantor from granting other licences or working the invention himself were also outside Article 85.1. The relative explanatory paragraph (20-10) appears somewhat equivocal. It leaves aside the question whether exclusive licences may restrict competition (because licences cannot be given to other people), and argues that such licences were then not capable of affecting inter-Member trade. Exclusivity seemed unobjectionable, being equivalent to an assignment of the patent rights. On this argument, exclusive manufacturing licences would be outside 85.1.

From the *Burroughs* and *Davidson* cases, however, it would seem that the Commission has now resiled from that view. In both cases, the Commission argued that an exclusive manufacturing licence could, in certain cases, be restrictive of competition. However, as there was no appreciable effect in the *Burroughs* case, negative clearance was given to both licences, and in the *Davidson* case exemption was granted as the exclusivity had been necessary to interest the licensees. In the *Raymond* case, it was also accepted by the Commission that exclusive manufacturing licences could be restrictive of competition, but negative clearance was granted in the rather special circumstances of that case.

It may be concluded, therefore, that an exclusive manufacturing licence will be considered to be restrictive of competition, either in object or effect, within 85.1 if its effect is appreciable, but that exemption may be granted if exclusivity is necessary to interest potential licensees (and the other requirements of 85.3 are satisfied).

8—31   *Sales licence* The interpretation of the Notice with regard to sales licences would seem to be the same as with regard to manufacturing licences, i.e. that they are outside 85.1.

Again, the *Davidson* case appears to evidence a change of mind on the part of the Commission as regards sales licences even greater than that with regard to manufacturing licences. The exclusive sales licences were modified to become non-exclusive (in effect a term was added that nothing in the licences would be used to prevent sales between Member States nor impose obligations contrary to the Rome Treaty), and in that form no objection was taken to them on that score.

In the *Raymond* case, Nagoya's manufacturing and sales licence in Japan was exclusive. The Commission considered that exclusive licences could restrict competition, but concluded that in the circumstances of that case there would be no appreciable effect within the Common Market.

It may be concluded, therefore, that exclusive sales licences, i.e. prohibiting trade in the patented articles between Member States, which have an appreciable effect will be treated as being within Article 85.1 (contrary to the view expressed in the Notice) and are unlikely to be exempted except for very cogent reasons.

8—32    *Ban on exports* For the same reason, a licence which, although not exclusive in that several licences are allowed to operate in the territory, nevertheless bans the licensees from exporting from that territory, is likely to be treated as infringing Article 85.1 if there is an appreciable effect on inter-Member trade, particularly if the territory in question is one of the Member States.

### Terms relating to the product or process

8—33    *Restrictions on the method of exploitation* These include such things as a licence to make only one product where the invention relates to several products, or to use the patented process for one purpose and not for others. Or again, a licence to supply one industry's requirements, and not another. In effect, such restrictions represent a sharing by the patent owner of part of his monopoly, and therefore not within Article 85.1, as recognised by the Notice in A2. This approach was confirmed in the *Davidson* case, in that no objection was taken to the licence agreement with STAR which authorised the latter to make seat cushions, and negative clearance was granted.

8—34    *Quantitative obligations* These include obligations to produce a minimum quantity or not to produce more than a maximum (or similar requirements with regard to the use of a patented process). An obligation to produce a minimum number is not likely to be restrictive of competition. In the *Burroughs* case, the licensees were to produce in quantity sufficient to meet the demand, a term which the Commission regarded as not restrictive.

The Notice also implies, in A3, that a restriction on the quantity to be produced (or the use of the process), i.e. a restriction as to the maximum, is not within 85.1. This might be so if there were sufficient licensees to ensure that expected demand was satisfied, but the possibility cannot be disregarded that the Commission might now consider that restrictions as to the maximum to be produced, where there is a limited number of licensees, did have the object or effect of restricting competition.

8—35   *Qualitative obligations* As the Notice explains (20-08), an obligation on the licensee to comply with necessary quality standards is not objectionable and cannot restrict competition where they are aimed at preventing misuse of the invention. In the *Burroughs* case, the licensees were required to conform to Burroughs' technical instructions, a term held not to restrict competition because it was aimed at a technically adequate exploitation of the patent rights.

8—36   *Purchase of materials* An obligation to procure materials from a particular source is acceptable if quality standards cannot be laid down for them. As the Notice recognises (20-08) such an obligation in those circumstances would be equivalent to quality standards.

By contrast, such an obligation, where there is no question of protecting standards, would presumably be restrictive of competition and capable of falling within 85.1.

8—37   *Marking* In some legal systems, damages cannot be recovered for *innocent* infringement of a patent. To make it difficult to prove innocent infringement, patented articles are marked with the patent number and licensees are required to comply with a marking obligation. Moreover, if the products are given an identifying mark, control and policing of the patent are facilitated.

The Notice accepts that such a requirement does not restrict competition. In the *Burroughs* case the licensees were required to put an identifying mark on the products, which the Commission accepted was for control purposes and not restrictive of competition.

8—38   *Prohibition on competing products or processes* A restriction imposed upon the licensee not to make a competing product or to use a competing process might be reasonable in practice. It might be difficult for the licensee to give his full effort and support to both — "a man cannot serve two masters". Such a restriction would restrict competition, but might not do so to an appreciable extent if there were a sufficient number of firms using the competing processes or making the competing products. The point is not covered in the Notice, and has not arisen in Commission decisions published to date. On analogy with Regulation 67/67 in relation to restrictions on distributors, it would seem reasonable to assume that negative clearance or exemption would be available in suitable cases.

### Terms as to the relations between the grantor and licensee

8—39   *Life of the licence* A licence for a period up to the life of the patent is indicated as being unobjectionable, in the Notice. In the *Davidson* case, the licences were for the respective lives of the patents except in the case of the sub-licence to CIM which ran from year to year. Negative clearance was granted to the CIM sub-licence, and no objection was taken to the other licences on this score.

The Notice specifically excludes from its scope terms exceeding the life of the patent. A licence extending beyond the life of the patent and containing terms acceptable only in a patent licensing situation is not likely to be acceptable in so far as those items fall within Article 85.1.

8—40   *Royalty* An obligation upon the licensee to pay a royalty to the grantor is not, of itself, a restriction upon competition. Royalties on the net selling prices were provided for in the *Davidson* case. In the Burroughs-Delplanque licence, a minimum royalty was payable, while in the Burroughs-Geha licence the royalty rate was to be halved in respect of patents declared invalid or patent applications which were not granted. In the *Raymond* case, if the royalties after 1st May, 1971, did not reach a minimum, the exclusive licence would automatically become non-exclusive. None of these terms provoked objection from the Commission.

In certain circumstances, however, royalty terms can fall within Article 85.1. In March, 1971, the Commission issued a report dealing with a joint research case. The parties were not named, and the report is referred to as *"Re Research and Development"*. Two large firms, established in different Member States and with positions of comparable importance in an industry showing oligopolistic tendencies, entered into an agreement to set up a joint company, in which each would own 50% of the capital, to carry out research and development for both parties. In respect of any resulting patents, each party could claim a non-exclusive royalty-free ten-year licence in respect of its own primary marketing area, and a non-exclusive licence with a royalty not exceeding 2% of the selling price in respect of the other party's primary selling area and any other areas. The Commission objected to the differential royalty rates, as hindering the penetration by one party into the other party's area, and so tending to restrict competition particularly as any new products were likely to replace the traditional products to a large extent. The case was settled informally by the parties cancelling the agreement.

8—41   *Supply and exchange of information* An obligation on the grantor to supply the necessary initial technical information to the licensee, and to communicate subsequent information and improvements was accepted as unobjectionable by the Notice. Similar obligations on Burroughs and Davidson caused no difficulty.

According to the Notice, an obligation on the licensee to communicate to the grantor information about improvements made by the licensee are not contrary to 85.1 provided the obligation is non-exclusive and the grantor is under an obligation to give the licensee information as to his own improvements. The terms in the Burroughs and Davidson licences as to communication of improvements were non-exclusive and reciprocal, and raised no difficulty.

8—42   *Rights in improvements* The Notice also treats as outside Article 85.1 an obligation on the grantor to give the licensee a licence under any patents taken out by the grantor for improvements in the invention.

According to the Notice, an obligation on the licensee to grant a licence to the grantor in respect of patents for improvements taken out by the licensee must be non-exclusive and balanced by a corresponding obligation on the grantor.

The *Raymond* case gives a good indication of the Commission's current thinking as regards licensee's improvements. Where Nagoya made improvements within Raymond's techniques, the licence agreement originally provided that the Nagoya improvements would become Raymond's property. On the Commission's intervention, this was amended so that the Nagoya improvements would become Raymond's property only if they were not patentable; in respect of patentable improvements, Raymond would be entitled only to a non-exclusive licence. An obligation on the licensee to grant a non-exclusive licence was accepted by the Commission in the *Davidson* case as well. As regards Nagoya's improvements outside Raymond's techniques, the original version gave Raymond an exclusive licence outside Japan, but this was amended to a non-exclusive licence.

It is by no means rare for licensees to be bound to transfer ownership of their improvements to the owner of the original patent. This is not as onerous as may appear at first sight. The owner of the original basic patent is in a better position to protect and enforce all rights in the invention and improvements if they are all in his hands. In so doing, he can act for all those interested in the invention, i.e. all the licensees. And the obligation on the grantor to communicate improvements to the licensee and to grant licences in respect of improvements without further royalty (terms commonly found in licence agreements) means that improvements made by one licensee enure to the benefit of all. In so far as each licensee is put in the position to make his improvements by the original work and know-how of the grantor and shares in the benefits of the work done by his co-licensees and in the protection of the invention by the grantor, the system has much to commend it in practice. However, the Commission does not seem to accept these practical considerations. The system can lose its attractions if each licensee can grant licences to outsiders, and if the grantor has to involve licensees in any infringement actions he may bring to protect the invention (where parties in different countries are concerned in taking joint legal action in third countries, the procedural and other difficulties are multiplied).

8–43  *Patent validity* Some legal systems adopt the principle that one cannot both claim a benefit under a right and at the same time question the validity of that right — one cannot "both approbate and reprobate". For example, a tenant who has accepted a lease from his landlord and thereby accepted the landlord's title cannot in proceedings against the landlord allege that that title is invalid. Similarly, a licensee under a patent agreement, having accepted the benefit of the patent, is not at liberty during the continuance of the agreement to challenge the validity of the patent in proceedings under the agreement. He is "estopped" from denying the validity of the patent.

Apart from the legal principles, there is a sound practical reason involved as well. It is usually to the interest of both grantor and licensee that the former should make a full disclosure to the latter of all the relevant technical information. In some instances, this might put the licensee in a position to challenge the validity of the patent, or put him on a line of enquiry which might lead him to the same position. Consequently, and also to overcome any limitations in the doctrine of "estoppel" (or corresponding concept in the particular legal system), it is common for licence agreements to include a provision that the licensee will not call in question the validity of the grantor's patents.

In the *Raymond* case, the Commission took the view that an obligation not to challenge the validity of the grantor's patent rights could restrict the competitive freedom of the licensee because it prevented him from freeing himself of restrictions and reducing the royalties payable and also freeing third parties from the restrictions on them. In the particular circumstances of that case, there was held to be no effect upon inter-Member trade, and the Commission granted negative clearance despite the clause. In the *Davidson* case, however, a similar clause appeared in all the licences (except that with STAR) and, at the Commission's instigation, it was removed.

In short, therefore, it would seem that the restrictions imposed by the legal system on the freedom of the licensee to challenge the validity of the patent will remain (under Articles 36 and 222 of the Treaty), but that the Commission will oppose a term in a licence agreement which is wider in scope. For the practical reasons mentioned above, it may be hoped that the Commission will be reasonably flexible in applying its views in practice.

8—44 *Arbitration* Where the remaining provisions of an agreement present no difficulty as regards Article 85.1, either by reason of their being outside 85.1 or by reason of exemption under 85.3, an obligation on the parties to submit their differences to settlement by arbitration seems to be acceptable. In the Burrough's licences the arbitration clause did not, in the Commission's view, constitute a restraint upon competition. And in the Davidson licences, the arbitration clause did not have the object or effect of restricting competition because, in the light of the exempted restrictions and of the provisions that nothing in the agreements was to be allowed to interfere with sale between Member States, an arbitration decision would not be likely to modify the position from the point of view of Article 85.

## Terms as to relations with third parties

8—45 *Prohibition on assignments or sub-licences* The Notice acknowledged that a prohibition on the licensee transferring his rights to somebody else or granting sub-licences is not forbidden by Article 85.1. Such a ban appeared in the Raymond/Nagoya licence and caused no difficulty. A ban on granting sub-licences without Davidson's consent appeared in the licences in that case (the sub-licence from Maglum to CIM was granted with Davidson's consent), and the Commission's view was that it was part of the monopoly accorded by the patent to the patent owner (and necessary to protect his know-how).

8—46 *Selling prices* In theory, as the patent owner, when granting a licence, is thereby sharing with the licensee the monopoly granted by the patent, the patent owner can also bind the licensee as to the prices at which the latter sells the patented product (or which the licensee charges for applying the patented process). Provisions in patent licences to that effect are permitted in some legal systems. However, no reference is made to the point in the Notice, and it seems reasonable to assume that such a term would be regarded by the Commission as restricting competition (except possibly where it could be shown that the price insisted upon was relatively low, perhaps to make the product available as widely as possible).

8—47 In conclusion, the comments in II of the Notice should be borne in mind. Terms which may be permissible in other patent licences may not be allowable in special situations, such as agreements relating to patents in common ownership, reciprocal licences, and multiple parallel licences (although the *Davidson* case is a precedent as to what may be acceptable in the latter situation).

Further guidance as to clauses in patent agreements may be available when the Commission issues "bloc" exemption regulations under Regulation 2821/71, in the shape of terms which must, and those which must not, appear.

## 3. Trade Marks

8—48 A trade mark is a mark placed upon the goods to indicate a trade connection between the goods and the owner of the mark, usually that the goods have been made or supplied by the owner of the mark. Most legal systems provide machinery whereby trade marks can be registered. Usually, registration gives the trade mark owner the exclusive right to use that mark on the goods for which it is registered.

8—49 Some systems make provision for the trade mark owner to allow his mark to be used by other firms, by a method known as "registered user". The registered user is allowed to put the trade mark on his goods, but is usually bound to comply with instructions laid down by the trade mark owner and to allow the latter to exercise technical control. Examples of such use by persons other than the trade mark owner occur in the textile industry. The proprietor of a process for treating textiles (such as flame-proofing, shrink-resisting, or drip-drying, treatments) may have registered a trade mark to be used to identify goods which have been treated with his process. The textile manufacturer or garment maker will then be authorised by a registered-user agreement to apply the mark to his goods. In essence, a registered-user agreement is akin to a patent licence.

8—50 Some legal systems also permit "quality" or "certification" marks. These are trade marks designed to show to the buyer that the goods comply with some quality or other standard. The right to use the mark may be granted by the body owning the mark to a manufacturer who can satisfy the body that his goods will comply with the relevant standards.

8—51 Trade mark registrations are usually for a particular period, such as fourteen years, but are usually renewable, so that trade marks, unlike patents, can have an almost unlimited life.

8—52 As with patents, the relationship between Community competition law and trade mark rights falls into three subjects:

     (i)    the existence of trade mark rights;
     (ii)   the exercise of trade mark rights;
     (iii)  agreements relating to trade mark rights.

## Existence and exercise of trade mark rights

8—53 The European Court ruled upon the existence and use of trade mark rights in the *Grundig* case. The arrangements between Grundig and Consten included an agreement whereby the latter was enabled to register the "GINT" mark in France, with an obligation to cancel the registration or transfer it to Grundig if Consten ceased to be Grundig's exclusive distributor. The Commission's decision had required Consten not to use its trade mark rights in such a way as to stop parallel imports. The Court held that this requirement did not touch the *existence* of those rights, but only their *exercise*, and that the Commission had not exceeded its powers in imposing the requirement. Moreover, the agreement between Grundig and Consten allowing the latter to register and use the mark had the object of restricting competition, and consequently could come within Article 85.1.

8—54 The Court followed the same line of reasoning in the *Sirena* case. Mark Allen, an American company, in 1933 registered a mark "Prep" in respect of shaving cream. By an agreement in 1937, Mark Allen transferred the Italian registration to Sirena. Sirena thereafter made and marketed the product in Italy under that mark. At a later date, Mark Allen allowed a German company to use the mark in West Germany. No problem arose until the German company began to market its product under the "Prep" mark in Italy, and at a lower price than the Sirena product. Sirena instituted proceedings in the Italian courts against the German company. The Italian court sought a ruling from the European Court upon the application of Articles 85 and 86.

The Court held that the *exercise* of trade mark rights is liable to contribute to the insulation of markets from each other. Article 85.1 applies where trade mark rights are used to prevent parallel imports and the right to use the mark has been acquired by those concerned either by agreement with each other or with a third party.

As regards Article 86, the Court held that the owner of a trade mark does not have a dominant position merely because he is able to prevent imports. He must, in addition, be in a position to prevent the maintenance of effective competition in a substantial part of the Common Market, taking into account similar or substitute goods.

### Parallel imports

8–55  In two cases in 1968, *Levers' Zeep* and *Nederlandse Persil*, the Dutch court considered cases relating to "OMO" and "Persil". In each case the company owning the Dutch registration was seeking to prevent imports of goods manufactured and put into circulation in Germany by the company owning the German mark. Despite arguments based upon relationship between the Dutch and German companies in each case, as subsidiaries of a common parent (Unilever), the Dutch court held that the Dutch and German companies concerned were separate and distinct legal entities and that the Dutch company in each case could stop the imports from Germany.

8–56  In view of the decision in the *Grundig* and *Sirena* cases, together with that in the *Deutsche Grammophon* case, it is doubtful if these Dutch decisions now represent the true state of the law. Taking the principles laid down by the European Court in the *Grundig* and *Sirena* cases, and taking account of those in the *Parke, Davis* and *Deutsche Grammophon* cases, the extent to which trade mark rights can be used to prevent imports must now be regarded as being the same as for patent rights:

(a)  *Trade mark registered in importing Member State, but not in exporting Member.*

Where the imported goods bearing the mark were not marketed or put in circulation in the exporting Member by the trade mark owner, either directly or indirectly, it would seem that he can stop the imports (on analogy with the *Parke, Davis* judgment).

But where the imported goods were put into circulation by him, either directly or indirectly, i.e. they are "genuine" goods, he cannot stop the imports. This conclusion arises from the "exhaustion of rights" doctrine as well as from Community competition law.

(b)  *Mark registered both in importing and exporting Member.*

Where the ownership of both registrations is held by the same person, either directly or indirectly, they will be "genuine" goods, and he cannot stop the imports. This conclusion derives from the "exhaustion of rights" doctrine and also from Articles 36 and 85, as in the *Grundig* and *Deutsche Grammophon* cases.

Where the registrations in each country are owned by different persons, but have derived from agreements between the owners or from a common previous owner, Article 85.1 may apply to the agreements and Article 36 to the exercise of the trade mark rights (*Sirena* case). (Bearing in mind that trade marks can have lives up to and over 100 years, it would be unfair if this principle is applied inflexibly. If A owns in Member X and B in Member Y a mark which 70 years ago was in common ownership but has not been thereafter, it would seem unreasonable not to allow A and B to exercise their normal exclusive rights to the mark in their country especially where there are quality differences in the product.)

Finally, where the registrations are and always have been in completely separate ownership and there are no agreements within 85.1, it would appear that imports of goods bearing the mark put into circulation by the other owner can be stopped.

### *Abuse of dominant position*

8—57    In the light of the *Sirena* judgment the application of Article 86 to trade mark rights is the same as to patent rights:

    (a)    The owner of a trade mark registration does not automatically hold a dominant position, even if he can prohibit imports.

    (b)    To constitute a dominant position, there must be power to prevent the maintenance of effective competition in a substantial part of the Common Market, taking into account similar or substitute goods.

    (c)    A higher price for the branded article as against similar unbranded goods does not itself prove abuse, but may do so if the difference is substantial and cannot be justified objectively.

### Agreements relating to trade mark rights

8—58    Agreements relating to the assignment of trade mark rights or granting registered-user rights may fall within the ambit of Article 85.1 if its conditions are satisfied.

8—59    Article 4.2 (1) of Regulation 17 applies to relieve from the obligation to notify if all the parties belong to one Member and the terms do not relate to imports or exports between Members, although the parties can notify the agreement if they wish. Article 4.2 (2)(b) applies if it is a two-party agreement and the terms are concerned solely with restrictions on the rights of the assignee or user to use the marks. In addition, it is expected that, towards the end of 1972 or in the beginning of 1973, a regulation granting "bloc" exemption to two-party agreements and concerted practices relating to trade mark agreements will be made by the Commission under the power granted to it in Regulation 19/65 (Appendix F).

8—60    If the agreement comes within the limits prescribed in the "Notice Concerning Minor Agreements" (Appendix J), it is deemed not to have appreciable effect, and to be outside 85.1.

Individual negative clearance is available if there is no, or no appreciable, effect upon competition within the Common Market or inter-Member trade. Thus, in the *Nicholas* case, when Nicholas sold to the British company Vitapro the business formerly carried on in the Commonwealth by Vitapointe the agreement, while allowing Vitapro to use the relevant trade marks in the Commonwealth, prohibited it from using those marks in the Common Market. However, Nicholas was not among the largest firms in that trade in the E.E.C. and was in lively competition with numerous other suppliers. In the circumstances, the Commission concluded that negative clearance could be given.

### Clauses in agreements relating to trade marks

8—61    As already noted, because of the possibility of repeated renewal of trade mark registrations, trade marks can have almost unlimited lives, unlike patents. This means that agreements granting the right to use a trade mark can continue for a long time.

Except for this question of period, the other comments with regard to clauses in patent agreements (8-15 — 8-20) are generally applicable to trade mark agreements also. In particular:

(a)    *Non-exclusive licence* In the *Burroughs* case, the licences to use the two trade marks were non-exclusive, and held not to restrict competition. The licensees remained free to use other marks on the goods if they wished.

(b)    *Ban on exports* In the *Burroughs* case there was no restriction on inter-Member trade.

(c)    *Quality control* The Burroughs' licensees were required to comply with Burroughs' technical instructions. This was considered not to be restrictive. Control of quality is permitted in relation to common quality marks (8-62 — 8-64).

(d)    *Marking* The Burroughs licensees were required to add the words "Made under licence from Burroughs Corporation" on goods bearing the two Burroughs trade marks. On agreement goods not bearing the trade marks, an identifying mark had to be placed, for control purposes. These requirements were not held to be restrictive.

(e)    *Royalty* An obligation to pay a royalty, with a minimum in the case of Delplanque, caused no difficulty in the grant of negative clearance to the Burroughs licences.

(f)    *Arbitration* Settlement of disputes by arbitration was also provided for in the Burroughs licences.

**"Quality" or "certification" marks**

8—62 In paragraph 8 of the "Notice Concerning Co-operation between Enterprises" (Appendix H), the Commission indicated its view that agreements relating to quality (and presumably also certification) marks do not come within Article 85.1, even if there is quality control provided non-members can use the mark on the same terms as members. But the agreement may restrict competition, for example if the member can manufacture or sell only products of the particular quality, or if there are obligations about prices, etc.

8—63 In the *Transocean Paint* case, the object was to market a marine paint to a single formula and with a common trade mark in such a way that it would be generally available as a standard product. The trade mark registration in each country was held by a member in that country. Each member was free to fix his own selling price, and could sell in other members' territories subject to payment of a commission. The Commission held the agreement to be within Article 85.1, but granted exemption as it contributed to the improvement of distribution and gave consumers the advantage of being able to buy a standard product which was widely available.

8—64 A similar case was *V.V.V.F.*, a Dutch association of paint and varnish manufacturers. It was an export group fixing a minimum export price for a branded product with quality conditions. As regards exports to other E.E.C. countries, only the marking and ancillary quality conditions applied. Members were free to market higher or lower quality products under different marks, i.e. the association marks could not be used. The Commission granted negative clearance.

## 4. Registered Designs

8—65 In essence, patents are to protect inventions relating to utility or function, such as a new product or a new way of making an existing product. Consequently, patents are granted for new ideas which relate to the function or utility of an article, but not for ideas relating to its aesthetic features, its features which appeal to and are judged solely by the eye. Non-functional creations of this sort can be registered as designs and models, such as textile designs, and patterns for wallpaper, lace, etc.

The intellectual property in respect of which Nagoya was licensed in the *Raymond* case, included utility models.

8—66 Like trade marks, registrations of designs, etc., are usually for an initial period, but renewable on expiry. This means that agreements relating to the use of such designs are not so strictly tied as to period as patent agreements are.

The comments given above in respect of trade marks can be taken as indicating the position as regards registered designs, etc.

## 5. Copyright, Performing Rights, and Analogous Rights

8—67 This group of intellectual property rights is probably the most complex as regards the relationships to which they can give rise. Take a novel, for example. There may be an agreement involved in its creation, if the author is commissioned to write it. Once it has been written, there are many rights in it, which can be the subject of separate dealing. There is the copyright, i.e. the right to reproduce it in print in book form, which may be divided into rights in its publication as a hard-back and those in paper-back form. Then there is the possibility of serialization. Then film rights. And T.V. rights. The right to turn it into a play. And so on. All these separate rights can exist and be dealt in separately in every country in which copyright is obtained.

There are the corresponding rights in a play. In music, there are the right to copy the music, and the right to perform it. And so on.

The period for which these rights run is governed by the law of the country in which the right is claimed. The periods can be fairly lengthy, such as the life of the author plus twenty-five years.

8—68 There is one characteristic of this category of intellectual property which is significant from the point of view of Community competition law. Somebody once claimed that if a certain number of monkeys played with another number of typewriters for sufficient millions of years, given sufficient supplies of paper, ribbons, etc., one of them would eventually produce the Bible. On the practical human scale, however, it is most unlikely that two people in different countries will independently write the same book or play, or compose the same piece of music. (It is quite otherwise with inventions — frequently patent applications touching upon the same basic idea are filed in different countries quite independently and about the same time.) Consequently, in almost every case, these rights will derive from a common owner.

8—69 As with other forms of intellectual property, it will be simpler to consider this group from the point of view of:

(i) existence;
(ii) exercise;
(iii) agreements.

### Existence and exercise

*Deutsche Grammophon case*

8—70 The judgment of the European Court in the *Deutsche Grammophon* case, establishes Community law in this context. The German Copyright Statute grants to record manufacturers an original protective right, analogous to copyright. The manufacturer has the "exclusive right to reproduce and distribute the recording". Deutsche Grammophon ("D.G.") was a German company producing gramophone records, having a number of artistes under exclusive contracts. D.G. marketed its records under various brand names including "Polydor". In Germany, the "Polydor" records were subject to a resale price maintenance system, so that D.G. had to ensure that the system was "water-tight". Metro, a German retailer, had sold "Polydor" records which it brought direct from D.G. but had not observed the r.p.m. As Metro was not prepared to sign the r.p.m. undertakings, business relations between Metro and D.G. were terminated.

8—71    D.G. sold its "Polydor" records in France through a French company, Polydor S.A., owned as to 99.55% by D.G. A licence agreement between D.G. and Polydor gave the latter the exclusive right to market D.G. recordings in France and to use the related marks. In 1970, Metro obtained a supply of "Polydor ' records made by D.G., and sold them in Germany at prices below the fixed r.p.m. price. These records were held to have been marketed by Polydor in France, and had reached Metro through Switzerland. D.G. sued in the German courts to prevent Metro selling at below the fixed price, in order to preserve the "water-tightness" of the r.p.m. system, on the ground that unauthorised sale of the records by Metro infringed the rights given to D.G. by the German Copyright Statute. The first German court, holding that D.G.'s rights had not been "exhausted" by sale in France by D.G.'s subsidiary, made an order against Metro, who appealed, relying upon Articles 85.1 and 86. The German appeal court sought rulings from the European Court.

8—72    The European Court ruled that Article 36 of the Treaty permits restrictions on imports and exports by virtue of intellectual property rights, but only to the extent justified for the protection of those rights. Accordingly, it would conflict with the Treaty provisions regarding the free movement of goods within the Common Market if a German record manufacturer used the rights granted by the German Copyright Statute to prohibit the sale in Germany of records marketed by him or with his consent in another Member State solely because that marketing had not taken place in Germany.

8—73    As to Article 86, the Court followed the same line as in the *Parke, Davis* and *Sirena* cases. The exclusive distribution right in Germany granted by the German Statute does not give the record manufacturer a dominant position, unless he can prevent effective competition and in this context any exclusive contracts with artistes must be taken into account. A higher price for the protected records in Germany, as compared with imported records, does not constitute abuse, but may do so if the price difference is large enough and not justifiable.

8—74    In effect, D.G. could not prevent import into Germany of its own records marketed by it or with its consent in other Members. This broke the "water-tightness" of its German r.p.m. system, and the system was brought to an end.

8—75    *Parallel imports* As regards parallel imports of goods subject to protection in the importing country by intellectual property rights of the group under discussion, the position is simpler than in the case of patents or trade marks:

(a)   *Protection in the importing Member State, but no protection in the exporting Member.*

If the goods were marketed in the exporting Member either directly or indirectly by the owner of the intellectual property rights, he cannot prevent imports.

If they were not marketed by him, directly or indirectly, he can prevent imports (on analogy with *Parke, Davis*.)

(b)   *Protection in both importing and exporting Member.*

In view of the nature of the intellectual property rights in question, the rights in both must have derived originally from the one owner. In these circumstances, it is unlikely that parallel imports can be prevented where the marketing in the exporting Member was legitimate.

8—76   *Abuse of dominant position* As in the case of other types of intellectual property, the position under Article 86 is as follows, as laid down by the European Court in the *Deutsche Grammophon* judgment:

(a)   The ownership of an exclusive right granted by the national law, such as the exclusive distribution right given by the German Copyright Statute to record manufacturers, does not of itself constitute a dominant position.

(b)   To constitute a dominant position there must be the ability to prevent effective competition in a substantial part of the Common Market.

(c)   A higher price for the protected article as compared with an imported article is not necessarily proof of abuse of a dominant position, but may be if the difference is sufficiently large and not justifiable objectively.

In the *GEMA* case, which involved performing rights, there was the ability to eliminate competition. GEMA had a monopoly in Germany, and by its arrangements with the corresponding organizations in other Member States affected inter-Member trade. The abuses included discrimination against nationals in other Members.

### Agreements relating to copyright, etc.

8—77   These agreements are capable of coming within Article 85.1 if its conditions are satisfied. Article 4.2 of Regulation 17 relieves the parties of the obligation to notify where the parties all belong to the one Member State and imports and exports between Member States are not involved (4.2 (1)), and where there are only two parties and the restrictions relate only to the exercise of his rights by the assignee or licensee (4.2 (2)(b)). "Bloc" exemption may be given to certain two-party agreements if the Commission makes a regulation pursuant to the power granted to it in Regulation 19/65 (Appendix F) — the Commission regulation is expected towards the end of 1972 or early in 1973.

8—78    Agreements falling within the limits set out in the "Notice Concerning Minor Agreements" (Appendix J) are considered by the Commission to fall outside Article 85.1 as being of no "appreciable" effect. Individual negative clearance may be obtained for agreements where those limits are exceeded if the effect is still not appreciable.

### Clauses in agreements

8—79    The comments upon clauses in trade mark agreements will serve as some indication of the position, pending publication of decisions involving agreements relating to the particular type of intellectual property under discussion.

## 6. Know-how

8—80    As intellectual property, know-how differs from patents in a most important respect. Essentially, both consist of information. In the case of a patent, full details of the invention are or should be set out in the patent specification which is available to the public (except for inventions of military significance). Making the information public and so adding to the available stock of public knowledge is the price the patentee has to pay, and in return for it he is granted his patent, i.e. a monopoly to make, use, and sell the invention and its products in that country for the life of the patent.

Conversely, know-how consists of secret information. Its value lies in the fact that it is not publicly or generally available. Legal systems will protect industrial and trade secrets and confidential information, but only so long as they remain secret and confidential. Consequently, a know-how agreement is essentially one which provides for one firm to pass over secret manufacturing information to another. And although legal systems may protect industrial secrets, such secrets do not give the owner a legal monopoly as does a patent.

Several important consequences flow from these differences.

### Existence and exercise

8—81    In the first place, the existence and exercise of know-how do not raise the same problems as regards competition law as in the case of patents, registered designs, copyright, and other monopolies granted by law. Although the owner of know-how may have a *de facto* monopoly, this can arise only because other people do not possess the relevant secrets. Once other people come into possession of the information legitimately, the know-how owner cannot by legal means prevent them from using it. Thus he is in no position to stop parallel imports or competition.

Possession of know-how will not, of itself, constitute a dominant position, although if the owner of the know-how is the only manufacturer with that information he may have a *de facto* monopoly and not be exposed to competition. There would then be a dominant position.

### Agreements relating to know-how

8—82    Turning now to agreements relating to know-how, these are capable of falling within Article 85.1. Regulation 17 gives relief from the obligation to notify, although the parties may notify if they so wish, where all the parties are in one Member and the agreement, etc., does not relate to inter-Member imports or exports (4.2 (1)), and to two-party know-how agreements (4.2 (2)(b)). If an agreement comes within the limits set out in the "Notice Concerning Minor Agreements" (Appendix J), it will be deemed to have no appreciable effect. And the Commission's regulation to be made pursuant to the power given in Council Regulation 19/65 to grant "bloc" exemption may be relevant when made.

### Clauses in know-how agreements

8—83    As regards the terms of agreements relating to know-how, its special character means that certain terms must be treated differently than the corresponding patents agreements clauses.

8—84    *Agreement period* A patent has a fixed life span varying from country to country, about sixteen to eighteen years, with limited possibilities of extension. As already noted (8-39), the period of a patent licence containing terms within Article 85.1 must not exceed the life of the relevant patent. In the case of know-how, there is no such time-limit, and the parties have greater flexibility as to the period they adopt, although it may be prudent to assume that once the information has entered the public domain (otherwise than through breach of the agreement) the justification for any restrictive provisions may be treated as having disappeared.

8—85    *Secrecy* It is reasonable for the grantor to insist upon the licensee (this is a slightly inaccurate but convenient term to use for the recipient of the know-how) keeping the information secret. The secrecy obligation may apply not only during the "life" of the agreement but after its termination, because otherwise the licensee would have an incentive to end the agreement as soon as he could. (There is a technical inconsistency in a provision of an agreement continuing to apply after the agreement has been terminated, because then the provision would have terminated also — the inconsistency can be overcome by having an active "life" or "production period" which can end leaving the continuing provisions of the agreement in force.)

In the Davidson licences, which ran for the lives of the respective patents, the licensees were bound to keep the know-how secret both during the agreement and after. In the Burroughs-Delplanque licence the secrecy obligation on Delplanque ran for the life of the agreement and ten years thereafter, while in the Burroughs-Geha licence the obligation lasted only for the life of the agreement; in both cases, the licensee was bound to use the information during the secrecy periods only within and in conformity with the agreement. In the *Fabrique Nationale* agreement the secrecy obligation continued for five years after the agreement ended. All these provisions were accepted by the Commission.

8—86    *Sub-licences* In the Davidson licences, the obligation on the licensees not to grant sub-licences except with the consent of Davidson was accepted by the Commission as not having the object of restricting competition. The obligation was part of the justifiable interest of the grantor in ensuring that his know-how was not divulged without his consent.

8—87    *Ban on exports* Although industrial secrets may be protected by law, they do not convey any legal monopoly. Consequently, there is even less justification in know-how agreements for seeking to prohibit the licensee from exporting to other Member States. The know-how agreements between Happich/Gallino and Happich/Maglum were revised so that prohibitions on exports were removed.

8—88    In other respects, the comments with regard to clauses in patent agreements apply also to the corresponding provisions in know-how agreements. For example, the know-how agreements between Happich and Gallino and between Happich and Maglum contained provisions requiring the licensees to pay royalties to Happich, but once the ban on exports had been suppressed from the agreements they fulfilled the requirements of Article 85.3 and exemption was granted.

8—89    As with patent agreements, when the Commission issues a regulation under Regulation 2821/71 granting "bloc" exemption to research and development agreements, it may indicate which terms relating to know-how must be included, and which excluded.

## 7. Check List

8—90    (i)    The Note in paragraph 6-31 applies to this Check List.

(ii)    It would be unusual for intellectual property rights to be governed otherwise than by an agreement, but the following comments apply equally to "decisions" and "concerted practices".

(iii)    "Restriction" in relation to competition includes "prevention" and "distortion".

*Between undertakings*

1.    Are all the parties to the agreement inter-related companies (i.e. a parent and its subsidiaries, or subsidiaries of a common parent) and does the parent control the allocation of intellectual property rights?

     If so, Article 85.1 does not apply.

     If not, read on.

*Inter-Member trade*
2.　Does the agreement have no effect upon inter-Member trade?
　　　　If so, Article 85.1 does not apply.
　　　　If not, read on.

*Restriction upon competition*
3.　Has the agreement neither the object nor the effect of restricting competition within the Common Market?
　　　　If so, Article 85.1 does not apply.
　　　　If not, read on.

*No appreciable effect*
4.　Are the quantitative limits in the "Notice Concerning Minor Agreements" (Appendix J) satisfied?
　　　　If so, Article 85.1 does not apply.
　　　　If not, read on.
5.　Is any effect upon inter-Member trade or upon competition within the Common Market not appreciable?
　　　　If so, apply for negative clearance.
　　　　If not, read on.

*Relief from obligation to notify*
6.　Are all the parties from one Member State, and does the agreement relate neither to imports nor exports between Members?
　　　　If so, Article 4.2 (1) of Regulation 17(18–05) applies – the agreement need not be notified, but may be notified if the parties so wish.
　　　　If not, read on.
7.　Are there only two parties to the agreement and do the restrictions relate only to the right of the licensee or assignee to use the intellectual property rights?
　　　　If so, Article 4.2 (2)(b) of Regulation 17 (18-05) applies – the agreement need not be notified, but may be notified if the parties so wish.
　　　　If not, read on.

*"Bloc" exemption*
8.　When the Commission has made a regulation under Regulation 19/65 granting "bloc" exemption to two-party intellectual property agreements, is the agreement within the "bloc" exemption?
　　　　If so, it will be exempt for the period of the "bloc" exemption so long as the conditions of exemption are satisfied.
　　　　If not, read on.

*Individual exemption*
9.　Does the agreement satisfy the requirements of Article 85.3?
　　　　If so, notify for exemption.
　　　　If not, read on.

*Remainder*

10.   If the agreement has already been made, it may be worth
notifying it and discussing it with the Commission in case it can
be modified so as to qualify for negative clearance or exemption.
Otherwise, the agreement should be terminated.

If the agreement has not already been made, it may be worth
discussing the proposals with the Commission.

*Timing*

(a)   For "existing agreements" to which Article 85.1 applies "by
virtue of accession" − notification must be made between 1st
January, 1973, and 30th June, 1973.

(b)   For other agreements − notification must be made before the
restrictive terms come into operation.

# PART 3

# HORIZONTAL AGREEMENTS

# CHAPTER 9

# Joint Research Agreements

## 1. Introduction

9—01 Many, and perhaps most, industries are now technological in character. They are based upon a specialised technology or a specialised application of general technology. A firm which wishes to keep abreast of its rivals, and even more if it wishes to keep ahead, must invest effort and money in research and development.

Research and development is not just a matter of providing money, buildings, and equipment for scientists who then work in ivory-tower isolation and send out a one-way stream of ideas to their production and marketing colleagues. Problems arise in production and in the use of the products which are referred back to the research people for solution. Research and development is a two-way process. The feed-back from production and marketing can show what are the current problems and may stimulate new ideas or point to new lines for investigation.

9—02 The object of private industrial research and development is to keep the firm abreast or ahead of its rivals. The resulting inventions and developments are kept for the benefit of the firm, either as secret know-how or as patented inventions. If the firm keeps the benefits to itself, the corollary is that the firm must bear all the cost and have to rely upon its own resources for feed-back.

From this point of view, there is something to be said for joint research, where the costs are shared between the parties and the feed-back catchment area widened. Ideally, this arrangement is best suited to situations where two or more firms in different and non-competing industries are interested in the same inventions or developments. Such situations can arise, but more usually it is a question of competitors in the same industry. Joint research by competitors is probably most commonly found in research associations, i.e. joint bodies which usually concentrate on problems recognized as basic to the whole industry, while the individual firms deal with the application of the R.A.'s results to its own particular needs. Or there may be joint arrangements between two or more firms to pool their efforts, either by one working on one problem for both, or perhaps by setting up a joint research company. The advantage of joint research is that the costs are shared and the feed-back catchment area is widened. But the results have to be shared as well.

9—03 From the point of view of competition law, the method of sharing the cost will normally present no difficulty. The difficulties arise from the method of sharing out the benefit of the results of the research.

## 2. Regulations and Notices

*Regulation 17*

9—04 Article 4.2 (3)(b) of Regulation 17 recognized that restrictions upon competition were more likely to be encountered in the allocation of the rights to use the results of the research. In its original form, the Article gave relief from the obligation to notify in respect of agreements, etc., which have as their sole object:

"(b) joint research for improvement of techniques, provided the results are accessible to all parties thereto and may be used by each of them".

The parties were, and remain, free to notify such agreements, but are not obliged to do so. Agreements, etc., within Article 4.2 (3)(b) benefit from temporary validity as recognized in the *Bilger v. Jehle* case.

*"Notice Concerning Co-operation between Enterprises"*

9—05 The Notice issued in July, 1968, (Appendix H) followed the same general line as Article 4 of Regulation 17 in its original form. To dispose first of joint market research, the Commission considered that this would not restrict competition (1 (b)), being concerned with collecting information and facts and ascertaining market conditions; if there were any restrictions upon competition some more far-reaching co-operation between the firms concerned would be involved (24-15).

9—06 Section 3 of the Notice deals with technological research and development. Agreements having as their sole object the joint carrying out of r. and d. projects, or their sharing out between the parties, or the joint placing of r. and d. contracts, would not normally affect the competitive position of the parties, as between themselves. But if there were provisions restricting the freedom of the parties to carry out their own research separately, or restricting their freedom to use the results of the joint work, their competitive position might be affected. However, if a party's participation in the joint work were limited to one sector, or limited financially, a corresponding limitation on his access to the results of the joint work would not be restrictive of competition.

9—07 As the Notice makes clear (24-28), the legal form in which the joint research arrangement is clothed is immaterial. The form adopted may be a research association, or a joint company, or specialisation by one party in one aspect of the problem, etc.

### Regulations 2821/71 and 2822/71

9—08  To deal first with Regulation 2822/71 (Appendix L), it made a significant alteration to Article 4.2 (3)(b) of Regulation 17. Instead of reading as in 9-04, it now relieves from the ban in Article 1, agreements, etc., which "have as their sole object:

(b)  joint research and development" (28-02)

omitting the requirement that the results must be available to all parties to use freely. This omission was presumably intended to widen the exemption, as compared with the original wording, because the preamble contains the comment "agreements, decisions and concerted practices which, as much as they restrict competition, only have a bearing on joint research and development, do not present, in general, dangers of such a nature as to make their notification necessary" (28-01).

However, the extent of the widening of the exemption is not clear. If an agreement provides for joint research and also for, say, one party to have the exclusive right to use the results of the research in one sector and the other party the exclusive right in another sector, is joint research the sole object of the agreement, or does the object, in so far as it includes the exclusive utilisation of the results, go beyond research? It would seem advisable for parties to such agreements to consult the Commission. Under Article 4 of Regulation 17 the parties remain free to notify if they so wish.

9—09  Regulation 2821/71 (Appendix K) gives the Commission power to issue a "bloc" exemption for joint r. and d. agreements. The regulation granting the "bloc" exemption must specify what agreements, etc., are within it, and what provisions are, and what are not, allowable.

## 3. Cases

9—10  An interesting illustration of what the Commission regards as permissible, and what not permissible, can be obtained by comparing two recent announcements by the Commission, the first entitled *"Re Research and Development"* and the second dealing with the *Henkel/Colgate* case.

### "Re Research and Development"

9—11  This announcement in March, 1971, related to a case which had been settled informally. After being advised of the Commission's views, the parties withdrew their notification. The case gave the Commission an opportunity to clarify the position as regards restrictions upon the exploitation by the parties of the results of the research, but without disclosing the identities of the parties.

9—12  Two large firms, in different Member States, of comparable importance in an oligopolistic industry, communicated to the Commission an agreement between them for the establishment of a joint company to carry out certain research and development projects. The parties considered that the agreement did not exceed the permissible limits set out in the 1968 Notice.

Each party was to hold half of the company's capital and have an equal share in its management. The company would decide whether to apply for patents in respect of any inventions resulting from its research. In respect of such patents, each party could claim a non-exclusive, ten-year, royalty-free, licence in respect of its own primary marketing area, and in respect of the primary marketing area of the other party, a non-exclusive licence subject to a royalty not exceeding 2% of the net selling price. For all other areas each party had the right to a non-exclusive licence subject to a royalty not exceeding 2%.

9–13    The Commission regarded the royalty arrangements as restricting competition, in that they were likely to hinder one party penetrating the other's area. Such a restriction would be serious as the newly developed products were likely to replace the traditional ones to a large extent. Moreover, as the differential royalty arrangement was not indispensable to the achievement of joint research, exemption under Article 85.3 would not be available.

Furthermore, while it could reasonably be assumed that each party would claim a licence for its own primary area, there was no certainty that it would claim a licence in the other's area. And as to other countries, it might be that only one party would claim a licence in a particular country. There was, therefore, a possibility of one party operating in each country, and perhaps preventing parallel imports between Member States by patent infringement actions or threats of such proceedings.

9–14    Finally, the Commission pointed out that, in the event of the joint company considering whether to take action in respect of infringements of any of its patents, in so far as the management of the company was shared equally by both parties, a decision by the company to institute proceedings would amount to either an agreement or a concerted practice between the parties. There could, consequently, be an agreement or concerted practice between them to stop parallel imports between Members, amounting to a disguised restriction on inter-Member trade within Article 36 (17-08).

Similar considerations would arise with regard to any unpatented know-how.

### Henkel/Colgate-Palmolive agreement

9–15    In October, 1971, the Commission issued an announcement setting out the gist of the agreement between Henkel and Colgate-Palmolive, in compliance with Article 19.3 of Regulation 17. The parties had applied for negative clearance and had also notified for exemption under 85.3. The summary of the agreement was published as the Commission proposed "to come to a favourable decision" (when publishing summaries, the Commission refrains from indicating which course it proposes to adopt, i.e. negative clearance or exemption).

9—16     The Henkel/Colgate agreement has points of similarity, and points of difference, when compared with the case discussed in the last section. Subject to a condition that the Commission adopted a favourable view, the agreement provided for the establishment of a joint company to carry out research into washing preparations for textiles. Each party would share equally in the capital and management. A decision whether to apply for a patent and the fees to be required from the parties or third parties, would be taken by the managing director with the authorisation of the board of directors. If the board so authorised, each party would be entitled to a non-exclusive licence at a royalty not exceeding 2% of the net selling price (gross value, less transport costs, rebates and charges). Non-exclusive licences could be granted to third parties on terms decided by the company; if the terms to a third party were better than those of a licence granted to one of the parties, that party could claim equal treatment. Royalties would be calculated in respect of each patent separately, and could not continue after expiry of the patent. Royalties for unpatented know-how could not be charged after expiry of a fixed period not exceeding the period allowed in the particular country for a patent. Each party remained free to carry out its own research based on the results of the joint research, to exploit commercially the results of its own research and to grant licences in respect of it (but not so as to infringe the joint company's rights). The agreement contained an arbitration clause. The parties emphasised that the agreement did not restrict the freedom of each to conduct its own trading operations, especially as to prices and areas, and its research activities.

9—17     The essential difference between the two agreements is that that between Henkel and Colgate gave each party equal access to the results of the joint research, and placed no handicap upon one party operating in the other's area.

### Fabrique Nationale

9—18     In contrast, the agreement between Fabrique Nationale and Cartoucherie Française in effect allowed each an exclusive right to use the results of joint research in its own sector of activity and its own sales area. That agreement (which is described more fully in paragraph 3-67) was essentially a specialisation agreement, providing for each party to specialise as to the items it produced, with exclusive purchase/supply arrangements in the balance of the joint range made by the other party, and also to specialise as to sales area. The provisions for joint research were ancillary, and as specialisation cannot be achieved without allocating areas of activity to the parties, this case is not inconsistent with the general approach to joint research and development.

*Eurogypsum*

9—19 This was an international trade association of manufacturers of plaster, gypsum, and anhydrite. It carried out research and studies into scientific, technical, economic, and legal matters relating to the industry and its products. The results of the research were available to all members equally. The Commission granted negative clearance.

# 4. Check List

9—20 (i) The Note in paragraph 6—31 applies to this Check List.

(ii) "Agreement" includes "decision" and "concerted practice".

(iii) "Restriction" in relation to competition includes "prevention" and "distortion".

*"Between undertakings"*

1. Are all the parties to the agreement inter-related companies (i.e. a parent and its subsidiaries, or subsidiaries of a common parent) and does the parent control research and development in the subsidiaries?

> If so, Article 85.1 does not apply.
>
> If not, read on.

*Inter-Member trade*

2. Does the agreement have no effect upon inter-Member trade?

> If so, Article 85.1 does not apply.
>
> If not, read on.

*Restriction upon competition*

3. Has the agreement neither the object nor the effect of restricting competition within the Common Market, taking account where appropriate of section 3 of the "Notice Concerning Co-operation between Enterprises" (Appendix H)?

> If so, Article 85.1 does not apply.
>
> If not, read on.

*No appreciable effect*

4. Are the quantitative limits in the "Notice Concerning Minor Agreements" (Appendix J) satisfied?

> If so, Article 85.1 does not apply.
>
> If not, read on.

5. Is any effect upon inter-Member trade or competition within the Common Market not appreciable?

> If so, apply for negative clearance.
>
> If not, read on.

*Relief from obligation to notify*

6. Are all the parties from one Member State, and does the agreement relate neither to imports nor exports between

Members?

        If so, Article 4.2 (1) of Regulation 17 (18-05) applies — the agreement need not be notified, but may be notified if the parties so wish.

        If not, read on.

7.    Is the sole object of the agreement joint research and development?

        If so, Article 4.2 (3)(b) of Regulation 17 applies — the agreement need not be notified, but may be notified if the parties so wish.

        If not, read on.

*"Bloc" exemption*

8.    When the Commission has made a regulation under the power granted to it by Article 1.1 (b) of Regulation 2821/71 (27-02) and gives "bloc" exemption to joint research and development agreements, is the agreement within the "bloc" exemption?

        If so, it will be exempt for the period of the "bloc" exemption so long as the conditions of exemption are satisfied.

        If not, read on.

*Individual exemption*

9.    Does the agreement satisfy the requirements of Article 85.3?

        If so, notify for exemption.

        If not, read on.

*Remainder*

10.    If the agreement has already been made, it may be worth notifying it and discussing it with the Commission in case it can be modified so as to qualify for negative clearance or exemption. Otherwise the agreement should be terminated.

        If the agreement has not already been made, it may be worth discussing the proposals with the Commission.

*Timing*

(a)    For "existing agreements" to which Article 85.1 applies "by virtue of accession" — notification must be made between 1st January, 1973, and 30th June, 1973.

(b)    For other agreements — notification must be made before the restrictive terms come into operation.

## CHAPTER 10

# Joint Production, Selling and Purchasing

## 1. Introduction

10—01 Research should lead on naturally to the purchase of materials, production, and selling. The possibility of joint research compatible with Community competition law was discussed in the last Chapter. The purpose of this Chapter is to consider the other three fields.

The logical sequence would be to deal with them in the order — joint purchasing, joint production, and joint selling. But as the two latter figure in the 1968 "Notice Concerning Co-operation between Enterprises" (Appendix H), it will be better to discuss them first, and deal with joint purchasing last.

## 2. Joint Production

10—02 The Notice deals first, in section 4, with the joint use of production facilities, including storage and transport. The mere fact that two competing concerns use the same facilities does not necessarily involve some restriction on their competition. If they drew their supplies from the same supplier, no such restriction would follow. If they jointly own that supplier, restriction on competition need not follow.

However, where the two concerns own the supplier, or own the production facilities jointly, there will have to be some agreement between them as to the extent to which each can draw on the supplier or facilities, and perhaps in what order. If the plant is the only one available, or demand exceeds supply, the arrangement as to "drawing rights" may determine the competitive position or market shares of the parties. The Notice draws attention to the risks of agreements or concerted practices in this context.

10—03 Joint production does not necessarily involve joint use of production facilities. Each party may use its own plant, etc., in fulfilment of a joint, co-ordinated, plan. This can happen where the parties are in different industries and are not competing, but have to ally their separate production skills to produce something which cannot be made otherwise. An example would be a consortium set up to tender for and erect a nuclear power station. Such a project involves three quite separate techniques — the handling of nuclear energy, the erection of large boilers for raising steam, and the building of large turbine-generators. A consortium of three firms drawn from each of these three industries, each firm having no involvement in the other two industries, would not restrict competition because the firms concerned would not be competing between themselves anyway. A term in the consortium agreement that each would not during the life of the agreement expand into one of the other two industries would merely be recognising the factual situation. Of course, if the concentration of each firm in its own industry resulted from an agreement or concerted practice, there would then, as the Notice points out, be a restriction of competition.

Separate use of separately owned facilities can also occur where the parties are competing. The joint Anglo-French Concorde project is probably an example of this — two aviation concerns which could compete joining together to manufacture a joint product. The Notice deals with this situation, when competitors execute orders in common with which, separately, they could not cope.

## 3. Joint Selling

10—04    In discussing joint selling agreements which are permissible under Community competition law, it is more convenient to take the conditions for the application of Article 85.1 and to group the cases according to the 85.1 condition which does *not* apply. If one of the 85.1 conditions is *not* satisfied, the prohibition in the Article cannot apply.

### *No effect on inter-Member trade*

10—05    The agreement will not affect inter-Member trade if it relates exclusively to trade outside the Common Market or to trade within one Member only, or both.

10—06    This point is exemplified by the *Cobelaz* decision (Cobelaz No.1), involving two Belgian co-operative societies and six Belgian manufacturers of nitrogenous fertilisers. Cobelaz was the joint selling organization for sales within Belgium and for sales in export markets outside the E.E.C. (in certain of the export markets the sales were through the international fertiliser organization Nitrex). The manufacturers were excluded from direct sales in Belgium and those export markets, but each retained the exclusive right to sell its own production within the other E.E.C. countries. In Belgium, Cobelaz fixed a monthly price for all its sales and each manufacturer was entitled to a quota. There were also quotas in the export markets outside the E.E.C. Despite the quotas, each manufacturer was free to decide for itself the quantities it would make available to Cobelaz for joint sale in Belgium and the export markets outside the E.E.C., and the quantities it would retain

185

for sale by itself in other E.E.C. countries. The sums obtained by Cobelaz from internal sales in Belgium were equalised so that the manufacturer received a single average price per unit of nitrogen. There were similar equalisation arrangements for each type of product in the export markets outside the E.E.C. Cobelaz had also operated a loyalty rebate scheme for buyers in Belgium, but this was terminated in response to comments by the Commission, as were several other provisions.

The Commission held that the Cobelaz arrangements did restrict competition within the Common Market because of the prohibition on individual sales in Belgium, but did not affect inter-Member trade. The agreements did not restrict the manufacturers' freedom to import from other Members or to export to other Members — increasingly important individual sales efforts in other Members had occurred after the arrangement for joint sales in other E.E.C. Members by Cobelaz had been terminated. There was no equalisation of prices as between internal Belgian sales and export sales outside the E.E.C. which could discourage exports to other Members. And each manufacturer was free to decide for itself how much it would export to other Members and how much it would make available to Cobelaz. Negative clearance was granted. Negative clearance was also given to a similar arrangement operated by Cobelaz for coking sulphate of ammonia (Cobelaz No.2).

10—07　Negative clearance has also been given to similar joint selling arrangements for the home market and for exports outside the E.E.C. relating to nitrogenous fertilisers in France (Comptoir Français de l'Azote-C.F.A.), and to phosphate fertilisers in France (Supexie). A French joint sales organization for cement, Cimfrance, was also modified to exclude from its purview export sales to other Members, leaving its export activities limited to non-E.E.C. markets.

10—08　In connection with price equalisation schemes, mention should be made of the *Belgaphos* case. Ten Belgian manufacturers of superphosphate had an agreement fixing quotas for sales in Belgium and in export markets, including other Members. Sales in Belgium and other E.E.C. countries were handled directly by each manufacturer, but sales in non-E.E.C. markets were handled by Belgaphos. Each year Belgaphos equalised the prices received by its members on all sales, by dividing total receipts by the amount sold; the members then paid to or received from each other balancing payments so that all received equal prices for equal amounts sold. The Commission condemned the quota and price equalisation arrangements, and the arrangement was cancelled. The Commission explained that Article 85.1 applies even when the parties have retained the right to sell individually and to decide their own prices if they subsequently pool the proceeds of their sales.

*Agreements which do not have the object or effect of restricting competition*

10—09 Clearly, the agreement will not have the *object* of restricting competition where it contains no restrictions. Even if it does include restrictions, it may not have the *object* or *effect* of restricting competition — its object and effect may be to re-inforce competition as in the *SAFCO* case, or the parties may in fact not be competitors as pointed out in the Notice (24-36) and as was the position in the *Alliance Machine Outils* and *Wild* cases. And even if the agreement does have the effect of restricting competition, that effect may not be appreciable.

10—10 *SAFCO case* This concerned an agreement between seven French producers of preserved vegetables. SAFCO was an organization ·to handle the exports of its members, one requirement being that no member could have a pay-roll of more than 500 employees nor a capital exceeding 5 million francs. Each member undertook not to export individually, not to join any other export group, and to deliver to SAFCO on request a certain proportion of its output. Previously, the members had not exported anything, or had exported only limited amounts and that sporadically. SAFCO had developed substantial exports, particularly to Germany, although nevertheless there remained many competitive concerns in the Common Market, some bigger than all the members of SAFCO put together. The Commission concluded that SAFCO did not have the object or effect of restricting competition, but rather re-inforced it. Negative clearance was granted.

10—11 *Alliance Machine Outils* In this case, the nine French machine tool manufacturers who participated in the Alliance specialized in different machines. They were all small or medium-sized undertakings. Each appointed the Alliance its exclusive agent for sales outside France. The Alliance negotiated export sales in the name of the manufacturer, who fixed the selling price. Each participant undertook not to make or sell machines which would compete with the products of any other participant — although each in fact specialized in different machines, this was not inevitable.

The Commission took the view that the exclusivity in sales outside France granted by the participants to the Alliance did not constitute a restriction of competition. The Alliance did not constitute an independent intermediate stage between the manufacturers and consumer — it did not affect the latter's interest whether he dealt with the manufacturer or the Alliance. Moreover, the machines handled by the Alliance did not compete with each other. As to the undertaking by the manufacturers not to make or sell machines competing with the product of any other participant, their ranges did not in fact overlap. Each participant was free to leave the Alliance if he wished to extend his range to compete with any of the others, but the market situation was such that this was unlikely, specialization rather than diversification being the trend. Finally, the Alliance represented only a small proportion of machine tool manufactures and sales within the Common Market. In these circumstances negative clearance was granted.

10—12 *Wild case* A similar case was the agreement between Wild and Leitz, both French subsidiaries set up by their respective parent companies to market the latters' products, mainly microscopes, in France. The agreement related to those microscopes not duplicated in the two ranges, i.e. microscopes in Wild's range which Leitz did not make, and *vice versa*. The agreement provided for the technical-sales team in each company to receive instruction in the other company's agreement goods. When a representative of one of the companies called on a possible customer for the other's products, he drew up a special report which was passed on to that other, which then decided whether the report was "valid" using the utmost good faith. "Valid" meant that that partner had not been in touch with the customer within the six months preceding the report. If the report were "valid" and any sales of the other partner's products resulted in the following twelve months, a commission of 7% was to be paid to the partner whose representative drew up the report. The agreement provided for joint after-sales service, joint publicity, etc. As the two companies were not competing in the agreement products, negative clearance was granted.

10—13 *No appreciable effect* As the Notice also points out (24-37), even if the parties are in competition with each other, a joint selling arrangement may not have any appreciable effect if the parties are small or medium-sized concerns. The Notice specifically refrained from indicating any quantitative limits for "small" or "medium-sized". That omission has now been repaired by the "Notice Concerning Minor Agreements" (Appendix J), expressing the Commission's view that there is no appreciable effect where the agreement products represent not more than 5% of the market and the parties' turnover does not exceed 15 million units of account (or 20 million for commercial concerns).

*Exemption*

10—14 Exclusive distributorship arrangements between competitors can be regarded as a form of joint selling. This was the situation in the *Sopelem* case, where individual exemption was accorded.

## 4. Joint Purchasing

10—15 Joint purchasing is not touched upon in the "Notice Concerning Co-operation between Enterprises", but has figured in two cases, *SPAR* and *SOCEMAS*.

10—16 *SPAR case* In April, 1972, the Commission published a summary of an application by SPAR for negative clearance, indicating that it intended to give a favourable decision. SPAR was an international organization of fourteen national SPAR organizations, voluntary chains of food wholesalers or retailers. Five of the national organizations were in the Common Market, in Belgium, Holland, Germany, France, and Italy. The international SPAR arrangements included research into and purchasing of certain products. SPAR's International Marketing Centre negotiated prices and terms with suppliers, placed orders, etc. The contracts were, however, concluded in the name of the national organization or wholesaler to whom the goods were consigned. In all cases, the national organization decided the prices at which the goods would be re-sold. The International Marketing Centre did not enjoy any exclusive rights as regards its purchasing activities.

The particular grounds upon which the Commission feels able to give a favourable decision are not indicated in the summary (it is not the Commission's practice to do so), and will not be known until a formal decision has been issued. It would, however, seem that the proposed favourable view is based on the absence of any competitive restriction in the arrangements.

10—17 *SOCEMAS case* SOCEMAS was a joint purchasing organization acting on behalf of some 69 chains of food shops in France. The chains were of medium size, and comprised altogether about 20,000 shops scattered throughout France. SOCEMAS passed on to its members information about foodstuffs available for purchase in other countries. If sufficient members were interested and the orders they gave to SOCEMAS warranted it, SOCEMAS would make a contract with the foreign supplier. If not, SOCEMAS would put any interested member in direct touch with the supplier. Members were not bound to buy through SOCEMAS. The Commission therefore concluded that the agreement did not have the *object* of restricting competition. As to *effect*, SOCEMAS' purchases represented only a minor part of the market in each product, so that its activities did not have a noticeable effect on competition. The Commission granted negative clearance.

## 5. Check List

10—18   (i)     The Note in paragraph 6-31 applies to this Check List.

     (ii)    "Agreement" includes "decision" and "concerted practice".

    (iii)   "Restriction" in relation to competition includes "prevention" and "distortion".

*"Between undertakings"*

1.     Are all the parties to the agreement inter-related companies, (i.e. a parent and its subsidiaries, or subsidiaries of a common parent), and does the parent control the relevant activity (production/ selling/purchasing) in the subsidiaries?

        If so, Article 85.1 does not apply.

        If not, read on.

*Inter-Member trade*

2.     Does the agreement have no effect on inter-Member trade?

        If so, Article 85.1 does not apply.

If not, read on.

*Restriction upon competition*

3. Has the agreement neither the object nor the effect of restricting competition within the Common Market, taking account where appropriate of sections 4, 5, and 6 of the "Notice Concerning Co-operation between Enterprises" (Appendix H)?

If so, Article 85.1 does not apply.

If not, read on.

*No appreciable effect*

4. Are the quantitative limits in the "Notice Concerning Minor Agreements" (Appendix J) satisfied?

If so, Article 85.1 does not apply.

If not, read on.

5. Is any effect upon inter-Member trade or competition within the Common Market not appreciable?

If so, apply for negative clearance.

If not, read on.

*Relief from obligation to notify*

6. Are all the parties from one Member State, and does the agreement relate neither to imports nor exports between Members?

If so, Article 4.2 (1) of Regulation 17 (18-05) applies – the agreement need not be notified, but may be notified if the parties so wish.

If not, read on.

*Individual exemption*

7. Does the agreement satisfy the requirements of Article 85.3?

If so, notify for exemption.

If not, read on.

*Remainder*

8. If the agreement has already been made, it may be worth notifying it and discussing it with the Commission in case it can be modified so as to qualify for negative clearance or exemption. Otherwise, the agreement should be terminated.

If the agreement has not already been made, it may be worth discussing the proposals with the Commission.

*Timing*

(a) For "existing agreements" to which Article 85.1 applies "by virtue of accession" – notification must be made between 1st January, 1973, and 30th June, 1973.

(b) For other agreements – notification must be made before the restrictive terms come into operation.

# CHAPTER 11

# Standardization Agreements

## 1. Introduction

11—01   If a nut comes off a machine and has to be replaced, a nut made to different dimensions or one with a thread of different dimensions will be useless. The relacement must be to the same dimensions and design as the original, and must complement the bolt. The same principle applies to all replacements. If all manufacturers of the replacements work to the same standards, their products will be interchangeable, an item made by one can be used to replace an item made by another.

Interchangeability is a considerable convenience for the user. It also has the merit that the manufacturers of the spare parts are in competition with each other, whereas if they were each making to separate designs and standards they would each have a smaller, but insulated, market.

11—02   There are other advantages in standardization. A host of different, specialized, items means that production runs will tend to be shorter. Fewer, standard, items means longer production runs and usually lower costs. Moreover, the manufacturer can then carry stocks and deliver from stock, whereas with specialized items ordered infrequently it may be uneconomic to carry stocks.

Standard items also ease the stock problem for the user. If he can obtain quick delivery ex-stock from the manufacturer, he need carry no or only small stocks. But if the item is made specially for him, he may have to carry large stocks to tide him over until his supplier can make some more.

There can, of course, be disadvantages in standardization, such as loss of variety and flexibility. But, on balance, standardization is desirable, and standardization agreements have been accorded favourable treatment in German and British cartel law, for example.

11—03   So far as the E.E.C. is concerned, there is a special argument for standardization. If within each separate Member there were and continued to be separate national standards, inter-Member trade would

191

be severely hindered. For example, if the United Kingdom worked only to inches and feet interchange with Continental industries using metric dimensions would be negligible. In short, retention of different national systems of standards would maintain market insulation. Creation of one unified market requires adoption of common standards throughout E.E.C. industries, and anything which leads in that direction is desirable.

## 2. Regulations and Notices

11—04    From the outset, Regulation 17 gave temporary exemption to standardization agreements. Article 4.2 (3)(a) removes the obligation to notify in respect of agreements, decisions, and concerted practices which have as their sole object "the development or uniform application of standards or types". Any such agreement which falls within Article 85.1 need not be notified, although the parties can notify it if they so wish.

11—05    Regulation 2821/71 gives the Commission power to grant "bloc" exemption to agreements, etc., where the sole object is "the application of standards and patterns".

11—06    Finally, the quantitative levels specified in the "Notice Concerning Minor Agreements" (Appendix J), apply to standardization agreements. Where those limits are satisfied, the agreement is deemed to have no appreciable effect, and consequently falls outside 85.1.

## 3. Cases

11—07    *Transocean case* The Transocean Marine Paint Association comprised eighteen medium-sized paint manufacturers in eighteen different countries, five of them Members of the E.E.C. The members manufactured a standard marine paint to a single formula, and sold it in the same form and under the same trade mark. The aim was that ship-owners could obtain supplies of the paint at ports throughout the world. Members could not sell the same paint under a different mark, but only paints of higher or lower quality. They had to comply with quality controls. Each member had a "territory", i.e. the country in which it was established.

Each member was free to fix its selling price for Transocean paint. If an order was received for delivery in another member's territory, the order could be supplied on payment of a commission to the member whose territory it was. In the case of orders from another member's territory for non-Transocean paint, delivery could be made with the latter's agreement (which should normally be given if the Association's interest were not harmed) and on payment of a commission. A member could manufacture paint for a non-member as sub-contractor only if the central office were notified to obtain the agreement of any other member concerned. And the members could not make paints in another member's territory or have them made there by somebody else.

The Commission held that the agreement came within Article 85.1. Trade between Member States was affected, because five of the Member countries were the "territories" of five of the members of the Association. The agreement had the object or effect of ,restricting competition for a variety of reasons. The obligation to pay commissions on sales in other members' territories put the selling member at a competitive disadvantage. The qualified export prohibition on non-Transocean paints limited competition, as did the restriction on manufacture. Some of the members were of sufficient size to compete against each other in the Common Market, so that the restriction of competition within the E.E.C. was appreciable.

The agreement improved distribution, by making a standard product widely available under the same mark and in the same form. Consumers obtained a fair share of these advantages. The agreement did not contain unnecessary restrictions − the restrictions on export, for example, had been essential at the start to give each member a territory which it could develop. And the members were exposed to lively competition within the Common Market, so that the agreements did not allow competition to be eliminated. As the requirements of Article 85.3 were satisfied, exemption was granted from 15th June, 1966, to 31st December, 1972, on condition that the Commission was informed immediately of any changes in the membership or the agreement and of any decisions of the managing board on matters relevant to the Commission's decision. An annual report had also to be submitted to the Commission.

(The agreement was made in 1959, and notified in due time. It was amended on 15th June, 1966, to exclude certain provisions which were not "indispensable", such as an absolute prohibition on making paint for non-members, and a much wider prohibition on exports to other members' territories. The exemption ran only from the 15th June, 1966, but the Commission exercised its power under Article 7.1 of Regulation 17 to declare that Article 85.1 did not apply to the agreement for the period 13th March, 1962, to 15th June, 1966.)

11−08    *V.V.V.F. case* V.V.V.F. was an association of Dutch paint manu-facturers, and the case related to its export agreement. The export agreement was concerned with a standard paint made to a fixed formulation and sold under a common brand name. So far as exports to other Member States were concerned, the Members could fix their own prices, so that the only restrictions related to the quality of the paint and to marking. There were provisions relating to exports to non-Members, such as a minimum price, an obligation to make a monthly report to the secretariat of sales, prices received, etc. In fact, the minimum prices were fixed at a fairly low level compared with effective prices. There was strong competition between members and with third parties. There was strong competition within the Common Market. The Commission concluded that there was no appreciable effect on competition within the Common Market and granted negative clearance as from 8th June, 1968, (when the export agreement had been amended — the Commission also declared Article 85.1 not to apply for the period 13th March, 1962, to 8th June, 1968).

11—09 *Other cases* Standardization has been a factor in two other, specialization, cases. The specialization agreement between Fabrique Nationale and Cartoucherie Française, dealing mainly with cartridges, was found by the Commission to have led to a standardization of the dimensions and ballistic characteristics of the products. The MAN/SAVIEM agreement, especially the joint research and development, contributed to the adoption by the parties of a common range of vehicles conforming to a uniform conception and design and to the achievement of standardization of components and assemblies.

## 4. Check List

11—10   (i)    The Note in paragraph 6-31 applies to this Check List.

     (ii)   "Agreement" includes "decision" and "concerted practice".

   (iii)  "Restriction" in relation to competition includes "prevention" and "distortion".

*"Between undertakings"*

1.    Are all the parties to the agreement inter-related companies (i.e. a parent and its subsidiaries, or subsidiaries of a common parent), and does the parent control standardization in the subsidiaries?
       If so, Article 85.1 does not apply.
       If not, read on.

*Inter-Member trade*

2.    Does the agreement have no effect on inter-Member trade?
       If so, Article 85.1 does not apply.
       If not, read on.

*Restriction upon competition*

3.    Has the agreement neither the object nor the effect of restricting competition within the Common Market?
       If so, Article 85.1 does not apply.
       If not, read on.

*No appreciable effect*

4.    Are the quantitative limits in the "Notice Concerning Minor Agreements" (Appendix J) satisfied?
       If so, Article 85.1 does not apply.
       If not, read on.

5.    Is any effect upon inter-Member trade or competition within the Common Market not appreciable?
       If so, apply for negative clearance.
       If not, read on.

*Relief from obligation to notify*

6.    Are all the parties from one Member State and does the agreement relate neither to imports nor exports between

Members?
> If so, Article 4.2 (1) of Regulation 17 (18-05) applies — the agreement need not be notified, but may be notified if the parties so wish.
>
> If not, read on.

7. Does the agreement have as its sole object the development or uniform application of standards or types?
> If so, Article 4.2 (2)(3)(a) of Regulation 17 applies — the agreement need not be notified, but may be notified if the parties so wish.
>
> If not, read on.

*"Bloc" exemption*

8. When the Commission has made a regulation under the power granted to it by Article 1.1(a) of Regulation 2821/71 (27-02) — does the agreement conform to the requirements of that regulation?
> If so, the agreement is exempt while the regulation is in force and so long as the agreement conforms to those requirements.
>
> If not, read on.

*Individual exemption*

9. Does the agreement satisfy the requirements of Article 85.3?
> If so, notify for exemption.
>
> If not, read on.

*Remainder*

10. If the agreement has already been made, it may be worth notifying it and discussing it with the Commission in case it can be modified so as to qualify for negative clearance or exemption. Otherwise, the agreement should be terminated.

   If the agreement has not already been made, it may be worth discussing the proposals with the Commission.

*Timing*

(a) For "existing agreements" to which Article 85.1 applies "by virtue of accession" — notification must be made between 1st January, 1973, and 30th June, 1973.

(b) For other agreements — notification must be made before the restrictive terms become operative.

# CHAPTER 12

# Specialization Agreements

## 1. Introduction

12—01 As with almost all sets of rules devised to govern complex human activities, competition policy is not without its internal inconsistencies. The basic principle of competition policy is that if several or many suppliers are vying with each other, none will be in a position to abuse economic power — and the striving of each to be ahead of his rivals will ensure efficiency, progress, and the best satisfaction of buyers' needs.

On the other hand, there are the wastes of competition — six producers working at less than optimum capacity where four working at optimum capacity could meet requirements; the expenditure of resources to persuade buyers to take Brand X instead of Brand Y where both are identical; the duplication of effort, and waste of resources, where six laboratories are pursuing the same research and exploring the same blind alleys; and so on. Even if all producers in the market are working at full capacity, if all are producing short runs, changing production frequently from one item to another and then to a third, and so on, efficiency could be improved with economy in the resources used if each specialized his production, giving fewer changes and longer runs.

12—02 It has to be recognized that specialization can bring economic benefits, to the producers, to consumers, and to the community by avoiding waste of scarce resources. But specialization almost always involves agreement and planning. Specialization by agreement is the antithesis of competition. Where there is "atomistic" competition, many small producers, an agreement between two to specialise may be acceptable even if the benefits may only be small. But as the market becomes more oligopolistic, the benefits to justify permissible specialization must be greater. Where the market is atomistic, specialization may be encouraged; where the market is oligopolistic, specialization may be less welcome. It is a matter of degree, and policy.

## 2. Regulations and Notices

12—03  Perhaps because of this inherent conflict, specialization agreements did not, until December, '1971, qualify for special treatment. Exemption was available under Article 85.3 where the relevant conditions were satisfied, and Article 4.2 (1) of Regulation 17 relieved from the obligation to notify any agreements where all the parties were in one Member State and the provisions related neither to imports nor exports. If the quantitative limits in the "Notice Concerning Minor Agreements" (Appendix J) were satisfied, the agreement would be deemed not to have an appreciable effect on competition within the Common Market or inter-Member trade, so that 85.1 would not apply.

12—04  Regulation 2822/71 made in December, 1971, changed this. The Regulation added a third category to Article 4.2 (3) of Regulation 17, so that the relief from the obligation to notify now applies additionally to agreements, etc., which have as their sole object specialization in manufacture, provided they are within generous quantitative limits. Those limits are that, first, the products governed by the agreement must not exceed 15% of the market in those products or substitutes in a substantial part of the Common Market, and, secondly, the turnover of the parties must not exceed 200 million units of account. The agreement may, of course, be notified if the parties so wish.

These quantitative limits are much wider than those allowed generally for "minor agreements" (Appendix J). The market share can go up to 15% as against 5%, and the parties' turnover up to 200 million units as against 15 million units. Moreover, it would seem that in calculating turnover, only the turnover of the parties is taken, not that of associated undertakings as is required in the case of "minor agreements" (26-08).

By agreements which "have as their sole object" specialization is meant, presumably, agreements with the object of specialization in which all the provisions, or all the provisions restricting competition, relate only to specialization.

12—05  Regulation 2821/71 was also made on the 20th December, 1971. It gives the Commission power to make a regulation granting "bloc" exemption to agreements, etc., which have the object of specialization (Article 1.1 (b)). In this case, any specialization is included, in contrast to Regulation 2822/71 which confines "specialization" to "specialization in the manufacture of products". Presumably, therefore, a "bloc" exemption regulation under 2821/71 could include specialization as regards the supply of services — for example, an agreement between research laboratories that each will concentrate on ône particular line or branch of research.

## 3. Cases

12—06  Prior to the December, 1971, Regulations, there had been a series of specialization cases in which individual exemption had been granted under Article 85.3. Four of the more important ones are outlined in the following paragraphs.

12—07 *A.C.E.C./Berliet agreement* A.C.E.C. of Brussels had developed a low-weight, high-yield, system of electric transmission, mainly for buses. It consisted in using the engine to generate electricity which in turn powered electric motors in each wheel. It made an agreement with Berliet in France, under which A.C.E.C. was to continue with developing the transmission system and to study its adaptation to Berliet's vehicles, while Berliet would concentrate on developing a bus to take the new transmission. If their joint development was successful, Berliet would buy all its electrical transmissions from A.C.E.C. who would supply nobody else in France; the price would be as mutually agreed, but Berliet would be entitled to the benefit of any better price allowed by A.C.E.C. to any other buyer. A.C.E.C. was to supply only one vehicle manufacturer in each of the other Members (except Belgium).

The agreement restricted competition within the Common Market. The freedom of the parties was limited — Berliet could buy electrical transmissions only from A.C.E.C. while the latter could supply only Berliet in France and only one manufacturer in each of the other Members (except Belgium). The competitive freedom of third parties was also limited — other manufacturers of electrical transmissions could not supply Berliet, only the selected manufacturers in other Members could buy from A.C.E.C. and not non-selected manufacturers, etc. Inter-Member trade was also affected. As only Berliet in France could buy from A.C.E.C., other French vehicle manufacturers could not buy and export to other Members. Non-selected manufacturers in other Members could not buy, and equally could not export. Consequently, the Commission held that Article 85.1 applied.

As to the application of Article 85.3, the agreement allowed each party to specialize in its research and production, A.C.E.C. on the transmission system, Berliet on the engine, chassis, etc. Thus, the agreement contributed to improving production and technical progress. In assessing whether consumers would have a fair share of the resultant benefits, the Commission recognized that it was dealing with future events, and could work only on probabilities. If the new system was successful, it would be competing with buses of traditional design, so that the parties could not exploit their position. And the agreement envisaged no restrictions on the vehicle manufacturers in selling the buses, so that there would be competition between them. It seemed reasonable to conclude that consumers would obtain a fair share of the benefits.

The exclusive supply and purchase arrangements between A.C.E.C. and Berliet were necessary to give each sufficient assurance to justify the investment. As regards the restriction on A.C.E.C. to supply only one bus manufacturer in each other Member, at the beginning the output would be small, and a new manufacturer would require some assurance as to his market to justify his investment. The restrictions were necessary to achieve the object of the agreement.

Finally, the new buses would be in competition with buses of traditional design, so that the agreement did not eliminate competition.

Exemption was granted from March, 1966, to July, 1973, with an obligation on the parties to present a report on the working of the agreement at the end of 1971.

12–08 *Jaz agreement* A French clock manufacturer, Jaz, made a specialization agreement with a German manufacturer, Peter-Uhren. Each would specialize upon its principal product — electric clocks and alarm clocks in the case of Jaz, and mechanical alarm clocks in the case of Peter — and would give up making the other's specialty products. Jaz would supply its specialty items only to Peter in Germany (apart from three other old-established German customers), and Peter would supply only Jaz in France with its specialty items (and stop watches, which did not compete with but extended Jaz' stop watch range). Each party was bound not to buy from anybody else the other's specialty products for resale in its territory. Each was free to fix its own selling prices in its own territory, and there was no restriction upon exports or upon parallel imports.

Article 85.1 applied because inter-Member trade was affected, the parties being in different Members, and competition was restricted by the obligations to give up making the other party's specialty items and to buy them exclusively from the other. But the agreement had increased productivity and achieved cost savings by longer runs from specialized production. Despite the production specialization, each party could offer for sale items in their joint range. The agreement improved both production and distribution. There were a large number of competitors, so that the parties could not keep all the resultant benefits to themselves but would have to pass on at least part of them to consumers. There were no unnecessary restrictions, and the parties could not eliminate competition. Exemption was granted for ten years, from 1967 to 1977.

12–09 *Clima Chappée agreement* This was an agreement between Clima Chappée in France and Buderus in Germany. The former was a specialist in manufacturing air-conditioning apparatus, the latter in hot-air generators. The object of the agreement was that each would concentrate upon its special line, supplying only the other for distribution in the latter's territory. Article 85.1 applied because the prohibition on making the other party's specialty and the exclusive purchase and supply arrangements constituted a restriction of competition, and inter-Member trade was affected as the parties were in different Members.

The rationalization of production and sale of the joint range improved production and distribution. The existence of numerous competitors meant that the parties would have to share any resulting benefits with consumers and could not eliminate competition. And no unnecessary restrictions were included. Exemption was granted for eleven years, from 1968 to 1979.

12—10 *MAN/SAVIEM agreement* This agreement between a German (MAN) and a French (SAVIEM) motor manufacturer provided for their collaboration in research and development, and also in manufacturing and selling industrial vehicles. The object was for the parties to put on world markets a joint range of vehicles weighing 7½ tons and above. SAVIEM was to play the main role in medium-sized vehicles, i.e. the range 7½ to 12 tons, and MAN in the larger-sized vehicles of 12 to 24 tons. The agreement provided for specialization in manufacture of components; for example, SAVIEM was to make the engines for the medium-sized range, and MAN for the larger sizes. For delivery in France, SAVIEM would assemble both ranges, and MAN would assemble both for delivery in Germany. For other countries, SAVIEM would assemble the medium-sized range, and MAN the larger. Except for replacements, neither party was to sell to third parties components of its own production or bought from the other, without the latter's consent. Together, the parties represented about 7.4% of vehicle production in Western Europe, ranking sixth out of eleven manufacturers.

The agreement provided a number of competitive restrictions. As regards research and development, neither party could work on items assigned to the other. As regards production, neither could manufacture anything in the other's range, nor use in the common range of vehicles components not accepted by both. As to marketing, MAN could not sell vehicles in France, nor SAVIEM in Germany; and neither could sell to third parties components of its own production or bought from the other party, except as replacements. Inter-Member trade was affected, as the parties were in different Members and had divided up their common range between themselves. So that the agreement came within Article 85.1.

The Commission held that the agreement contributed to technical progress, to production, and to distribution (each party used its own national network of distributors to sell and provide after-sales service in the joint range). Competition from other vehicle manufacturers would ensure that consumers enjoyed a share of the benefits, and prevented the parties from eliminating competition. The agreement contained no unnecessary restrictions. Exemption was granted for ten years from March, 1968, to March, 1978, on condition that the parties presented a report to the Commission every three years, and also advised the Commission of any agreements entered into with other vehicle manufacturers touching upon competitive conduct.

## 4. Check List

12—11 (i)   The Note in paragraph 6-31 applies to this Check List.

(ii)    "Agreement" includes "decision" and "concerted practice".

(iii)   "Restriction" in relation to competition includes "prevention" and "distortion".

*"Between undertakings"*

1.      Are all the parties to the agreement inter-related companies (i.e. a parent and its subsidiaries, or subsidiaries of a common parent), and does the area in which specialization has been adopted come within the parent's control?

        If so, Article 85.1 does not apply.

        If not, read on.

*Inter-Member trade*

2.      Does the agreement have no effect on inter-Member trade?

        If so, Article 85.1 does not apply.

        If not, read on.

*Restriction upon competition*

3.      Has the agreement neither the object nor effect of restricting competition within the Common Market?

        If so, Article 85.1 does not apply.

        If not, read on.

*No appreciable effect*

4.      Are the quantitative limits in the "Notice Concerning Minor Agreements" (Appendix J) satisfied?

        If so, Article 85.1 does not apply.

        If not, read on.

5.      Is any effect upon inter-Member trade or competition within the Common Market not appreciable?

        If so, apply for negative clearance.

        If not, read on.

*Relief from obligation to notify*

6.      Are all the parties from one Member State and does the agreement relate neither to imports nor exports between Members?

        If so, Article 4.2 (1) of Regulation 17 (18-05) applies – the agreement need not be notified, but may be notified if the parties so wish.

        If not, read on.

7.      Does the agreement have manufacturing specialization as its sole object, and are the quantitative limits in Article 4.2 (3)(c) of Regulation 17 satisfied?

        If so, Article 4.2 (3)(c) applies – the agreement need not be notified, but may be notified if the parties so wish.

        If not, read on.

*"Bloc" exemption*

8.      When the Commission has made a regulation under the power granted to it by Article 1.1 (c) of Regulation 2821/71 (27-02) – does the agreement conform to the requirements of that

regulation?

If so, the agreement is exempt while the regulation is in force, so long as the agreement conforms to those requirements.

If not, read on.

*Individual exemption*

9.   Does the agreement satisfy the requirements of Article 85.3?

If so, notify for exemption.

If not, read on.

*Remainder*

10.   If the agreement has already been made, it may be worth notifying it and discussing it with the Commission in case it can be modified so as to qualify for negative clearance or exemption. Otherwise, the agreement should be terminated.

If the agreement has not already been made, it may be worth discussing the proposals with the Commission.

*Timing*

(a)   For "existing agreements" to which Article 85.1 applies "by virtue of accession" — notification must be made between 1st January, 1973, and 30th June, 1973.

(b)   For other agreements — notification must be made before the restrictive terms become operative.

# CHAPTER 13

# Exchange of Information Agreements

## 1. Introduction

13—01    In order to analyse the working of a market economy, theoretical economics developed the "perfect competition" model. If all the conditions of the model are satisfied in all parts of the economy, there will be the optimum distribution of goods and services, the optimum use of available resources, immediate adjustment to changing situations, and so on.

One of the conditions of perfect competition is complete and immediate knowledge of all facts relating to the market. Each buyer and seller knows all the prices being offered by buyers or asked by sellers. Each knows immediately there is any change anywhere and can adjust his own policy immediately. If one seller lowers his price, all buyers know of it immediately and can flock to him. Then, either his supplies run out and the price goes up, or other suppliers have to adjust their prices downwards. If one buyer offers a higher price, the reverse happens.

13—02    These ideal conditions do not obtain in real life. For speedy knowledge of prices and price changes, organized commodity markets probably present the closest approach to the perfect competition model — in the London Metal Exchange, offers to sell or to buy are made in the "ring", i.e. in the presence of the other dealers who may be either buyers or sellers.

In many instances, information does not come to the knowledge of competitors until much later. If one firm has decided to extend its capacity, the existence of the new capacity may not become known until after it has been in use. If several competitors all think the demand is going up and individually increase their capacity, the result may be excess capacity: or they may each think the other is expanding capacity and each decides not to put down new plant, with the result that there is insufficient capacity.

Some information may never become known. Secret prices, or

special discounts, may never become known to competitors.

13—03 Consequently, there is an argument for "market transparency", for trying to collect and collate as much information as possible and to make it available to all, or to all interested in the particular market or industry. Eddy's "open price" system was an early move in this direction. Some "open price" schemes have passed judicial scrutiny, such as the American *Tag Manufacturers* case.

13—04 Every businessman wants as much information as he can get bearing upon the particular market he is interested in. Some information is available from official sources. Governments collect information as to production, employment, investment, imports, exports, etc. In the nature of things, these official statistics cannot deal separately with every product or subdivision of a product. If a firm makes only one product, a chemical, the official statistics will not be very helpful if that chemical is grouped with several others, so that the figures for it are not available. Different countries may adopt different classifications, so that it may be impossible to build up a picture from, say, import and export statistics from several countries. And official statistics are notoriously slow in publication.

13—05 For reasons such as these, many industries arrange for the collection and distribution of information, and many firms exchange information between themselves. The methods used vary. Each participant may send his information to a central office (or to one participant who acts as a central office), where the information is collated and published or distributed to participants or held so as to be available to those with access to it. Or each participant may merely send his information to each of the others.

13—06 It may be of interest to look quickly at the sort of information which a manufacturer or supplier will quite legitimately want.

As to his *competitors*, who are they? What is each producing or selling, both in terms of qualities and of quantities? What are their selling prices and terms for each quality of each product, and for each· type of customer? What are their future plans, for new products, for new processes, etc.?

As to the *buyers*, who are they? How much does each buy of each quality of the product? What prices do they pay? Is the offtake of each going up or going down? What is the credit-worthiness of each?

As to *future planning,* is demand going up or going down? If he supplies industrial raw materials, is demand going up or down in the industries he supplies? Is one quality of the product expanding while others are contracting?

As to *technical matters,* how do his efficiency and costs compare with those of his competitors? Are there any new processes or products in the wind, and if so are they likely to be successful, are the claims made for them valid? Is standardization of his products with those of his competitors possible and likely to be acceptable to buyers, and will it pay? In some industries, are the hygiene precautions in his factory capable of improvement, do his competitors have better systems which he could instal?

13—07 Obviously, the mere exchange of information cannot in itself restrict competition. On the other hand, the furnishing or receipt of the information may be ancillary to some agreement, decision, or concerted practice which is restrictive. As the "Notice Concerning Co-operation between Enterprises" explains (24-13), if each firm remains free to decide independently its own future market behaviour, an agreement whose sole purpose is the joint procurement of the relevant information will not have the object or effect of restricting competition. But if the freedom of the firm is limited in some way, or its behaviour co-ordinated with that of its competitors, either by an express arrangement or through a co-ordinated practice, there may be a restraint of competition. The essential point is that there should be no express or understood restriction upon each firm's freedom to arrive at its own independent decision upon the facts before it.

It is probably broadly true that the further the information is from the commercial field, the less likely it is that the agreement will be restrictive in relation to competition. And conversely, the closer the information is to commercial matters, the greater the risk that competition may be restricted. It may be useful to look in more detail at certain types of information which might be the subject of an exchange scheme.

13—08 *Costs* Knowledge of competitors' costs can provide a stimulus to efficiency, and a very effective antidote to complacency. It is best to have costs broken down into individual processes and individual items, such as the separate figures for raw materials or for labour in each process. It is unlikely that one manufacturer will have the lowest figure in each category. A low figure in one category may be counterbalanced by a higher one elsewhere. Of course, cost information is of little use for comparative purposes if it has not been prepared on the same basis, so that standardization of costing methods is probably a necessary pre-condition of exchange of cost information.

If the figures are merely presented to each participant without comment, there is unlikely to be any restriction of competition. But the addition of some comments may alter the situation. For example, a comment that the cost changes over all participants showed an increase of X% might be an implied recommendation to the participants to raise their prices by X%, a conclusion which would be more cogent if in fact such a comment had been followed by such price increases.

13—09 *Credit information* If a buyer is facing cash liquidity problems, he will try to postpone paying his bills. He will still want to draw supplies, so that the supplier finds that he is giving longer and longer credit to the buyer. If the supplier seeks to remedy the position by refusing or limiting supplies, or insisting upon cash with order or against *pro-forma* invoice, the buyer will turn to other suppliers. The latter may feel that they are being competitively successful, and welcome the newcomer, whereas in fact they may be only incurring bad debts.

This situation can be met by suppliers exchanging information as to their customers' credit. For example, each supplier might notify the others of any customer whose payments are overdue. If another supplier then receives an order from a new customer, and that customer is one who is overdue, the supplier knows he may be taking a greater risk than usual if he supplies. But the decision must be left to him, there must be no agreement or arrangement not to supply. Moreover, the definition of what is "overdue" must be left to each supplier. For one, it may be payment more than one month after the invoice, for another two months, and so on. If there is an agreed definition of what is "overdue" that could involve an agreement or concerted practice as to credit terms.

13—10 *Turnover* Turnover is usually thought of in money terms, i.e. the total amount received for goods or services supplied during the period in question. But it can also mean quantities, i.e. the amount of goods supplied.

An accurate idea of the size of the market may be essential to establishing the correct commercial policy. A firm may have an increasing turnover and be satisfied with its efforts; but if it had the total market figures and found that its share of the market was falling, i.e. that the total market had been increasing at a greater rate than its turnover, that satisfaction should disappear. Conversely, if a firm found its sales declining, it might feel impelled to take desperate action, but the total market figures might show that total demand had fallen to a greater extent, and that by comparison with its competitors, the firm had been successful. A firm with expanding sales might be inclined to put down more capacity — but if the total figures for the industry were falling, investment in new plant might be disastrous and only make larger the eventual surplus capacity. Information as to the total supplies by the industry, divided into the various types or qualities of the product, is usually one of the main desiderata for efficient and sound policy-making. Similar information for imports and exports is necessary to give the complete picture for each market.

As already mentioned, some statistics are available from various governments, but frequently they are not sufficiently detailed, and in most cases are late in publication. Differences of classification and grouping can reduce their value. For such reasons, many industries collect and prepare their own statistics, which are published in many cases.

It must be recognized that exchange of information as to turnover can be used as part of an agreement or concerted practice as to market sharing. If the firms concerned have an understanding as to their respective shares of the market, collection and distribution to all of statistics showing the deliveries of each will show whether the shares are being adhered to, and if not who is the culprit. This is not possible where all that the individual firm receives is a statement of the total figures, so that it has only its own figures and the total.

13—11 *Prices* Information as to competitors' prices (including credit and other terms) is essential for deciding a firm's pricing policy. Otherwise, it is working in the dark. It is also necessary to deal with "buyers' tales" (1-13). That information is difficult to acquire in industries where there are no "shop windows", no published price lists. Even in a trade where price lists are used, extensive "off-list" prices and rebates may make the list itself useless, if not positively misleading. In the *Tag Manufacturers* case, a substantial proportion of the prices reported were in respect of transactions at "off-list" prices. In some trades, rebates according to purchases over a period (six months, or one year) are the practice, and it is impossible to tell what each supplier is charging to each customer — a price can be lowered by according a buyer a higher "rating" than he actually achieves.

For these reasons, price-reporting schemes have been adopted. Clearly, merely knowing the prices charged by competitors does not restrict competition. But again, such a system may be used as part of some restrictive arrangement. An agreement or concerted practice involving the automatic adoption of the prices charged by one firm could be operated through a price-reporting system. And where the scheme requires the reporting of prices *before* they take effect there is a restriction — a new price cannot be put into force until it has been notified.

## 2. Regulations and Notices

13—12 There are no regulations dealing specifically with agreements to exchange information, but the "Notice Concerning Co-operation between Enterprises" (Appendix H) deals with some four groups of agreements of this type (24-12), i.e. agreements which have as their sole object:

(a)  an exchange of opinion or experience;

(b)  joint market research;

(c)  joint execution of comparative studies of enterprises or economic sectors;

(d)  joint preparation of statistics and standardized calculation systems.

Although (a) is clearly concerned with exchange of information, the other groups could also include it. For example, joint market research might involve the parties pooling their separate information as to their markets (as was the case in the *Clima Chappée* agreement).

13—13 The Notice, while recognizing that the mere exchange of information does not restrict competition so that agreements within the four groups can be considered as falling outside Article 85.1, draws attention to four types of information where a general clearance cannot be given, i.e. orders, turnover, investment, and prices (24-14). As mentioned in paragraphs 13-10 and 13-11, schemes for exchanging information as to turnover and prices may be part and parcel of restrictive arrangements. Where orders are reported, there is the same risk of market-sharing. And where information is exchanged as to investment plans, there could be some arrangement as to future markets. The Notice underlines the possible restraint exchange of such information might have in oligopolistic markets for homogeneous products. Where agreements include the exchange of information as to orders, turnover, investment, and prices, they should be made the subject of an application for individual negative clearance.

13—14 The Notice also draws attention to the risk of recommendations restricting competition where standardized calculation systems specify such things as rules to be adopted. For example, to specify a rate of depreciation to be used in calculating costs in a standardized costing system would be equivalent to fixing one item of costs and so one component of prices.

13—15 In addition to the Notice, Article 4.2 (1) of Regulation 17 applies to relieve from the obligation to notify agreements where all the parties are from one Member State and the provisions do not relate to imports or exports between Members. The "Notice Concerning Minor Agreements" (Appendix J) also applies to information agreements which satisfy its quantitative limits.

## 3. Cases

13—16 Exchange of information as to technical matters figured in the *Fabrique Nationale* agreement. The parties systematically exchanged all their documents and plans concerning the agreement products, tools, and processes. This was not regarded by the Commission as restraining competition, but more as one of the benefits flowing from the agreement.

13—17 Turning to commercial matters, the Commission in 1969 objected to a practice carried on by insurance companies in four Member States. The companies, which operated in a specialized field, had an agreement dealing with the situation when responsibility for covering a risk was transferred from one Member State to another. Under the agreement, the company taking over the risk was required to seek comprehensive information from the company which had previously carried the risk, including the rate of premium charged, the effective rate obtained, the financial results of the insurance, and so on. The Commission objected to the exchange of this information, on the ground that its supply was liable to distort competition, and the companies cancelled the agreement.[1]

[1] Commission Press Release, 1st April, 1969.

13—18    Commercial information figured also in the *V.V.V.F.* case. The original version of the agreement required the members to give the secretariat of the association any information which the secretariat might request as to the composition of products, prices, and terms and conditions of sale. In addition, each member had to report every month to the secretariat the exports made during the preceding month and to include copies of the relevant invoices, and also to report agreements made with agents abroad. The agreement was amended so that these provisions did not apply in respect of exports to other Members, and negative clearance was given.

## 4. Check List

13—19    (i)    The Note in paragraph 6-31 applies to this Check List.
    (ii)    "Agreement" includes "decision" and "concerted practice".
    (iii)    "Restriction" in relation to competition includes "prevention" and "distortion".
*"Between undertakings"*
1.    Are all the parties to the agreement inter-related companies (i.e. a parent and its subsidiaries, or subsidiaries of a common parent) and does the parent require the exchange of the particular information?
        If so, Article 85.1 does not apply.
        If not, read on.
*Inter-Member trade*
2.    Does the agreement have no effect upon inter-Member trade?
        If so, Article 85.1 does not apply.
        If not, read on.
*Restriction upon competition*
3.    Has the agreement neither the object nor the effect of restricting competition within the Common Market, taking account where appropriate of section 1 of the "Notice Concerning Co-operation between Enterprises" (Appendix H)?
        If so, Article 85.1 does not apply.
        If not, read on.
*No appreciable effect*
4.    Are the quantitative limits in the "Notice Concerning Minor Agreements" (Apendix J) satisfied?
        If so, Article 85.1 does not apply.
        If not, read on.
5.    Is any effect upon inter-Member trade or upon competition within the Common Market not appreciable?
        If so, apply for negative clearance.
        If not, read on.
*Relief from obligation to notify*
6.    Are all the parties from one Member State, and does the agreement relate neither to imports nor exports between

Members?

> If so, Article 4.2 (1) of Regulation 17 (18-05) applies — the agreement need not be notified, but may be notified if the parties so wish.
>
> If not, read on.

*Individual exemption*

7.    Does the agreement satisfy the requirements of Article 85.3?

> If so, notify for exemption.
>
> If not, read on.

*Remainder*

8.    If the agreement has already been made, it may be worth notifying it and discussing it with the Commission in case it can be modified so as to qualify for negative clearance or exemption. Otherwise, the agreement should be terminated.

If the agreement has not already been made, it may be worth discussing it with the Commission.

*Timing*

(a)    For "existing agreements" to which Article 85.1 applies "by virtue of accession" — notification must be made between 1st January, 1973, and 30th June, 1973.

(b)    For other agreements — notification must be made before the restrictive terms come into operation.

# CHAPTER 14

# Other Forms of Co-operation

## 1. Introduction

14—01  A course of competition law can leave the impression that any contact between competitors is dangerous, except for a few permitted areas. This impression would be almost, although not entirely, erroneous. Contact between competitors can be dangerous if those involved allow the contacts to develop in ways which restrict or distort competition, into areas prohibited by Community competition law (and also by national competition law in those countries which have such laws). But provided those forbidden areas are avoided, there are many fruitful and proper fields for inter-firm co-operation. From the point of view of Community competition law, everything is permitted except restraint of competition within Article 85.1 (or abuse of market dominance). But it is dangerously easy to stray over the boundary between what is licit and what is illicit. In contacts between competitors eternal vigilance is necessary to make sure that the boundary is not crossed.

## 2. Regulations and Notices

14—02  All the types of agreements, etc., given special treatment in the Regulations issued to date have been dealt with in the preceding chapters, and most of those referred to in the "Notice Concerning Co-operation between Enterprises" (Appendix H). There are some types of agreements in the Notice and also some in cases decided to date which do not fall within the foregoing chapters, and it is the purpose of this Chapter to cover this rather heterogeneous residue.

14—03  Section 2 of the Notice mentions four types of agreement which do not restrict competition, i.e. those relating to co-operation in accounting matters, credit guarantees, collection of accounts, and provision of organizational and fiscal advice. In connection with the joint collection of debts, the Notice brings out a point discussed in connection with exchange of information as to customers' credit (13-09). The joint collection office must take the terms of sale and credit adopted independently by each firm, and not try to standardize or reach common, agreed, terms. This would be a form of restriction of competition.

Section 7 refers to forms of joint advertising which are permissible. Joint advertising was one of the joint activities between the two parties to the *Fabrique Nationale* agreement.

14—04 This is a convenient stage at which to draw attention to a significant omission in the Articles of the Treaty and the Regulations and Notices issued in connection with them. A feature of industrial development is the growth of trade unions. The individual employee is economically weak, and his organization into trade unions is an economically desirable form of "countervailing power". With the extension of workers' unions to cover whole industries and whole countries, there has been a corresponding growth of employers' associations to deal with labour-relations negotiations. Joint negotiation and settlement of wages and other conditions of employment are now the rule.

Clearly, workers' unions do not fall within Articles 85 and 86, because they are not "undertakings". But what about employers' associations? If employers agree between themselves the wages they will pay and the other conditions of employment, are they not restricting competition between themselves, both in their offers for labour in the labour market and in their costs and so in one element in prices in the markets for their products? And as the unified common market becomes an economic reality, so it must be expected that workers' unions and employers' associations will cross inter-Member boundaries until wage negotiations are eventually on an E.E.C. basis. In that event, are workers' unions to be treated as being outside Articles 85 and 86, while employers' associations are held to be within the Articles?

Joint negotiation of wages and conditions of employment are regarded as being outside competition law (as in the United Kingdom, for example), and it would seem not unreasonable that that is the position in the Common Market also. Some authoritative guidance by the Commission seems to be required.

### 3. Cases

14—05 Two other forms of inter-firm co-operation have been dealt with in cases decided to date, i.e. rationalization, and reciprocal supply.

*Rationalization*

14—06 Specialization agreements (Chapter 12) necessarily involve some degree of rationalization, but rationalization is possible without specialization. This can be seen from the *CECIMO* and *CEMATEX* cases.

14—07 *CECIMO case* CECIMO was an international association of twelve European national associations of machine tool manufacturers. Its activities included the organization every other year of a European machine tool exhibition (EEMO) in one of its member countries. Each manufacturer was free to decide whether or not to take part in an EEMO, but if he did take part he was bound not to participate during that year in any other machine tool exhibition in a CECIMO country and his machines could not be used in any other such exhibition (so that his distributors could not take part on his behalf in non-CECIMO exhibitions during an EEMO year). In non-EEMO years, all manufacturers belonging to the CECIMO national associations were free to exhibit their machines without restriction.

The Commission held that the EEMO arrangements infringed Article 85.1. They restricted competition within the Common Market. Competition between the organizers of exhibitions was restricted because during EEMO years machine tools exhibited at the EEMO were not available for exhibition elsewhere. Competition between machine tool manufacturers and between their distributors was also restricted in EEMO years for the same reason. The national associations in five of the Member States belonged to CECIMO, so that the restrictions upon competition affected inter-Member trade.

The Commission also concluded that the restrictions on exhibiting elsewhere during the EEMO year rationalized participation in exhibitions. An EEMO brought together almost all the available machines in one place for confrontation and comparison. Although costs of taking part in an EEMO would always be higher than participating in a local exhibition, there would be an overall reduction in costs by avoiding the need to participate in a whole series of local exhibitions. The rotation of EEMO's through each member country gave a chance to participate to those manufacturers who would not normally exhibit outside their own country. On balance, the Commission held that the CECIMO arrangements improved distribution and promoted economic progress, so that the first requirement of Article 85.3 was met. Consumers shared the benefits, because in EEMO years they need only go to one exhibition so avoiding numerous journeys, and the avoidance of duplication of publicity expenditure on the part of the manufacturers would keep their costs and prices down. The second requirement of Article 85.3 was met. There were no unnecessary restrictions, and competition was not eliminated — other forms of publicity were not affected, and there was no restriction in non-EEMO years. All the conditions of Article 85.3 were satisfied, and exemption granted as from 13th March, 1962, to 31st December, 1978.

14—08 *CEMATEX case* CEMATEX was an international association of seven European national associations of textile machinery manufacturers. One of the functions was to organize an international textile machinery exhibition (ITMA) every four years in each member country in rotation. The CEMATEX arrangements allowed each manufacturer to decide freely whether he would take part in an ITMA or not, but if he did he was under an obligation not to take part in any other exhibition of textile machinery during the ITMA year and the preceding and succeeding years in any country in Western Europe. In practice, almost all the manufacturers concerned took part in the ITMAs and refrained from participating in other exhibitions during the forbidden years. In 1968, a recommendation was made that they should not participate in exhibitions during the fourth, free, year, and most complied with the recommendation as well. On the Commission's intervention, the CEMATEX rules were changed, so that the prohibition on participation in other exhibitions applied only during the ITMA year and the preceding year, leaving manufacturers entirely free in the other two years.

Following a similar reasoning to that in the CECIMO case, the Commission held that the amended CEMATEX rules satisfied the conditions of Article 85.3, and granted exemption from 30th November, 1967, until 1982. The Commission also declared that the prohibition in Article 85.1 was not applicable for the period 13th March, 1962, to 30th November, 1967, so granting protection from the possibility of private suit.

### Reciprocal supply

14—09 *Dunlop/Pirelli agreements* This case involved two agreements. The first was made on the 27th February, 1959, and related to France — Dunlop (France) was the manufacturer and undertook to supply tyres, inner tubes, etc., to Pirelli (France) as the buyer. The second was made on the 9th November, 1959, and related to Italy — Pirelli (Italy) was the manufacturer and undertook to supply Dunlop (Italy) as the buyer. At that time, there still remained customs duties between the two countries, and there were technical differences in the tyres, etc., used. The purpose of the agreement was to enable each buyer to extend its sales in the country in question.

In their original versions, the main provisions of the agreements were as follows:

(a) Each manufacturer would make for the buyer, but only standard, not special, products.

(b) The buyer would order at least 60% of the annual figure, and not less than a monthly minimum — if the latter was not reached, the buyer would bear any extra costs arising from the reduced production.

(c) The products supplied could be used only as replacements, and not as original equipment (i.e. sold to the vehicle manufacturer).

(d) The buyers were each to limit their imports into each country to 50% of their respective purchases, and if they wished to import more the manufacturer would be given an opportunity to supply.

(e) The prices charged were to be those to the manufacturer's lowest-priced customer, with an extra allowance fixed in the agreement.

(f) The buyers were not to make similar purchase agreements with other manufacturers within the country.

Provisions (c), (d), and (f), were eventually deleted, and a new term added so that each manufacturer would have the right to supply any requirements of the buyer in excess of the agreed maxima if the buyer matched the prices offered by competing suppliers.

The Commission held that the purpose of the agreements was to enable each buyer to penetrate the other party's market. For such penetration to be possible, without the reciprocal supply permitted by the agreements, the buying group would have had to have sufficient excess capacity in its production country to change over to making products with the technically different characteristics required in the other country. Consequently the agreements did not have the *object* of restricting competition. Although the agreements fixed maximum quantities to be supplied, in fact these figures were regarded as guide lines and were greatly exceeded in practice. The agreements did not, therefore, have the *effect* of restricting competition. As one of the conditions for the application of Article 85.1 was not satisfied, the Commission granted negative clearance to the agreements in their amended form. The Commission also declared that the prohibition in Article 1 of Regulation 17 did not apply to the agreements from the 13th March, 1962, up to the date when the amended versions came into force.

## 4. Check List

14—10  (i)    The Note in paragraph 6-31 applies to this Check List.

(ii)   "Agreement" includes "decision" and "concerted practice".

(iii)  "Restriction" in relation to competition includes "prevention" and "distortion".

*"Between undertakings"*

1.     Are all the parties to the agreement inter-related companies (i.e. a parent and its subsidiaries, or subsidiaries of a common parent) and does the parent control the particular activity which is the subject of the agreement?

       If so, Article 85.1 does not apply.

       If not, read on.

*Inter-Member trade*

2.     Does the agreement have no effect on inter-Member trade?

       If so, Article 85.1 does not apply.

       If not, read on.

*Restriction upon competition*

3.     Has the agreement neither the object nor effect of restricting competition within the Common Market, taking account wherever appropriate of sections 2 and 7 of the "Notice Concerning Co-operation between Enterprises" (Appendix H)?

       If so, Article 85.1 does not apply.

       If not, read on.

*No appreciable effect*

4.  Are the quantitative limits in the "Notice Concerning Minor Agreements" (Appendix J) satisfied?

    If so, Article 85.1 does not apply.

    If not, read on.

5.  Is any effect upon inter-Member trade or competition within the Common Market not appreciable?

    If so, apply for negative clearance.

    If not, read on.

*Relief from obligation to notify*

6.  Are all the parties from one Member State, and does the agreement relate neither to imports nor exports between Members?

    If so, Article 4.2 (1) of Regulation 17 (18-05) applies — the agreement need not be notified, but may be notified if the parties so wish.

    If not, read on.

*Individual exemption*

7.  Does the agreement satisfy the requirements of Article 85.3?

    If so, notify for exemption.

    If not, read on.

*Remainder*

8.  If the agreement has already been made, it may be worth notifying it and discussing it with the Commission in case it can be modified so as to qualify for negative clearance or exemption. Otherwise the agreement should be terminated.

    If the agreement has not already been made, it may be worth discussing the proposals with the Commission.

*Timing*

(a) For "existing agreements" to which Article 85.1 applies "by virtue of accession" — notification must be made between the 1st January, 1973, and the 30th June, 1973.

(b) For other agreements — notification must be made before the restrictive terms come into operation.

# PART 4

# MERGERS AND ABUSES
# OF DOMINANT POSITIONS

# CHAPTER 15

# Mergers

## 1. Introduction

15—01 The merging of two or more undertakings can take many forms. At its simplest, shopkeeper A takes over the business of shopkeeper B next door, and runs the two shops as one. To fall within the ambit of competition law, larger enterprises have to be involved, and these will usually be in the form of companies. The merging of two companies can also take many forms. Strictly speaking, it is extremely rare for the *companies* themselves to merge. The undertakings carried on by the companies may merge, or the companies may come into common ownership, but only in exceptional cases will the companies themselves actually merge.

15—02 For example, companies A and B may agree that the undertaking of A will be sold to B, either for a cash payment or shares in B or a mixture of both. When the transaction has been completed A and B will remain quite separate as before, except that instead of having assets in the form of its undertaking, A will now have assets consisting of cash or shares in B, or both. The two *enterprises* will have merged, but not the companies. However, this type of transaction is not usually adopted, because it would involve transferring from A to B the rights and liabilities under contracts to which A was party — for example, contracts of employment with A's employees, etc.

15—03 Because of these practical difficulties, it is easier and more common to proceed by way of transfer of shares. Thus, if companies A and B decide to merge, in the sense of bringing their undertakings under common control, a new company A/B could be set up which offers its shares to the shareholders in A and B in return for their holdings. If the offer is accepted, company A/B will finish up holding all the shares in A and B, and so be able to run both undertakings as one, while the old shareholders in A and B will now hold A/B shares in place of their previous holdings. Companies A and B have now become subsidiaries of A/B. Another method would be for A to offer to buy all the shares in

219

B, either for cash or for its own shares or a mixture of cash and "paper". In the event of acceptance by the B shareholders, they would end up holding cash or A shares (or both) and A would be holding all the shares in B. A would then be able to run both enterprises as one.

15—04 In these methods, one or more of the companies concerned loses its independence, but that need not always be the case. If A and B are both large undertakings, each with only a small part of its undertaking in one particular branch of industry, they may wish to merge those two parts into one but without affecting the remainder of their separate enterprises. They might then set up a new company X, each transferring to X the relevant part of its undertaking in return for shares in X. A and B will then be left independent as before, with X as a company jointly owned by the two of them.

15—05 Mergers can take place without any formal offer for the shares of the company taken over. If A buys up all the shares of B on the Stock Exchange, it has achieved the same result as if it had made an offer to B's shareholders which had been accepted. Nor is purchase of all the shares necessary. In most cases, purchase of 50% of the voting shares will give control, and in some cases a purchase of a smaller proportion than 50% — when the balance is in a lot of small holdings and the owners use the right to vote only infrequently, or when the existing management is prepared to work in with the main shareholder which is likely to be the case if that shareholder is itself a large company or group of companies.

15—06 In essence, even when carried through as a result of an agreement between the parties, a merger aims at modifying the ownership of undertakings, i.e. it changes the structure of the industry. A merger is directed towards altering the structure of the parties, rather than altering their behaviour or conduct. In contrast, a cartel, whether involving an agreement or not, is aimed, not at changing the ownership of the parties, the structure of the industry, but at modifying the behaviour or conduct of the undertakings concerned.

This is not to say that particular situations cannot arise which both alter the structure and the behaviour of the parties. One can conceive of a merger deal in which group A sells a subsidiary company X to group B and undertakes not to engage in the industry in which X operated.

15—07 The Commission recognized, in its study *Le Problème de la Concentration dans le Marché Commun*,[1] that the Common Market needs enterprises of a European scale, in order to give research and production adapted to a market of 180 million consumers, and to enable European enterprises to compete on equal terms with their rivals in other developed areas. Enterprises could reach the desired scale of operations either by internal growth or by mergers with other enterprises. The policy implications of this need for larger groups were

[1] European Economic Community. Série Concurrence 3. Brussels, 1966.

twofold. First, legal and fiscal obstacles hindering the merger process should be removed. Second, the merging of independent enterprises could have a detrimental effect upon competition.

The merger boom of the 1960s still lay in the future when the Rome Treaty was being drafted, so that it does not contain any provisions dealing specifically with control of mergers. The Commission therefore considered whether and if so how far Articles 85 and 86 were applicable in the merger field. The Commission's views were set out in the Study, and, as will be seen, the development of those Articles into a means of controlling mergers is still in progress.

## 2. Application of Article 85 to mergers

15—08  Bearing in mind that Article 85 is aimed at agreements, decisions, and concerted practices which restrict the competitive conduct of the parties, the Commission concluded that it is not an appropriate means for controlling mergers, which are concerned with changes in the ownership of the parties. The technique of control incorporated into Article 85 is not adapted to dealing with mergers. For example, exemptions under 85.3 can be given for a specified period. Where the ownership of an enterprise is to be changed, it would not be consistent with the aims of the parties to tell them that the change could be permitted only for a limited period after which ownership may have to be transferred back again.

15—09  It is, however, possible for merger deals to include aspects which come within Article 85. This can happen where the deal includes restrictions upon the competitive freedom of the parties. For example, if company A sells part of its enterprise to company B, either by selling a subsidiary or by selling part of its business, the terms of the transaction may include an undertaking by A not to engage in that particular activity in the future. Or, if A and B both have parts of their enterprises engaged in a particular industry and wish to unite those parts into one separate enterprise, they might set up a jointly owned company and transfer the separate parts to it. The terms of such a transaction could well include prohibitions on A and B competing with the joint company, and also upon the latter from competing with A and B in the remaining activities.

15—10  If it is proposed to include in a merger deal terms restricting competition, the possible impact of Article 85.1 must be considered. Where the quantitative limits in the "Notice Concerning Minor Agreements" (Appendix J) are met, Article 85.1 will not apply. If those limits are exceeded, but it is thought that any effect upon competition within the Common Market or upon inter-Member trade will not be appreciable, negative clearance can be sought.

But if Article 85.1 does apply to a merger agreement, the parties must recognize that any form of exemption they obtain will be limited in period. The possibilities are:

221

(a) *Relief from the obligation to notify*

Even if paragraphs (1), 3(b), and 3(c) of Article 4.2 of Regulation 17, applied, it is unlikely that the parties would wish to rely upon them, because of the risk of private suit when the relief no longer applied unless the particular terms qualified for full exemption.

(b) *"Bloc" exemption*

It is conceivable that a "bloc" exemption issued by the Commission under Regulation 2821/71 (Appendix K) in respect of specialization agreements might apply to some merger cases.

(c) *Individual exemption*

It is also conceivable that some merger agreements containing restrictions upon competition might qualify for exemption under Article 85.3.

The limited period of exemption available under (b) and (c) might not be an obstacle if the restrictive terms were intended to operate only for a period. If two large concerns, A and B, hived off into a joint company their interests in a particular industry, they might be prepared to limit to a specified period any restriction upon their freedom to enter that industry again — the specified period would have served its purpose if it enabled the joint company to become established and was long enough for other parts of A and B to lose contact with that industry.

## 3. Application of Article 86 to mergers

15—11   As explained in Chapter 5, for Article 86 to apply there must be a dominant position and an abuse of that position. Consequently, Article 86 can apply to a merger only if a dominant position is involved and also an abuse of it. In what respect can a merger be an "abusive exploitation" of a dominant position?

15—12   The Commission solved this difficulty, in the Study, by arguing that the Rome Treaty sets out to establish a regime of competition. Anything contrary to that policy is an abuse. It is not permitted to independent concerns to eliminate competition between themselves by means of cartels or concerted practices, and neither should it be permitted to dominant firms to use that dominance to eliminate competition. The elimination of competition can, therefore, be an abuse of a dominant position, and so can the reduction or elimination of the freedom of consumer choice. Mergers by dominant firms can, therefore, infringe Article 86 in so far as they increase that dominance and eliminate competition or restrict consumer choice. The closer a firm comes to monopoly the more likely it is that a merger by it will infringe the Article. The vice lies, not in the merger itself, but in the reduction of competition and of consumer choice.

15—13   The Commission has applied this interpretation of Article 86 in practice. During 1969, it considered a number of merger cases, and after investigation came to the conclusion that there was no need to apply Article 86. However, a merger scheme in the glass industry was dropped because it might have infringed the Article.[1] During 1970, investigations into mergers and proposed mergers continued, including cases in the metal cans, motor tyre and electrical equipment industries. Finally, in 1971, the Commission issued its first decision formally applying Article 86 to a merger case — the *Continental Can* case.

15—14　The various aspects of the *Continental Can* case have already been discussed in Chapter 5. Suffice it to say that Continental Can, through its wholly-owned subsidiary Europemballage, held 85% of the share capital of Schmalbach. Schmalbach had a dominant position in the German markets for "open top" tins for meat and charcuterie and for fish and shellfish, and also in the supply of metal lids for glass containers. Thomassen was the main supplier of metal containers in Benelux, having 100% of the supply in Belgium and Holland of "open top" tins for meat products, and in Holland for fish and shellfish. Although the areas they supplied were adjacent to each other, Schmalbach and Thomassen did not compete with each other in practice — the former exported only 0.7% of its turnover to Benelux, and the latter only 2.5% to Germany (including business passed to it by Schmalbach). As a result of a bid by Europemballage, the Continental Can/Europemballage holding in Thomassen was raised to 91.07%. The sale of the shares to Europemballage was entirely voluntary, without any pressure being exerted by Continental Can or Europemballage, so that there was no abuse of dominant position in that respect. The dominant position, in any event, was held by Schmalbach, but following the doctrine of "enterprise entity" the Commission held that this could be imputed to Continental Can and Europemballage. The Commission held that the elimination of the potential competition between Schmalbach and Thomassen (there being no actual competition) and the consequent restriction of consumer choice in the supply of the products in question constituted abuse within Article 86. The Commission addressed its decision to Continental Can, requiring that Company to put forward proposals before the 1st July, 1972, to bring the infringement of Article 86 to an end. The European Court refused an application by Continental Can for a stay of execution, but an appeal by that Company on the substantive issues involved in the Commission's decision is before the Court. The Court's decision will, it is hoped, establish whether Article 86 can be extended as sought by the Commission to control mergers (and also whether the doctrine of "enterprise entity" is good E.E.C. law).

15—15　Pending the Court's decision, what advice can be given to firms contemplating a merger? It is more convenient to treat separately each of the three main types of merger, i.e.:

(i)　　Horizontal mergers — between two or more firms at the same

---

[1]　Third General Report on the Activities of the Communities — 1969. Brussels, 1970. p.58.

level in the economic chain, say two manufacturers, or two distributors

(ii) Vertical mergers — where the firms are at different levels in the economic chain, as where a manufacturer takes over a distributor or *vice versa*. Where a firm takes over another lower down the chain, nearer the consumer, it is known as "forward integration", as in the case of a manufacturer taking over a distributor. The converse is "backward integration", such as a distributor taking over a manufacturer, or a manufacturer taking over a supplier of a raw material

(iii) Conglomerate mergers — where neither (i) nor (ii) applies. These may be motivated by the desire to diversify (e.g. tobacco firms seeking other activities to make up for any decline in tobacco sales) or as a vehicle for breaking into another industry.

### Horizontal mergers

15—16 This is the area where Article 86 is most likely to apply. Bearing in mind that the presence of a dominant position is a pre-requisite for the application of the Article, it follows that a merger in which none of the parties has a dominant position, and neither will the resultant undertaking, is not within Article 86. It is impossible to give any precise quantitative level below which a merger is not likely to be within the ambit of the Article, but taking guidance from the limits laid down in Regulation 2822/71 (Appendix L), it would seem reasonable to assume that where the resultant undertaking has not more than 15% of the relevant market nor a turnover exceeding 200 million units of account, there is not likely to be an infringement of Article 86 except in special circumstances. (The Regulation does not itself apply to mergers as envisaged here, because they are concerned only with changes in ownership, i.e. they do not have any terms restrictive of competition — if a merger does have such terms, restricting the freedom of competition of independent undertakings, Article 85.1 may apply and also Regulation 2822/71, as discussed in paragraph 15-10.)

15—17 Where none of the parties has a dominant position but the resultant undertaking is likely to have one, the answer is not quite so straightforward. As Article 86 applies only where there is a dominant position and abuse of that position, in principle where the dominant position emerges only after the merger, the merger cannot be said to infringe the Article. But, following this reasoning, if there were twenty firms in the market, none with a dominant position, a merger involving all twenty would be outside the Article even though the resultant undertaking had 100% of the market. The logic is impeccable, and the conclusion unacceptable! Where a dominant position is likely to emerge as a result of a merger, the parties might well consider the desirability of seeking clearance from the Commission, bearing in mind the Commission's aim of encouraging the growth of enterprises of

European scale.

15—18   Finally, where one party to a merger does hold a dominant position, the effect of a merger must, if it is a horizontal merger, be to increase that market dominance. The parties would, therefore, be well advised to discuss their proposals with the Commission. If adequate and active competition will continue between the remaining firms clearance may well be given, especially if the merger helps to create a unit which is more viable in world markets.

### Vertical mergers

15—19   Article 86 is less likely to apply to vertical mergers. If neither of the parties has a dominant position in its markets, such a position is unlikely to be created by the merger, so that no question of infringements is likely to arise.

15—20   Where one party does have a dominant position, there may be a reduction in competition. For example, if firm A having a dominant position in the supply of an industrial raw material takes over B, one of the firms it supplies, and if A insists upon supplying all B's requirements, the market available to A's competitors has to that extent been reduced, i.e. foreclosed. There may, however, be counter-vailing considerations. Normally, businessmen do not like buying supplies from a concern which is itself competing with them. It might be, therefore, that such a take over might result in business being transferred from A to its competitors. This can be an important factor in a forward merger, but is not likely to apply in a backward integration case. If B were dominant in its field and took over its supplier A, it is unlikely that A's competitors would refuse to supply B, although the possibility of their market being reduced is great if B can increase A's capacity so as to meet all B's requirements. Where one of the parties does have a dominant position in its market, the wiser course would seem to be to consult the Commission.

### Conglomerate mergers

15—21   Article 86 is least likely to apply in this field. If none of the parties has a dominant position, a conglomerate merger is unlikely to create one, so that no question of infringement of Article 86 is likely to arise.

15—22   Where any party does have a dominant position, it seems unlikely that a conglomerate merger would eliminate competition, so that again Article 86 would not appear likely to apply.

### Limitation

15—23   As already explained (4-101), a draft regulation has been issued which, if adopted, would provide periods of limitation after the end of which the Commission cannot take action (Appendix N). For infringements of Article 86 the period is five years. However, the limitation period starts to run from the day the infringement was terminated. Consequently, in the case of a merger which infringes Article 86, it would appear unlikely that the limitation period will apply (assuming the regulation is adopted without change in this respect) because the infringement will not be brought to an end unless the merger is undone, or perhaps the market rendered more competitive by the growth of other firms or the advent of new ones. Unless the infringement is ended, the limitation period will not begin to run.

# CHAPTER 16

# Other Abuses of a Dominant Position

16—01 Concentration upon the merger problem and the possibility that the elimination of competition may constitute an "abuse" within Article 86 should not obscure the fact that there are many other possible abuses of dominant position. Seven have already been identified in paragraphs 5-22 — 5-34:

(1) those mentioned in Article 86 itself:
    (i) imposing unfair prices or terms;
    (ii) limiting production, markets, or development;
    (iii) discrimination;
    (iv) imposing tying conditions;

(2) those mentioned in the Study:
    (v) price cutting to eliminate a financially weaker competitor;
    (vi) price cutting to impose a merger, or one on unfavourable terms;

(3) other possible abuses:
    (vii) refusal to supply.

Not all of these have arisen in the cases to date of which full details have been published. The *GEMA* decision identified six specific abuses. Two, binding its members by obligations which were not essential and exacting a copyright fee in respect of non-copyright work, were of the nature of (i) above — imposing unfair terms. A third was the prevention of the establishment of a single market in music publishing, i.e. elimination of competition. The other three were different forms of discrimination — discriminating against nationals of other Member States, discriminating against independent importers of gramophone records into Germany, and discriminating against independent importers of tape recorders into Germany.

16—02 Discrimination has been identified as an abuse under Article 86 in two other cases.

16—03 The first case, *Union de Remorquage*, involved tug companies in

227

Antwerp. The three established companies had formed themselves into a cartel having a complete monopoly of the business. A new company, S.S.B., was formed in 1963, to start operating in July, 1964. Before S.S.B. could start, the cartel members introduced new terms offering substantial loyalty rebates and reductions for shipowners who entered into exclusive contracts with them for one, two, or three years. In litigation between S.S.B. and the cartel members, the court pointed out that, pending the start of operations by S.S.B., shipowners were forced to use the services of the cartel members, with the result that any who wished to use S.S.B.'s services when available would incur a substantial financial loss as compared with their rivals who made longer term contracts with the cartel members and obtained the benefit of the rebates and reduced rates. The court held that this was discrimination between contractual and non-contractual shipowners. As the cartel had a monopoly, its members had a dominant position, and the discrimination was an abuse of that position. The cartel members were ordered to terminate the abuse.

16—04 The second, the *Brinkhof* case, was a decision by a Dutch court. Of eight forwarding agents specialising in the despatch of cut flowers from Holland to Germany, seven had formed themselves into a co-operative known as C.B.A. and negotiated new terms with the Dutch Railways, obtaining a rate reduction from 17 to 7 florins. The Dutch Railways voluntarily granted the same reduced rate to the outsider, Brinkhof. However, after certain business formerly done by C.B.A. members was transferred to Brinkhof, the Railways withdrew the reduced rates from the latter when their currect contract expired. Brinkhof applied to the Commission, and also to the Dutch court for an interim injunction pending completion of the Commission's investigation. The court prohibited the Railways from allowing *via* C.B.A. terms which it did not allow to Brinkhof.

### Private suit

16—05 The *Union de Remorquage* and *Brinkhof* cases bring out an important point. The application of Article 86 is not something reserved exclusively to the Commission or the competent national authorities. In appropriate cases private citizens, including companies and business undertakings, can use it to defend themselves against abuse of a dominant position, provided the abuse affects inter-Member trade. A trader in Member A who exports to Member B and has to pay his supplier in A a higher price than the supplier charges in B may be able to use the Article against the supplier if the latter has a dominant position. And if a supplier with a dominant position imposed a tying clause on an exporter which made it more difficult for the latter to export to other Members, the exporter might be able to free himself from the clause by appealing to the Commission, or to use Article 86 as a defence if the supplier sued him for breach of the tying clause.

16—06 It is also possible that in some Member States a private person may be able to sue undertakings in a dominant position for any damage caused to him by abuse of that position. This depends upon the national law of the particular Member, as discussed in paragraphs 3-56 and 5-42.

# APPENDICES

# A. Extracts from the Rome Treaty.

## PRINCIPLES

17—01 *ARTICLE 1*
By this Treaty, the High Contracting Parties establish among themselves a EUROPEAN ECONOMIC COMMUNITY.

17—02 *ARTICLE 2*
The Community shall have as its task, by establishing a common market and progressively approximating the economic policies of Member States, to promote throughout the Community a harmonious development of economic activities, a continuous and balanced expansion, an increase in stability, an accelerated raising of the standard of living and closer relations between the States belonging to it.

17—03 *ARTICLE 3*
For the purposes set out in Article 2, the activities of the Community shall include, as provided in this Treaty and in accordance with the timetable set out therein:

  (a) the elimination, as between Member States, of customs duties and of quantitative restrictions on the import and export of goods, and of all other measures having equivalent effect;

  (b) the establishment of a common customs tariff and of a common commercial policy towards third countries;

  (c) the abolition, as between Member States, of obstacles to freedom of movement for persons, services and capital;

  . . . . . . . . . . . . . . . . . . . . . . . . . . . . . . . . . . . . . . . . . . . . . . . . . . . . . . . . . .

  (f) the institution of a system ensuring that competition in the common market is not distorted;

  . . . . . . . . . . . . . . . . . . . . . . . . . . . . . . . . . . . . . . . . . . . . . . . . . . . . . . . . . .

17—04  *ARTICLE 4*
1. The tasks entrusted to the Community shall be carried out by the following institutions:
    —an ASSEMBLY,
    —a COUNCIL,
    —a COMMISSION,
    —a COURT OF JUSTICE.
Each institution shall act within the limits of the powers conferred upon it by this Treaty.
2. The Council and the Commission shall be assisted by an Economic and Social Committee acting in an advisory capacity.

17—05  *ARTICLE 5*
Member States shall take all appropriate measures, whether general or particular, to ensure fulfilment of the obligations arising out of this Treaty or resulting from action taken by the institutions of the Community. They shall facilitate the achievement of the Community's tasks.
    They shall abstain from any measure which could jeopardise the attainment of the objectives of this Treaty.

## ELIMINATION OF QUANTITATIVE RESTRICTIONS BETWEEN MEMBER STATES

17—06  *ARTICLE 30*
Quantitative restrictions on imports and all measures having equivalent effect shall, without prejudice to the following provisions, be prohibited between Member States.

17—07  *ARTICLE 34*
1. Quantitative restrictions on exports, and all measures having equivalent effect, shall be prohibited between Member States.

17—08  *ARTICLE 36*
The provisions of Articles 30 and 34 shall not preclude prohibitions or restrictions on imports, exports or goods in transit justified on grounds of public morality, public policy or public security; the protection of health and life of humans, animals or plants; the protection of national treasures possessing artistic, historic or archaeological value; or the protection of industrial and commercial property. Such prohibitions or restrictions shall not, however, constitute a means of arbitrary discrimination or a disguised restriction on trade between Member States.

*Appendix A*

# RULES ON COMPETITION

## Section 1: Rules applying to undertakings

17—09 *ARTICLE 85*

1. The following shall be prohibited as incompatible with the common market: all agreements between undertakings, decisions by associations of undertakings and concerted practices which may affect trade between Member States and which have as their object or effect the prevention, restriction or distortion of competition within the common market, and in particular those which:

(a) directly or indirectly fix purchase or selling prices or any other trading conditions;

(b) limit or control production, markets, technical development, or investment;

(c) share markets or sources of supply;

(d) apply dissimilar conditions to equivalent transactions with other trading parties, thereby placing them at a competitive disadvantage;

(e) make the conclusion of contracts subject to acceptance by the other parties of supplementary obligations which, by their nature or according to commercial usage, have no connection with the subject of such contracts.

2. Any agreements or decisions prohibited pursuant to this Article shall be automatically void.

3. The provisions of paragraph 1 may, however, be declared inapplicable in the case of:

—any agreement or category of agreements between undertakings;

—any decision or category of decisions by associations of undertakings;

— any concerted practice or category of concerted practices:

which contributes to improving the production or distribution of goods or to promoting technical or economic progress, while allowing consumers a fair share of the resulting benefit, and which does not:

(a) impose on the undertakings concerned restrictions which are not indispensable to the attainment of these objectives;

(b) afford such undertakings the possibility of eliminating competition in respect of a substantial part of the products in question.

17—10 *ARTICLE 86*

Any abuse by one or more undertakings of a dominant position within the common market or in a substantial part of it shall be prohibited as incompatible with the common market in so far as it may affect trade between Member States. Such abuse may, in particular, consist in:

(a) directly or indirectly imposing unfair purchase or selling

235

prices or other unfair trading conditions;
(b)  limiting production, markets or technical development to the prejudice of consumers;
(c)  applying dissimilar conditions to equivalent transactions with other trading parties, thereby placing them at a competitive disadvantage;
(d)  making the conclusion of contracts subject to acceptance by the other parties of supplementary obligations which, by their nature or according to commercial usage, have no connection with the subject of such contracts.

17—11  *ARTICLE 87*

1. Within three years of the entry into force of this Treaty the Council shall, acting unanimously on a proposal from the Commission and after consulting the Assembly, adopt any appropriate regulations or directives to give effect to the principles set out in Articles 85 and 86.

If such provisions have not been adopted within the period mentioned, they shall be laid down by the Council, acting by a qualified majority on a proposal from the Commission and after consulting the Assembly.

2. The regulations or directives referred to in paragraph 1 shall be designed, in particular:
(a)  to ensure compliance with the prohibitions laid down in Article 85 (1) and in Article 86 by making provision for fines and periodic penalty payments;
(b)  to lay down detailed rules for the application of Article 85 (3), taking into account the need to ensure effective supervision on the one hand, and to simplify administration to the greatest possible extent on the other;
(c)  to define, if need be, in the various branches of the economy, the scope of the provisions of Articles 85 and 86;
(d)  to define the respective functions of the Commission and of the Court of Justice in applying the provisions laid down in this paragraph;
(e)  to determine the relationship between national laws and the provisions contained in this Section or adopted pursuant to this Article.

17—12  *ARTICLE 88*

Until the entry into force of the provisions adopted in pursuance of Article 87, the authorities in Member States shall rule on the admissibility of agreements, decisions and concerted practices and on abuse of a dominant position in the common market in accordance with the law of their country and with the provisions of Article 85, in particular paragraph 3, and of Article 86.

17–13 *ARTICLE 89*

1. Without prejudice to Article 88, the Commission shall, as soon as it takes up its duties, ensure the application of the principles laid down in Articles 85 and 86. On application by a Member State or on its own initiative, and in co-operation with the competent authorities in the Member States, who shall give it their assistance, the Commission shall investigate cases of suspected infringement of these principles. If it finds that there has been an infringement, it shall propose appropriate measures to bring it to an end.

2. If the infringement is not brought to an end, the Commission shall record such infringement of the principles in a reasoned decision. The Commission may publish its decision and authorise Member States to take the measures, the conditions and details of which it shall determine, needed to remedy the situation.

17–14 *ARTICLE 90*

1. In the case of public undertakings and undertakings to which Member States grant special or exclusive rights, Member States shall neither enact nor maintain in force any measure contrary to the rules contained in this Treaty, in particular to those rules provided for in Article 7 and Articles 85 to 94.

2. Undertakings entrusted with the operation of services of general economic interest or having the character of a revenue-producing monopoly shall be subject to the rules contained in this Treaty, in particular to the rules on competition, in so far as the application of such rules does not obstruct the performance, in law or in fact, of the particular tasks assigned to them. The development of trade must not be affected to such an extent as would be contrary to the interests of the Community.

3. The Commission shall ensure the application of the provisions of this Article and shall, where necessary, address appropriate directives or decisions to Member States.

## Section 3: Aids granted by States

17–15 *ARTICLE 92*

1. Save as otherwise provided in this Treaty, any aid granted by a Member State or through State resources in any form whatsoever which distorts or threatens to distort competition by favouring certain undertakings or the production of certain goods shall, in so far as it affects trade between Member States, be incompatible with the common market.

# THE COURT OF JUSTICE

17—16 *ARTICLE 173*

The Court of Justice shall review the legality of acts of the Council and the Commission other than recommendations or opinions. It shall for this purpose have jurisdiction in actions brought by a Member State, the Council or the Commission on grounds of lack of competence, infringement of an essential procedural requirement, infringement of this Treaty or of any rule of law relating to its application, or misuse of powers.

Any natural or legal person may, under the same conditions, institute proceedings against a decision addressed to that person or against a decision which, although in the form of a regulation or a decision addressed to another person, is of direct and individual concern to the former.

The proceedings provided for in this Article shall be instituted within two months of the publication of the measure, or of its notification to the plaintiff, or, in the absence thereof, of the day on which it came to the knowledge of the latter, as the case may be.

17—17 *ARTICLE 177*

The Court of Justice shall have jurisdiction to give preliminary rulings concerning:

   (a)   the interpretation of this Treaty;
   (b)   the validity and interpretation of acts of the institutions of the Community;
   (c)   the interpretation of the statutes of bodies established by an act of the Council, where those statutes so provide.

Where such a question is raised before any court or tribunal of a Member State, that court or tribunal may, if it considers that a decision on the question is necessary to enable it to give judgment, request the Court of Justice to give a ruling thereon.

Where any such question is raised in a case pending before a court or tribunal of a Member State, against whose decisions there is no judicial remedy under national law, that court or tribunal shall bring the matter before the Court of Justice.

17—18 *ARTICLE 184*

Notwithstanding the expiry of the period laid down in the third paragraph of Article 173, any party may, in proceedings in which a regulation of the Council or of the Commission is in issue, plead the grounds specified in the first paragraph of Article 173, in order to invoke before the Court of Justice the inapplicability of that regulation.

# PROVISIONS GOVERNING THE INSTITUTIONS OF THE COMMUNITY

17—19  *ARTICLE 191*

Regulations shall be published in the Official Journal of the Community. They shall enter into force on the date specified in them or, in the absence thereof, on the twentieth day following their publication.

Directives and decisions shall be notified to those to whom they are addressed and shall take effect upon such notification.

## GENERAL AND FINAL PROVISIONS

17—20  *ARTICLE 222*

This Treaty shall in no way prejudice the rules in Member States governing the system of property ownership.

# B.  Council Regulation No. 17/62.

## FIRST REGULATION IMPLEMENTING ARTICLES 85 AND 86 OF THE TREATY

18—01  THE COUNCIL OF THE EUROPEAN ECONOMIC COMMUNITY,

HAVING REGARD to the Treaty establishing the European Economic Community, and in particular Article 87 thereof;

HAVING REGARD to the proposal from the Commission;

HAVING REGARD to the Opinion of the Economic and Social Committee;

HAVING REGARD to the Opinion of the European Parliament;

WHEREAS in order to establish a system ensuring that competition shall not be distorted in the common market, it is necessary to provide for balanced application of Articles 85 and 86 in a uniform manner in the Member States;

WHEREAS in establishing the rules for applying Article 85(3) account must be taken of the need to ensure effective supervision and to simplify administration to the greatest possible extent;

WHEREAS it is accordingly necessary to make it obligatory, as a general principle, for undertakings which seek application of Article 85(3) to notify to the Commission their agreements, decisions and concerted practices;

WHEREAS, on the one hand, such agreements, decisions and concerted practices are probably very numerous and cannot therefore all be examined at the same time and, on the other hand, some of them have special features which may make them less prejudicial to the development of the common market;

WHEREAS there is consequently a need to make more flexible arrangements for the time being in respect of certain categories of agreements, decisions and concerted practices without prejudging their validity under Article 85;

240

WHEREAS it may be in the interest of undertakings to know whether any agreements, decisions or practices to which they are party, or propose to become party, may lead to action on the part of the Commission pursuant to Article 85(1) or Article 86;

WHEREAS, in order to secure uniform application of Articles 85 and 86 in the common market, rules must be made under which the Commission, acting in close and constant liaison with the competent authorities of the Member States, may take the requisite measures for applying those Articles;

WHEREAS for this purpose the Commission must have the cooperation of the competent authorities of the Member States and be empowered, throughout the common market, to require such information to be supplied and to undertake such investigations as are necessary to bring to light any agreement, decision or concerted practice prohibited by Article 85(1) or any abuse of a dominant position prohibited by Article 86;

WHEREAS in order to carry out its duty of ensuring that the provisions of the Treaty are applied the Commission must be empowered to address to undertakings or associations of undertakings recommendations and decisions for the purpose of bringing to an end infringements of Articles 85 and 86;

WHEREAS compliance with Articles 85 and 86 and the fulfilment of obligations imposed on undertakings and associations of undertakings under this Regulation must be enforceable by means of fines and periodic penalty payments;

WHEREAS undertakings concerned must be accorded the right to be heard by the Commission, third parties whose interests may be affected by a decision must be given the opportunity of submitting their comments beforehand, and it must be ensured that wide publicity is given to decisions taken;

WHEREAS all decisions taken by the Commission under this Regulation are subject to review by the Court of Justice under the conditions specified in the Treaty; whereas it is moreover desirable to confer upon the Court of Justice, pursuant to Article 172, unlimited jurisdiction in respect of decisions under which the Commission imposes fines or periodic penalty payments;

WHEREAS this Regulation may enter into force without prejudice to any other provisions that may hereafter be adopted pursuant to Article 87;

HAS ADOPTED THIS REGULATION:

18—02 *ARTICLE 1*
*Basic provision*
Without prejudice to Articles 6, 7 and 23 of this Regulation, agreements, decisions and concerted practices of the kind described in Article 85(1) of the Treaty and the abuse of a dominant position in the

market, within the meaning of Article 86 of the Treaty, shall be prohibited, no prior decision to that effect being required.

18—03 *ARTICLE 2*
*Negative clearance*
Upon application by the undertakings or associations of undertakings concerned, the Commission may certify that, on the basis of the facts in its possession, there are no grounds under Article 85(1) or Article 86 of the Treaty for action on its part in respect of an agreement, decision or practice.

18—04 *ARTICLE 3*
*Termination of infringements*
1. Where the Commission, upon application or upon its own initiative, finds that there is infringement of Article 85 or Article 86 of the Treaty, it may by decision require the undertakings or associations of undertakings concerned to bring such infringement to an end.
2. Those entitled to make application are:
    (a)    Member States;
    (b)    natural or legal persons who claim a legitimate interest.
3. Without prejudice to the other provisions of this Regulation, the Commission may, before taking a decision under paragraph 1, address to the undertakings or associations of undertakings concerned recommendations for termination of the infringement.

18—05 *ARTICLE 4 (as amended by Regulation 2822/71 — Appendix L)*
*Notification of new agreements, decisions and practices*
1. Agreements, decisions and concerted practices of the kind described in Article 85(1) of the Treaty which come into existence after the entry into force of this Regulation and in respect of which the parties seek application of Article 85(3) must be notified to the Commission. Until they have been notified, no decision in application of Article 85(3) may be taken.
2. Paragraph 1 shall not apply to agreements, decisions or concerted practices where:
    (1)    the only parties thereto are undertakings from one Member State and the agreements, decisions or practices do not relate either to imports or to exports between Member States;
    (2)    not more than two undertakings are party thereto, and the agreements only:
        (a)    restrict the freedom of one party to the contract in determining the prices for or conditions of business on which the goods which he has obtained from the other party to the contract may be resold; or
        (b)    impose restrictions on the exercise of the rights of the assignee or user of industrial property rights — in particular

patents, utility models, designs or trade marks — or of the person entitled under a contract to the assignment, or grant, of the right to use a method of manufacture or knowledge relating to the use and to the application of industrial processes;

(3) they have as their sole object:

    (a)  the development or uniform application of standards or types;

or    (b)  joint research and development;

or    (c)  specialisation in the manufacture of products, including agreements necessary for the achievement thereof;

        —  where the products which are the object of specialisation do not, in a substantial part of the common market, represent more than 15% of the volume of business done in identical products, or those considered by the consumers to be similar by reason of their characteristics, price and use, and

        —  where the total annual turnover of the participating undertakings does not exceed 200 million units of account.

These agreements, decisions and practices may be notified to the Commission.

18—06  *ARTICLE 5 (as amended by Council Regulation 59/62)*
*Notification of existing agreements, decisions and practices*
1. Agreements, decisions and concerted practices of the kind described in Article 85(1) of the Treaty which are in existence at the date of entry into force of this Regulation and in respect of which the parties seek application of Article 85(3) shall be notified to the Commission before 1 November 1962. However, notwithstanding the foregoing provisions, any agreements, decisions and concerted practices to which not more than two undertakings are party shall be notified before 1 February 1963.
2. Paragraph 1 shall not apply to agreements, decisions or concerted practices falling within Article 4(2); these may be notified to the Commission.

18—07  *ARTICLE 6*
*Decisions pursuant to Article 85(3)*
1. Whenever the Commission takes a decision pursuant to Article 85(3) of the Treaty, it shall specify therein the date from which the decision shall take effect. Such date shall not be earlier than the date of notification.
2. The second sentence of paragraph 1 shall not apply to agreements, decisions or concerted practices falling within Article 4(2) and Article 5(2), nor to those falling within Article 5(1) which have been notified

within the time limit specified in Article 5(1).

18—08 *ARTICLE 7*
*Special provisions for existing agreements, decisions and practices*
1. Where agreements, decisions and concerted practices in existence at the date of entry into force of this Regulation and notified before 1 August 1962 do not satisfy the requirements of Article 85(3) of the Treaty and the undertakings or associations of undertakings concerned cease to give effect to them or modify them in such manner that they no longer fall within the prohibition contained in Article 85(1) or that they satisfy the requirements of Article 85(3), the prohibition contained in Article 85(1) shall apply only for a period fixed by the Commission. A decision by the Commission pursuant to the foregoing sentence shall not apply as against undertakings and associations of undertakings which did not expressly consent to the notification.
2. Paragraph 1 shall apply to agreements, decisions and concerted practices falling within Article 4(2) which are in existence at the date of entry into force of this Regulation if they are notified before 1 January 1967 (as amended by Council Regulation 118/63).

18—09 *ARTICLE 8*
*Duration and revocation of decisions under Article 85(3)*
1. A decision in application of Article 85(3) of the Treaty shall be issued for a specified period and conditions and obligations may be attached thereto.
2. A decision may on application be renewed if the requirements of Article 85(3) of the Treaty continue to be satisfied.
3. The Commission may revoke or amend its decision or prohibit specified acts by the parties:
    (a)    where there has been a change in any of the facts which were fundamental in the making of the decision;
    (b)    where the parties commit a breach of any obligation attached to the decision;
    (c)    where the decision is based on incorrect information or was induced by deceit;
    (d)    where the parties abuse the exemption from the provisions of Article 85(1) of the Treaty granted to them by the decision.
In cases to which subparagraphs (b), (c) or (d) apply, the decision may be revoked with retroactive effect.

18—10 *ARTICLE 9*
*Powers*
1. Subject to review of its decision by the Court of Justice, the Commission shall have sole power to declare Article 85(1) inapplicable pursuant to Article 85(3) of the Treaty.

2. The Commission shall have power to apply Article 85(1) and Article 86 of the Treaty; this power may be exercised notwithstanding that the time limits specified in Article 5(1) and in Article 7(2) relating to notification have not expired.

3. As long as the Commission has not initiated any procedure under Articles 2, 3 or 6, the authorities of the Member States shall remain competent to apply Article 85(1) and Article 86, in accordance with Article 88 of the Treaty; they shall remain competent in this respect notwithstanding that the time limits specified in Article 5(1) and in Article 7(2) relating to notification have not expired.

18—11 *ARTICLE 10*

*Liaison with the authorities of the Member States*

1. The Commission shall forthwith transmit to the competent authorities of the Member States a copy of the applications and notifications together with copies of the most important documents lodged with the Commission for the purpose of establishing the existence of infringements of Articles 85 or 86 of the Treaty or of obtaining negative clearance or a decision in application of Article 85(3).

2. The Commission shall carry out the procedure set out in paragraph 1 in close and constant liaison with the competent authorities of the Member States; such authorities shall have the right to express their views on that procedure.

3. An Advisory Committee on Restrictive Practices and Monopolies shall be consulted prior to the taking of any decision following upon a procedure under paragraph 1, and of any decision concerning the renewal, amendment or revocation of a decision pursuant to Article 85(3) of the Treaty.

4. The Advisory Committee shall be composed of officials competent in the matter of restrictive practices and monopolies. Each Member State shall appoint an official to represent it who, if prevented from attending, may be replaced by another official.

5. The consultation shall take place at a joint meeting convened by the Commission; such meeting shall be held not earlier than fourteen days after dispatch of the notice convening it. The notice shall, in respect of each case to be examined, be accompanied by a summary of the case together with an indication of the most important documents, and a preliminary draft decision.

6. The Advisory Committee may deliver an opinion notwithstanding that some of its members or their alternates are not present. A report of the outcome of the consultative proceedings shall be annexed to the draft decision. It shall not be made public.

18—12 *ARTICLE 11*

*Requests for information*

1. In carrying out the duties assigned to it by Article 89 and by

provisions adopted under Article 87 of the Treaty, the Commission may obtain all necessary information from the Governments and competent authorities of the Member States and from undertakings and associations of undertakings.

2. When sending a request for information to an undertaking or association of undertakings, the Commission shall at the same time forward a copy of the request to the competent authority of the Member State in whose territory the seat of the undertaking or association of undertakings is situated.

3. In its request the Commission shall state the legal basis and the purpose of the request and also the penalties provided for in Article 15(1)(b) for supplying incorrect information.

4. The owners of the undertakings or their representatives and, in the case of legal persons, companies or firms, or of associations having no legal personality, the persons authorised to represent them by law or by their constitution, shall supply the information requested.

5. Where an undertaking or association of undertakings does not supply the information requested within the time limit fixed by the Commission, or supplies incomplete information, the Commission shall by decision require the information to be supplied. The decision shall specify what information is required, fix an appropriate time limit within which it is to be supplied and indicate the penalties provided for by Article 15(1)(b) and Article 16(1)(c) and the right to have the decision reviewed by the Court of Justice.

6. The Commission shall at the same time forward a copy of its decision to the competent authority of the Member State in whose territory the seat of the undertaking or association of undertakings is situated.

18—13 *ARTICLE 12*
*Inquiry into sectors of the economy*

1. If in any sector of the economy the trend of trade between Member States, price movements, inflexibility of prices or other circumstances suggest that in the economic sector concerned competition is being restricted or distorted within the common market, the Commission may decide to conduct a general inquiry into that economic sector and in the course thereof may request undertakings in the sector concerned to supply the information necessary for giving effect to the principles formulated in Articles 85 and 86 of the Treaty and for carrying out the duties entrusted to the Commission.

2. The Commission may in particular request every undertaking or association of undertakings in the economic sector concerned to communicate to it all agreements, decisions and concerted practices which are exempt from notification by virtue of Article 4(2) and Article 5(2).

3. When making inquiries pursuant to paragraph 2, the Commission

shall also request undertakings or groups of undertakings whose size suggests that they occupy a dominant position within the common market or a substantial part thereof to supply to the Commission such particulars of the structure of the undertakings and of their behaviour as are requisite to an appraisal of their position in the light of Article 86 of the Treaty.

4. Article 10(3) to (6) and Articles 11, 13 and 14 shall apply correspondingly.

18—14 **ARTICLE 13**

*Investigations by the authorities of the Member States*

1. At the request of the Commission, the competent authorities of the Member States shall undertake the investigations which the Commission considers to be necessary under Article 14(1), or which it has ordered by decision pursuant to Article 14(3). The officials of the competent authorities of the Member States responsible for conducting these investigations shall exercise their powers upon production of an authorisation in writing issued by the competent authority of the Member State in whose territory the investigation is to be made. Such authorisation shall specify the subject matter and purpose of the investigation.

2. If so requested by the Commission or by the competent authority of the Member State in whose territory the investigation is to be made, the officials of the Commission may assist the officials of such authority in carrying out their duties.

18—15 **ARTICLE 14**

*Investigating powers of the Commission*

1. In carrying out the duties assigned to it by Article 89 and by provisions adopted under Article 87 of the Treaty, the Commission may undertake all necessary investigations into undertakings and associations of undertakings. To this end the officials authorised by the Commission are empowered:

    (a)    to examine the books and other business records;

    (b)    to take copies of or extracts from the books and business records;

    (c)    to ask for oral explanations on the spot;

    (d)    to enter any premises, land and means of transport of undertakings.

2. The officials of the Commission authorised for the purpose of these investigations shall exercise their powers upon production of an authorisation in writing specifying the subject matter and purpose of the investigation and the penalties provided for in Article 15(1)(c) in cases where production of the required books or other business records is incomplete. In good time before the investigation, the Commission shall inform the competent authority of the Member State in whose

territory the same is to be made, of the investigation and of the identity of the authorised officials.

3. Undertakings and associations of undertakings shall submit to investigations ordered by decision of the Commission. The decision shall specify the subject matter and purpose of the investigation, appoint the date on which it is to begin and indicate the penalties provided for in Article 15(1)(c) and Article 16(1)(d) and the right to have the decision reviewed by the Court of Justice.

4. The Commission shall take the decisions referred to in paragraph 3 after consultation with the competent authority of the Member State in whose territory the investigation is to be made.

5. Officials of the competent authority of the Member State in whose territory the investigation is to be made may, at the request of such authority or of the Commission, assist the officials of the Commission in carrying out their duties.

6. Where an undertaking opposes an investigation ordered pursuant to this Article, the Member State concerned shall afford the necessary assistance to the officials authorised by the Commission to enable them to make their investigation. Member States shall, after consultation with the Commission, take the necessary measures to this end before 1 October 1962.

18—16    *ARTICLE 15*
*Fines*

1. The Commission may by decision impose on undertakings or associations of undertakings fines of from one hundred to five thousand units of account where, intentionally or negligently:

    (a)    they supply incorrect or misleading information in an application pursuant to Article 2 or in a notification pursuant to Articles 4 or 5; or

    (b)    they supply incorrect information in response to a request made pursuant to Article 11(3) or (5) or to Article 12, or do not supply information within the time limit fixed by a decision taken under Article 11(5); or

    (c)    they produce the required books or other business records in incomplete form during investigations under Article 13 or 14, or refuse to submit to an investigation ordered by decision issued in implementation of Article 14(3).

2. The Commission may by decision impose on undertakings or associations of undertakings fines of from one thousand to one million units of account, or a sum in excess thereof but not exceeding ten per cent of the turnover in the preceding business year of each of the undertakings participating in the infringement where, either intentionally or negligently:

    (a)    they infringe Article 85(1) or Article 86 of the Treaty; or

    (b)    they commit a breach of any obligation imposed pursuant to Article 8(1).

In fixing the amount of the fine, regard shall be had both to the gravity and to the duration of the infringement.

3. Article 10(3) to (6) shall apply.

4. Decisions taken pursuant to paragraphs 1 and 2 shall not be of a criminal law nature.

5. The fines provided for in paragraph 2(a) shall not be imposed in respect of acts taking place:

(a)    after notification to the Commission and before its decision in application of Article 85(3) of the Treaty, provided they fall within the limits of the activity described in the notification;

(b)    before notification and in the course of agreements, decisions or concerted practices in existence at the date of entry into force of this Regulation, provided that notification was effected within the time limits specified in Article 5(1) and Article 7(2).

6. Paragraph 5 shall not have effect where the Commission has informed the undertakings concerned that after preliminary examination it is of opinion that Article 85(1) of the Treaty applies and that application of Article 85(3) is not justified.

18–17    *ARTICLE 16*
*Periodic penalty payments*

1. The Commission may by decision impose on undertakings or associations of undertakings periodic penalty payments of from fifty to one thousand units of account per day, calculated from the date appointed by the decision in order to compel them:

(a)    to put an end to an infringement of Article 85 or 86 of the Treaty, in accordance with a decision taken pursuant to Article 3 of this Regulation;

(b)    to refrain from any act prohibited under Article 8(3);

(c)    to supply complete and correct information which it has requested by decision taken pursuant to Article 11(5);

(d)    to submit to an investigation which it has ordered by decision taken pursuant to Article 14(3).

2. Where the undertakings or associations of undertakings have satisfied the obligation which it was the purpose of the periodic penalty payment to enforce, the Commission may fix the total amount of the periodic penalty payment at a lower figure than that which would arise under the original decision.

3. Article 10(3) to (6) shall apply.

18–18    *ARTICLE 17*
*Review by the Court of Justice*

The Court of Justice shall have unlimited jurisdiction within the meaning of Article 172 of the Treaty to review decisions whereby the Commission has fixed a fine or periodic penalty payment; it may cancel, reduce or increase the fine or periodic penalty payment imposed.

18—19  *ARTICLE 18*
*Unit of account*
For the purposes of applying Articles 15 to 17 the unit of account shall be that adopted in drawing up the budget of the Community in accordance with Articles 207 and 209 of the Treaty.

18—20  *ARTICLE 19*
*Hearing of the parties and of third persons*
1. Before taking decisions as provided for in Articles 2, 3, 6, 7, 8, 15 and 16, the Commission shall give the undertakings or associations of undertakings concerned the opportunity of being heard on the matters to which the Commission has taken objection.
2. If the Commission or the competent authorities of the Member States consider it necessary, they may also hear other natural or legal persons. Applications to be heard on the part of such persons shall, where they show a sufficient interest, be granted.
3. Where the Commission intends to give negative clearance pursuant to Article 2 or take a decision in application of Article 85(3) of the Treaty, it shall publish a summary of the relevant application or notification and invite all interested third parties to submit their observations within a time limit which it shall fix being not less than one month. Publication shall have regard to the legitimate interest of undertakings in the protection of their business secrets.

18—21  *ARTICLE 20*
*Professional secrecy*
1. Information acquired as a result of the application of Articles 11, 12, 13 and 14 shall be used only for the purpose of the relevant request or investigation.
2. Without prejudice to the provisions of Articles 19 and 21, the Commission and the competent authorities of the Member States, their officials and other servants shall not disclose information acquired by them as a result of the application of this Regulation and of the kind covered by the obligation of professional secrecy.
3. The provisions of paragraphs 1 and 2 shall not prevent publication of general information or surveys which do not contain information relating to particular undertakings or associations of undertakings.

18—22  *ARTICLE 21*
*Publication of decisions*
1. The Commission shall publish the decisions which it takes pursuant

to Articles 2, 3, 6, 7 and 8.

2. The publication shall state the names of the parties and the main content of the decision; it shall have regard to the legitimate interest of undertakings in the protection of their business secrets.

18—23 **ARTICLE 22**

*Special provisions*

1. The Commission shall submit to the Council proposals for making certain categories of agreement, decision and concerted practice falling within Article 4(2) or Article 5(2) compulsorily notifiable under Article 4 or 5.

2. Within one year from the date of entry into force of this Regulation, the Council shall examine, on a proposal from the Commission, what special provisions might be made for exempting from the provisions of this Regulation agreements, decisions and concerted practices falling within Article 4(2) or Article 5(2).

18—24 **ARTICLE 23**

*Transitional provisions applicable to decisions of authorities of the Member States*

1. Agreements, decisions and concerted practices of the kind described in Article 85(1) of the Treaty to which, before the entry into force of this Regulation, the competent authority of a Member State has declared Article 85(1) to be inapplicable pursuant to Article 85(3) shall not be subject to compulsory notification under Article 5. The decision of the competent authority of the Member State shall be deemed to be a decision within the meaning of Article 6; it shall cease to be valid upon expiration of the period fixed by such authority but in any event not more than three years after the entry into force of this Regulation.

Article 8(3) shall apply.

2. Applications for renewal of decisions of the kind described in paragraph 1 shall be decided upon by the Commission in accordance with Article 8(2).

18—25 **ARTICLE 24**

*Implementing provisions*

The Commission shall have the power to adopt implementing provisions concerning the form, content and other details of applications pursuant to Articles 2 and 3, and of notifications pursuant to Articles 4 and 5, and concerning hearings pursuant to Article 19(1) and (2).

18—26 **ARTICLE 25 (added by the Treaty of Accession)**

1. As regards agreements, decisions and concerted practices to which Article 85 of the Treaty applies by virtue of accession, the date of accession shall be substituted for the date of entry into force of this Regulation in every place where reference is made in this Regulation to

this latter date.

2. Agreements, decisions and concerted practices existing at the date of accession to which Article 85 of the Treaty applies by virtue of accession shall be notified pursuant to Article 5(1) or Article 7(1) and (2) within six months from the date of accession.

3. Fines under Article 15(2)(a) shall not be imposed in respect of any act prior to notification of the agreements, decisions and practices to which paragraph 2 applies and which have been notified within the period therein specified.

4. New Member States shall take the measures referred to in Article 14(6) within six months from the date of accession after consulting the Commission.

18—27 This Regulation shall be binding in its entirety and directly applicable in all Member States.

*Done at Brussels, 6 February 1962.*

For the Council
The President
M COUVE DE MURVILLE

# C. Commission Notice relating to Sole Agency Contracts with Trade Representatives.*

19—01  1. The Commission is of opinion that contracts with trade representatives in which the representative undertakes, in respect of a specified
part of the territory of the Common Market:
- — to negotiate transactions on behalf of an enterprise,
- — to conclude transactions in the name and on behalf of the
enterprise, or
- — to conclude transactions in his own name and on behalf of
the enterprise,

are not prohibited by Article 85, paragraph 1 of the Treaty.

19—02  It is essential in such cases that the contracting party described in the
contract as trade representative must in fact discharge the function of a
trade representative and must neither undertake nor carry on any
activity as an independent trader in the course of business. The
Commission considers that the real test for distinguishing the trade
representative from the independent trader is the express or implied
agreement, as to which party bears the financial risks attaching to the
sale or to the performance of the contract. The Commission therefore
attaches no weight to the way in which a party is described. With the
exception of the customary "del credere" guarantee, it is not the
function of a trade representative to assume any risk arising out of the
transaction. If he does so, his function, from the economic point of
view, is that of an independent trader and he must therefore be treated
as such for the purposes of the legislation on competition. In such
circumstances, sole agency contracts must be deemed to be contracts
with independent traders.

19—03  The Commission considers in particular that a party described as trade
representative is in fact an independent trader where he:
- — is required to maintain, or in fact maintains, as owner a

---

* Published on 24 December 1962, in the Journal Officiel.

253

substantial stock of the products covered by the contract; or

— is required to organise, maintain, or provide at his own expense or in fact organises, maintains or provides a substantial free service to customers; or

— is entitled to determine, or in fact determines, prices or the conditions of the transactions.

19—04  2. Contrary to the case of contracts with trade representatives as referred to in this Notice, the possibility cannot be excluded of Article 85, paragraph 1 applying to sole agency contracts made with independent traders. In contracts of this kind, the restraint of competition consists either in the restriction of supply, when the seller undertakes to supply a particular product to one buyer exclusively, or in the restriction of demand, when the buyer undertakes to obtain a particular product from one seller exclusively. There is restraint of competition on both sides when such undertakings are entered into reciprocally. Whether a restraint of this kind is capable of affecting trade between Member States depends on the facts of the case.

19—05  On the other hand, in the opinion of the Commission, the conditions of the prohibition in Article 85, paragraph 1, are not satisfied by sole agency contracts with trade representatives, because these contracts are not designed to prevent, restrict or distort competition within the Common Market and do not have that effect. In the commodities market the function of the trade representative is purely that of an intermediary. He acts in the market on the instructions and in the interest of the enterprise on whose behalf he operates. Unlike the independent trader, he is neither buyer nor seller himself, but seeks buyers or sellers in the interest of his contracting partner, who is the seller or buyer. In this type of sole agency contract, the buying or selling enterprise is still present as a competitor; it merely makes use of an intermediary, the trade representative, in order to sell or buy commodities in the market.

19—06  The legal status of the trade representative is more or less similar throughout the Member States. In most of them it is fixed by legislation, in the others by judicial decisions. The common characteristic of all trade representatives is that they do business as intermediaries. The attributions of the trade representative are governed by the civil law rules or agency. Under these rules the representative's contracting partner, who is the party selling or buying, freely decides in respect of which commodity and which area he wished to transfer these attributions to his representative.

19—07  Besides the aspect of competition in those markets where the trade representative acts as an intermediary for his contracting partner, there is also the question of the particular market in which trade representatives offer their services for the negotiation or conclusion of business. The undertaking by the trade representative to work exclusively for one principal for a stipulated period involves a restriction of supply in this market; the undertaking by the principal to make the other his sole representative for a stated area implies a restriction of demand. The Commission, however, regards these restrictions as a consequence of the special obligation between the trade representative and his principal to protect each other's interests. For this reason, the Commission does not consider that they amount to a restraint of competition.

19—08 The object of this Notice is to inform enterprises of the considerations which will guide the Commission in interpreting Article 85, paragraph 1, of the Treaty in its application to sole distributor agreements with trade representatives. Accordingly, as a general rule, enterprises should no longer need to obtain negative clearance for such agreements, or to ascertain the legal position by means of an individual decision of the Commission. Similarly, it is no longer necessary to notify agreements of this kind. This Notice is not binding on other competent authorities, and in particular on the courts, in their interpretation.

# D. Commission Notice,
# relating to Patent Licence Agreements. *

20—01   1. The Commission is of opinion, on its present knowledge of the circumstances, that the following clauses in patent licence contracts are not prohibited by Article 85, paragraph 1 of the Treaty:

A.    Conditions imposed on the licensee with a view to:

    1.    Restricting the working of the invention to certain forms specified under patent law (manufacture, use, sale).

    2.    Restricting:

       (a)   the manufacture of a patented article, or

       (b)   the working of a patented process — to certain technical applications.

    3.    Restricting the quantity of articles to be manufactured or the number of occasions of working the invention or process.

    4.    Limiting the licence:

       (a)   in time (licence for a shorter term than the patent);

       (b)   in area (local licence for a part of the territory covered by the patent; licence limited to a specified place of business or factory);

       (c)   in respect of persons (restriction of the licensee's power of disposition, e.g. prohibiting the assignment of the licence or the grant of sub-licences).

B.    Conditions requiring the licensee to mention the patent on the article.

C.    Imposition on the licensee of standards of quality or of conditions as to the procurement of certain products, so far as such standards or conditions are essential to the sound technical working of the patent.

D.    Undertakings to disclose experience acquired in the working of

---

* Published on 24 December 1962, in the Journal Officiel.

the invention or to grant licences in respect of improvements or new applications; this does not, however, apply to undertakings by the licensee unless they are non-exclusive and the grantor has entered into similar undertakings.

E.    Undertakings by the grantor:

1.    not to authorise any other person to work the invention;

2.    not to work the invention himself.

20—02    2. This Notice does not purport to determine the legal effect of clauses other than those mentioned in points 1/A to E.

Furthermore, it does not seem possible to make a general ruling in the case of agreements relating to:

1.    patents in common ownership;

2.    reciprocal licences;

3.    multiple parallel licences.

The ruling in respect of the clauses referred to in points 1/A to E is limited to clauses not exceeding the period of validity of the patent.

20—03    3. The object of this Notice is to inform enterprises of the considerations which will guide the Commission in interpreting Article 85, paragraph 1 of the Treaty, in its application to a number of clauses which frequently appear in patent licence contracts. Provided that and so far as such contracts contain no restrictions other than those arising out of one or more of the clauses referred to above, the Commission is of opinion that they do not fall within the prohibition in Article 85, paragraph 1. Accordingly, as a general rule, enterprises should no longer need to obtain negative clearance for such agreements, or to ascertain the legal situation by means of an individual decision of the Commission. Similarly, it is no longer necessary to notify agreements of this kind.

20—04    This Notice is not binding on other competent authorities, and in particular on the courts, in their interpretation.

20—05    The question whether Article 85, paragraph 1 of the Treaty applies to any of the above clauses contained in contracts relating to patents in common ownership, the grant of reciprocal licences or multiple parallel licences, to agreements relating to the use of other rights of industrial property or of technological improvements not protected by law, and to all other clauses than those referred to above, will be dealt with in a later decision.

This Notice does not purport to interpret Article 4, paragraph 2, 2(b), of Regulation No. 17.

20—06    4. The conditions enumerated in point 1/A are not prohibited by Article 85, paragraph 1, because they are covered by the patent. They merely amount to the partial exercise against a licensee who is otherwise authorised to work the invention of the right of prohibition inherent in the patentee's exclusive right. The points listed under 1/A are not an exhaustive delimitation of the privileges conferred by the patent.

20—07    The condition requiring the licensee to mention the patent on the article (point 1/B) is justified by the patentee's legitimate interest that the protected article should be identified as originating from the patented invention. Since the licensee is equally entitled to put his own distinctive marks on the protected article, this condition cannot be designed to restrict competition, or have that effect.

20—08    The conditions mentioned in point 1/C requiring the licensee to conform to certain standards of quality in respect of protected articles, semi-finished products, raw materials or subsidiary materials cannot restrict competition insofar as their object is to ensure against a technically incorrect application of the invention. The condition as to the procurement of certain products arises only if quality cannot be determined by objective criteria. In such circumstances this condition has the same effect as standards of quality.

20—09    The licensee's undertakings referred to in point 1/D have in no case a restrictive effect on competition if the licensee retains the right to disclose experience acquired or grant licences to third parties and is entitled by the contract to share in future experience and inventions acquired by the grantor. As regards the grantor's undertakings referred to in point 1/D to disclose experience or grant licences, these seem unobjectionable from the point of view of the law on competition, even without such limitation. Point 1/D, therefore, applies to nothing more than the obligation to disclose experience or grant licences; it does not prejudge the assessment of the legal effect of any restrictions imposed on the parties concerning the use of such experience or inventions.

20—10    By the undertaking referred to in point 1/E not to authorize the working of the invention by any other person, the grantor loses the right to contract with other persons applying for licences. Leaving aside the unsettled question whether such exclusive undertakings are designed to restrict competition or have that effect, they are not, in the present situation of the Community, capable of affecting trade between Member States. The undertaking by the grantor not to work the patented invention himself is equivalent to the assignment of the patent rights and therefore seems unobjectionable.

# E. Commission Regulation
# No.99/63.

## ON THE HEARINGS PROVIDED FOR IN ARTICLE 19(1) AND (2) OF COUNCIL REGULATION NO 17

21—01 THE COMMISSION OF THE EUROPEAN ECONOMIC COMMUNITY,

HAVING REGARD to the Treaty establishing the European Economic Community, and in particular Articles 87 and 155 thereof;

HAVING REGARD to Article 24 of Council Regulation No 17 of 6 February 1962 (First Regulation implementing Articles 85 and 86 of the Treaty);

WHEREAS the Commission has power under Article 24 of Council Regulation No 17 to lay down implementing provisions concerning the hearings provided for in Article 19(1) and (2) of that Regulation;

WHEREAS in most cases the Commission will in the course of its inquiries already be in close touch with the undertakings or associations of undertakings which are the subject thereof and they will accordingly have the opportunity of making known their views regarding the objections raised against them;

WHEREAS, however, in accordance with Article 19(1) of Regulation No 17 and with the rights of defence, the undertakings and associations of undertakings concerned must have the right on conclusion of the inquiry to submit their comments on the whole of the objections raised against them which the Commission proposes to deal with in its decisions;

WHEREAS persons other than the undertakings or associations of undertakings which are the subject of the inquiry may have an interest in being heard; whereas, by the second sentence of Article 19(2) of Regulation No 17, such persons must have the opportunity of being heard if they apply and show that they have a sufficient interest;

WHEREAS it is desirable to enable persons who pursuant to Article 3(2) of Regulation No 17 have applied for an infringement to be terminated to submit their comments where the Commission considers that on the basis of the information in its possession there are insufficient grounds for granting the application;

WHEREAS the various persons entitled to submit comments must do so in writing, both in their own interest and in the interests of good administration, without prejudice to oral procedure where appropriate to supplement the written evidence;

WHEREAS it is necessary to define the rights of persons who are to be heard, and in particular, the conditions upon which they may be represented or assisted and the setting and calculation of time limits;

WHEREAS the Advisory Committee on Restrictive Practices and Monopolies delivers its Opinion on the basis of a preliminary draft decision; whereas it must therefore be consulted concerning a case after the inquiry in respect thereof has been completed; whereas such consultation does not prevent the Commission from re-opening an inquiry if need be;

HAS ADOPTED THIS REGULATION:

21—02 **ARTICLE 1**

Before consulting the Advisory Committee on Restrictive Practices and Monopolies, the Commission shall hold a hearing pursuant to Article 19(1) of Regulation No 17.

21—03 **ARTICLE 2**

1. The Commission shall inform undertakings and associations of undertakings in writing of the objections raised against them. The communication shall be addressed to each of them or to a joint agent appointed by them.

2. The Commission may inform the parties by giving notice in the *Official Journal of the European Communities*, if from the circumstances of the case this appears appropriate, in particular where notice is to be given to a number of undertakings but no joint agent has been appointed. The notice shall have regard to the legitimate interest of the undertakings in the protection of their business secrets.

3. A fine or a periodic penalty payment may be imposed on an undertaking or association of undertakings only if the objections were notified in the manner provided for in paragraph 1.

4. The Commission shall when giving notice of objections fix a time limit up to which the undertakings and associations of undertakings may inform the Commission of their views.

21—04 **ARTICLE 3**

1. Undertakings and associations of undertakings shall, within the appointed time limit, make known in writing their views concerning the objections raised against them.

2. They may in their written comments set out all matters relevant to their defence.

3. They may attach any relevant documents in proof of the facts set out. They may also propose that the Commission hear persons who may corroborate those facts.

21—05 *ARTICLE 4*

The Commission shall in its decisions deal only with those objections raised against undertakings and associations of undertakings in respect of which they have been afforded the opportunity of making known their views.

21—06 *ARTICLE 5*

If natural or legal persons showing a sufficient interest apply to be heard pursuant to Article 19(2) of Regulation No 17, the Commission shall afford them the opportunity of making known their views in writing within such time limit as it shall fix.

21—07 *ARTICLE 6*

Where the Commission, having received an application pursuant to Article 3(2) of Regulation No 17, considers that on the basis of the information in its possession there are insufficient grounds for granting the application, it shall inform the applicants of its reasons and fix a time limit for them to submit any further comments in writing.

21—08 *ARTICLE 7*

1. The Commission shall afford to persons who have so requested in their written comments the opportunity to put forward their arguments orally, if those persons show a sufficient interest or if the Commission proposes to impose on them a fine or periodic penalty payment.
2. The Commission may likewise afford to any other person the opportunity of orally expressing his views.

21—09 *ARTICLE 8*

1. The Commission shall summon the persons to be heard to attend on such date as it shall appoint.
2. It shall forthwith transmit a copy of the summons to the competent authorities of the Member States, who may appoint an official to take part in the hearing.

21—10 *ARTICLE 9*

1. Hearings shall be conducted by the persons appointed by the Commission for that purpose.
2. Persons summoned to attend shall appear either in person or be represented by legal representatives or by representatives authorised by their constitution. Undertakings and associations of undertakings may moreover be represented by a duly authorised agent appointed from among their permanent staff.

Persons heard by the Commission may be assisted by lawyers or university teachers who are entitled to plead before the Court of Justice of the European Communities in accordance with Article 17 of the Protocol on the Statute of the Court, or by other qualified persons.

3. Hearings shall not be public. Persons shall be heard separately or in the presence of other persons summoned to attend. In the latter case, regard shall be had to the legitimate interest of the undertakings in the protection of their business secrets.

4. The essential content of the statements made by each person heard shall be recorded in minutes which shall be read and approved by him.

21–11 *ARTICLE 10*

Without prejudice to Article 2(2), information and summonses from the Commission shall be sent to the addressees by registered letter with acknowledgement of receipt, or shall be delivered by hand against receipt.

21–12 *ARTICLE 11*

1. In fixing the time limits provided for in Articles 2, 5 and 6, the Commission shall have regard both to the time required for preparation of comments and to the urgency of the case. The time limit shall not be less than two weeks; it may be extended.

2. Time limits shall run from the day following receipt of a communication or delivery thereof by hand.

3. Written comments must reach the Commission or be dispatched by registered letter before expiry of the time limit. Where the time limit would expire on a Sunday or Public holiday, it shall be extended up to the end of the next following working day. For the purpose of calculating this extension, public holidays shall, in cases where the relevant date is the date of receipt of written comments, be those set out in the Annex to this Regulation, and in cases where the relevant date is the date of dispatch, those appointed by law in the country of dispatch.

21–13 This Regulation shall be binding in its entirety and directly applicable in all Member States.

*Done at Brussels, 25 July 1963.*

For the Commission
The President
WALTER HALLSTEIN

21–14 *ANNEX*

referred to in the third sentence of Article 11(3)
(List of public holidays)

| | |
|---|---|
| New Year | 1 Jan |
| Good Friday | |
| Easter Saturday | |

| | |
|---|---|
| Easter Monday | |
| Labour Day | 1 May |
| Schuman Plan Day | 9 May |
| Ascension Day | |
| Whit Monday | |
| Belgian National Day | 21 July |
| Assumption | 15 Aug |
| All Saints | 1 Nov |
| All Souls | 2 Nov |
| Christmas Eve | 24 Dec |
| Christmas Day | 25 Dec |
| Boxing Day | 26 Dec |
| New Year's Eve | 31 Dec |

# F. Council Regulation No. 19/65.

## ON APPLYING ARTICLE 85(3) OF THE TREATY TO CATEGORIES OF AGREEMENTS AND OF CONCERTED PRACTICES

22–01   THE COUNCIL OF THE EUROPEAN ECONOMIC COMMUNITY,

HAVING REGARD to the Treaty setting up the European Economic Community, and in particular Article 87 thereof;

HAVING REGARD to the proposal of the Commission;

HAVING REGARD to the Opinion of the Assembly;

HAVING REGARD to the Opinion of the Economic and Social Committee;

WHEREAS the declaration of inapplicability of the provisions of Article 85(1) of the Treaty may, in accordance with the provisions of paragraph 3 of the same Article, relate to categories of agreements, of decisions and of concerted practices which fulfil the conditions required by those provisions;

WHEREAS procedures for applying Article 85(3) must be adopted by way of a regulation, laid down on the basis of Article 87;

WHEREAS in view of the large number of notifications lodged in pursuance of Regulation No 17 it is advisable that the Commission be enabled, in order to facilitate its task, to declare by way of a Regulation that the provisions of Article 85(1) are inapplicable to certain categories of agreements and of concerted practices;

WHEREAS it should be laid down under what conditions the Commission, in close and constant liaison with the competent authorities of the Member States, may exercise such power when sufficient experience has been gained in the light of individual decisions and when it becomes possible to specify those categories of agreements and concerted practices in respect of which the conditions of Article 85(3) may be considered as being fulfilled;

WHEREAS the Commission, by its action and in particular by Regulation No 153, indicated that there can be no question of easing the procedures stipulated by Regulation No 17 in respect of certain types of agreements or concerted practices which are particularly liable to distort competition in the Common Market;

WHEREAS by virtue of Article 6 of Regulation No 17 the Commission may stipulate that a decision taken in accordance with Article 85(3) of the Treaty shall apply with retroactive effect; whereas the Commission should also be empowered to lay down such provision by way of a Regulation;

WHEREAS by virtue of Article 7 of Regulation No 17, agreements, decisions and concerted practices may be exempted from prohibition by decision of the Commission, particularly if they are so altered as to fulfil the requirements for applying Article 85(3); whereas it is advisable that the Commission be enabled to grant the same benefit, by means of a regulation, to such agreements and concerted practices if they are so altered as to fall within a category defined in an exempting regulation;

WHEREAS since there can be no exemption save when all the conditions set out in Article 85(3) are present, the Commission must have the power to prescribe, by decision, the requirements to be fulfilled by an agreement or concerted practice which owing to special circumstances has certain effects incompatible with Article 85(3);

HAS ADOPTED THIS REGULATION:

22–02 *ARTICLE 1*

1. Without prejudice to the application of the Council's Regulation No 17, the Commission may declare by means of a Regulation and in accordance with Article 85(3) of the Treaty, that Article 85(1) shall not apply to categories of agreements to which only two undertakings are parties and by which:

    (a)   one undertakes to supply the other alone with certain products with a view to their resale within a specified part of the Common Market territory,

or   one undertakes to purchase from the other alone certain products with a view to their resale,

or   sole supply or purchase commitments in respect of certain products with a view to resale, of the type envisaged in the two preceding sub-paragraphs, have been entered into by the two undertakings,

or which

    (b)   include limitations imposed in relation to the acquisition or use of industrial property rights — in particular of patents, utility models, industrial designs and models or trade marks — or to the rights arising out of contracts which include transfer of, or licence to use, manufacturing processes or knowledge relating to the use or application of industrial techniques.

2. The regulation shall define those categories of agreements to which it applies, and shall specify in particular:

(a)    the restrictions or clauses which may not be included in the agreements;

(b)    the clauses which must be included in the agreements, or other requirements which must be fulfilled.

3. Paragraphs 1 and 2 of this Article shall apply *mutatis mutandis* to categories of concerted practices to which only two undertakings are parties.

22—03   *ARTICLE 2*

1. A regulation in pursuance of Article 1 shall be adopted for a limited period.

2. It may be revoked or amended where circumstances have altered with respect to a factor essential in its adoption; in such case, a period of adaptation shall be laid down for the agreements and concerted practices referred to in the earlier regulation.

22—04   *ARTICLE 3*

A regulation laid down in accordance with Article 1 may stipulate that it shall apply with retroactive effect to agreements and concerted practices which could, at the date of its entry into force, have benefited by a decision issued with retroactive effect in pursuance of Regulation No 17, Article 6.

22—05   *ARTICLE 4 (as amended by the Treaty of Accession)*

1. A regulation pursuant to Article 1 may stipulate that the prohibition contained in Article 85(1) of the Treaty shall not apply, for such period as shall be fixed by that regulation, to agreements and concerted practices already in existence at the date of accession to which Article 85 applies by virtue of accession and which do not satisfy the conditions of Article 85(3), where:

—    such agreements and concerted practices are so amended, within three months from the coming into force of the regulation, that they fulfil the said requirements in accordance with the provisions of the regulation, and

—    the amendments are brought to the notice of the Commission within the time-limit fixed by the regulation.

2. Paragraph 1 shall not apply to agreements and concerted practices to which Article 85(1) of the Treaty applies by virtue of accession and which must be notified before 1 July 1973, in accordance with Articles 5 and 25 of Regulation No 17, unless they have been so notified before that date.

3. The benefit of the provisions laid down pursuant to paragraph 1 of this Article may not be invoked in cases pending at the date of entry into force of a regulation adopted pursuant to Article 1; neither may

such benefit be invoked in support of a claim for damages against third parties.

22—06 **ARTICLE 5**

When the Commission intends to adopt a regulation, it shall publish the draft thereof and shall invite all persons concerned to submit their comments within a time-limit which shall be fixed by the Commission and shall in no case be less than one month.

22—07 **ARTICLE 6**

1. The Commission shall consult the Consultative Committee on matters relating to cartels and monopolies:
    (a)   before publishing a draft regulation,
    (b)   before adopting a regulation.
2. Article 10(5) and (6) of Regulation No 17, relating to consultation with the Consultative Committee, shall apply *mutatis mutandis*, it being understood that the joint meetings with the Commission shall take place at the earliest one month after despatch of the notice convening them.

22—08 **ARTICLE 7**

Should the Commission, either on its own initiative or at the request of a Member State or of natural or legal persons establishing the fact of a legitimate interest, ascertain that in a given case agreements or concerted practices dealt with by a regulation laid down pursuant to Article 1 of this Regulation have nevertheless certain effects which are incompatible with the requirements laid down in Article 85(3) of the Treaty, it may withdraw the benefit of application of that regulation and may issue a decision, in accordance with Articles 6 and 8 of Regulation No 17, without the notification referred to in Article 4(1) of Regulation No 17 being required.

22—09 **ARTICLE 8**

The Commission shall, before 1st January, 1970, submit to the Council a draft regulation designed to amend this Regulation as shall appear necessary in the light of experience.

22—10 This Regulation shall be binding in all its parts and directly applicable in all Member States.

    *Done at Brussels, 2nd March, 1965.*
      By the Council
      The President
      M COUVE DE MURVILLE

# G. Commission Regulation No.67/67.

## ON THE APPLICATION OF ARTICLE 85(3) OF THE TREATY TO CERTAIN CATEGORIES OF EXCLUSIVE DEALING AGREEMENTS

23—01 THE COMMISSION OF THE EUROPEAN ECONOMIC COMMUNITY,

HAVING REGARD to the Treaty establishing the European Economic Community, and in particular Articles 87 and 155 thereof;

HAVING REGARD to Article 24 of Regulation No 17 of 6 February 1962;

HAVING REGARD to Regulation No 19/65/EEC of 2 March 1965 on the application of Article 85(3) of the Treaty to certain categories of agreements and concerted practices;

HAVING REGARD to the Opinions delivered by the Advisory Committee on Restrictive Practices and Monopolies in accordance with Article 6 of Regulation No 19/65/EEC;

WHEREAS under Regulation No 19/65/EEC the Commission has power to apply Article 85(3) of the Treaty by regulation to certain categories of bilateral exclusive dealing agreements and concerted practices coming within Article 85;

WHEREAS the experience gained up to now, on the basis of individual decisions, makes it possible to define a first category of agreements and concerted practices which can be accepted as normally satisfying the conditions laid down in Article 85(3);

WHEREAS since the adoption of such a regulation would not conflict with the application of Regulation No 17 the right of undertakings to request the Commission, on an individual basis, for a declaration under Article 85(3) of the Treaty would not be affected;

WHEREAS exclusive dealing agreements of the category defined in Article 1 of this Regulation may fall within the prohibition contained in Article 85(1) of the Treaty; whereas since it is only in exceptional cases that exclusive dealing agreements concluded within a Member State affect trade between Member States, there is not need to include them in this Regulation;

WHEREAS it is not necessary expressly to exclude from the category as defined those agreements which do not fulfil the conditions of Article 85(1) of the Treaty;

WHEREAS in the present state of trade exclusive dealing agreements relating to international trade lead in general to an improvement in distributing because the entrepreneur is able to consolidate his sales activities; whereas he is not obliged to maintain numerous business contacts with a large number of dealers, and whereas the fact of maintaining contacts with only one dealer makes it easier to overcome sales difficulties resulting from linguistic, legal, and other differences; whereas exclusive dealing agreements facilitate the promotion of the sale of a product and make it possible to carry out more intensive marketing and to ensure continuity of supplies, while at the same time rationalising distribution; whereas, moreover, the appointment of an exclusive distributor or of an exclusive purchaser who will take over, in place of the manufacturer, sales promotion, after-sales service and carrying of stocks, is often the sole means whereby small and medium-size undertakings can compete in the market; whereas it should be left to the contracting parties to decide whether and to what extent they consider it desirable to incorporate in the agreements terms designed to promote sales; whereas there can only be an improvement in distribution if dealing is not entrusted to a competitor;

WHEREAS as a rule such exclusive dealing agreements also help to give consumers a proper share of the resulting benefit as they gain directly from the improvement in distribution, and their economic or supply position is thereby improved as they can obtain products manufactured in other countries more quickly and more easily;

WHEREAS this Regulation must determine the obligations restricting competition which may be included in an exclusive dealing agreement; whereas it may be left to the contracting parties to decide which of those obligations they include in exclusive dealing agreements in order to draw the maximum advantages from exclusive dealing;

WHEREAS any exemption must be subject to certain conditions; whereas it is in particular advisable to ensure through the possibility of parallel imports that consumers obtain a proper share of the advantages resulting from exclusive dealing; whereas it is therefore not possible to allow industrial property rights and other rights to be exercised in an abusive manner in order to create absolute territorial protection; whereas these considerations do not prejudice the relationship between the law of competition and industrial property rights, since the sole object here is to determine the condition for exemption of certain categories of agreements under this Regulation;

WHEREAS competition at the distribution stage is ensured by the possibility of parallel imports; whereas, therefore, the exclusive dealing agreements covered by this Regulation will not normally afford any possibility of preventing competition in respect of a substantial part of the products in question;

WHEREAS it is desirable to allow contracting parties a limited period of time within which they may, in accordance with Article 4 of Regulation No 19/65/EEC, modify their agreements and practices so as to satisfy the conditions laid down in this Regulation, without it being possible, under Article 4(3) of Regulation No 19/65/EEC, to rely thereon in actions which are pending at the time of entry into force of this Regulation, or as grounds for claims for damages against third parties;

WHEREAS agreements and concerted practices which satisfy the conditions set out in this Regulation need no longer be notified; whereas Article 4(2)(a) of Regulation No 27, as amended by Regulation No 153, can be repealed, since agreements which it was possible to notify on Form B 1 would normally come within the scope of the exemption;

WHEREAS agreements notified on Form B 1 and not amended so as to satisfy the conditions of this Regulation should be made subject to the normal notification procedure, in order that they may be examined individually;

HAS ADOPTED THIS REGULATION:

23—02 *ARTICLE 1*

1. Pursuant to Article 85(3) of the Treaty and subject to the provisions of this Regulation it is hereby declared that until 31 December 1972 Article 85(1) of the Treaty shall not apply to agreements to which only two undertakings are party and whereby:

    (a)    one party agrees with the other to supply only to that other certain goods for resale within a defined area of the common market; or

    (b)    one party agrees with the other to purchase only from that other certain goods for resale; or

    (c)    the two undertakings have entered into obligations, as in (a) and (b) above, with each other in respect of exclusive supply and purchase for resale.

2. Paragraph 1 shall not apply to agreements to which undertakings from one Member State only are party and which concern the resale of goods within that Member State.

23—03 *ARTICLE 2*

1. Apart from an obligation falling within Article 1, no restriction on competition shall be imposed on the exclusive dealer other than:

    (a)    the obligation not to manufacture or distribute, during the duration of the contract or until one year after its expiration, goods which compete with the goods to which the contract relates;

    (b)    the obligation to refrain, outside the territory covered by the contract, from seeking customers for the goods to which the contract relates, from establishing any branch, or from maintaining any distribution depot.

2. Article 1(1) shall apply notwithstanding that the exclusive dealer undertakes all or any of the following obligations:

(a) to purchase complete ranges of goods or minimum quantities;

(b) to sell the goods to which the contract relates under trade marks or packed and presented as specified by the manufacturer;

(c) to take measures for promotion of sales, in particular
   − to advertise,
   − to maintain a sales network or stock of goods,
   − to provide after-sale and guarantee services,
   − to employ staff having specialised or technical training.

23−04 *ARTICLE 3*

Article 1(1) of this Regulation shall not apply where:

(a) manufacturers of competing goods entrust each other with exclusive dealing in those goods;

(b) the contracting parties make it difficult for intermediaries or consumers to obtain the goods to which the contract relates from other dealers within the common market, in particular where the contracting parties:

   (1) exercise industrial property rights to prevent dealers or consumers from obtaining from other parts of the common market or from selling in the territory covered by the contract goods to which the contract relates which are properly marked or otherwise properly placed on the market;

   (2) exercise other rights or take other measures to prevent dealers or consumers from obtaining from elsewhere goods to which the contract relates or from selling them in the territory covered by the contract.

23−05 *ARTICLE 4*

1. As regards agreements which were in existence on 13 March 1962 and were notified before 1 February 1963, the declaration contained in Article 1(1) of inapplicability of Article 85(1) of the Treaty shall have retroactive effect from the time when the conditions of application of this Regulation were fulfilled.

2. As regards all other agreements notified before the entry into force of this Regulation, the declaration contained in Article 1(1) of inapplicability of Article 85(1) of the Treaty shall have retroactive effect from the time when the conditions of application of this Regulation were fulfilled, but not earlier than the day of notification.

23—06　*ARTICLE 5 (as amended by the Treaty of Accession)*

As regards agreements, decisions or concerted practices for exclusive dealing already in existence at the date of accession to which Article 85(1) applies by virtue of accession, the prohibition in Article 85(1) of the Treaty shall not apply where they are modified within six months from the date of accession so as to fulfil the conditions contained in this Regulation. The notification shall take effect from the time of receipt thereof by the Commission. Where the notification is sent by registered post, it shall take effect from the date on the postmark of the place of despatch.

23—07　*ARTICLE 6*

The Commission shall examine whether Article 7 of Regulation No 19/65/EEC applies in individual cases, in particular when there are grounds for believing that:

(a) the goods to which the contract relates are not subject, in the territory covered by the contract, to competition from goods considered by the consumer as similar goods in view of their properties, price and intended use;

(b) it is not possible for other manufacturers to sell, in the territory covered by the contract, similar goods at the same stage of distribution as that of the exclusive dealer;

(c) the exclusive dealer has abused the exemption:

(1) by refusing, without objectively valid reasons, to supply in the territory covered by the contract categories of purchasers who cannot obtain supplies elsewhere, on suitable terms, of the goods to which the contract relates;

(2) by selling the goods to which the contract relates at excessive prices.

23—08　*ARTICLE 7*

1. Article 4(2)(a) of Regulation No 27 of 3 May 1962, as amended by Regulation No 153, is hereby repealed.

2. Notification, on Form B 1, of an exclusive dealing agreement which does not fulfil the conditions contained in Articles 1 to 3 of this Regulation shall, if such agreement is not amended so as to satisfy those conditions, be effected before 3 October 1967, by submission of Form B, with annexes, in accordance with the provisions of Regulation No 27.

23—09　*ARTICLE 8*

Articles 1 to 7 of this Regulation shall apply by analogy to the category of concerted practices defined in Article 1(1).

23—10  *ARTICLE 9*
This Regulation shall enter into force on 1 May 1967.

23—11  This Regulation shall be binding in its entirety and directly applicable in all Member States.

*Done at Brussels, 22 March 1967.*

For the Commission
The President
WALTER HALLSTEIN

# H.  Commission Notice, Concerning Agreements, Decisions and Concerted Practices in connection with Co-operation between Enterprises. *

24—01   Questions are frequently put to the Commission of the European Communities on the attitude it intends to take up, for purposes of implementation of the competition rules contained in the Treaties of Rome and Paris, with regard to co-operation between enterprises. In this Notice, it endeavours to provide guidance which, though not exhaustive, may prove useful to enterprises in the correct interpretation, in particular, of Article 85(1) of the EEC Treaty and Article 65(1) of the ECSC Treaty.

## I

24—02   The Commission welcomes co-operation among small and medium-sized enterprises in so far as it enables them to work more rationally and increase their productivity and competitiveness on a larger market. While considering that its duty is to facilitate co-operation among small and medium-sized enterprises in particular, the Commission recognises that co-operation among large enterprises, too, can be economically desirable without raising difficulties from the standpoint of competition policy.

24—03   Article 85(1) of the Treaty establishing the European Economic Community (EEC Treaty) and Article 65(1) of the Treaty establishing the European Coal and Steel Community (ECSC Treaty) provide that all agreements, decisions and concerted practices (hereafter referred to as "agreements") which have the object or effect of preventing, restraining or distorting competition within the common market (hereafter referred to as "restraints of competition") are incompatible with the common market and are prohibited; under Article 85(1) of the EEC Treaty this applies, however, only if such agreements are liable to

* Published 23rd July 1968.

impair trade between the Member States.

24—04 The Commission feels that, in the interests of the small and medium-sized enterprises in particular, it should make known the considerations by which it will be guided when interpreting Article 85(1) of the EEC Treaty and Article 65(1) of the ECSC Treaty and applying them to certain co-operation arrangements between enterprises, and should indicate which of these arrangements in its opinion do not come under provisions. This notice applies to all enterprises, irrespective of their size.

24—05 There may also be forms of co-operation between enterprises other than the forms of co-operation listed below which are not prohibited by Article 85(1) of the EEC Treaty or Article 65(1) of the ECSC Treaty. This applies in particular if the market position of the enterprises co-operating with each other is in the aggregate too weak for the co-operation agreement between them to lead to an appreciable restraint of competition in the common market and — where the agreements fall within the scope of Article 85 of the EEC Treaty — to impair trade between the Member States.

24—06 It is also pointed out that other forms of co-operation between enterprises or agreements containing additional clauses, to which the rules of competition of the Treaties apply, can be exempted pursuant to Article 85(3) of the EEC Treaty or be authorised pursuant to Article 65(2) of the ECSC Treaty.

24—07 The Commission intends to clarify without delay by means of suitable decisions in individual cases or by general notices, the status of the various forms of co-operation in relation to the provisions of the Treaties.

24—08 No general statement can be made at this stage on the application of Article 86 of the EEC Treaty on the abuse of dominant positions within the common market or within a part of it. The same applies to Article 66(7) of the ECSC Treaty.

24—09 As a result of this Notice, as a general rule, it should no longer be useful for enterprises to obtain negative clearance, as defined by Article 2 of Regulation No 17, for the agreements listed, nor should it be necessary to have the legal position clarified through a Commission decision on an individual case; this also means that notification with this end in view will no longer be necessary for agreements of this type. However, if it is doubtful whether in an individual case an agreement between enterprises restricts competition or if other forms of co-operation between enterprises which in the view of the enterprises do not restrict competition are not listed here, the enterprises are free to apply, where the matter comes under Article 85(1) of the EEC Treaty, for negative clearance, or to file as a precautionary measure, where Article 65(1) of the ECSC Treaty is the relevant provision, an application on the basis of Article 65(2) of the ECSC Treaty.

24—10 This Notice is without prejudice to any interpretation to be given by the Court of Justice of the European Communities.

## II

24—11    The Commission takes the view that the following agreements do not restrict competition.

24—12    1.    Agreements having as their sole object:
   (a)    An exchange of opinion or experience,
   (b)    Joint market research,
   (c)    The joint execution of comparative studies of enterprises or economic sectors,
   (d)    The joint preparation of statistics and standardized calculation systems.

24—13    Agreements whose sole purpose is the joint procurement of information which the various enterprises need to determine their future market behaviour freely and independently, or the use by each of the enterprises of a joint advisory body, do not have the object or effect of restraining competition. But if the freedom of action of the enterprises is limited or if their market behaviour is co-ordinated either expressly or through concerted practices, there may be restraint of competition. This is the case — for example — where concrete recommendations are made or where conclusions are given so specific a form that they induce at least some of the participating enterprises to behave in an identical manner on the market.

24—14    The exchange of information may take place between the enterprises themselves or through a body acting as an intermediary. It is, however, particularly difficult to distinguish between methods of information which are unexceptionable so far as competition is concerned on the one hand and behaviour in restraint of competition on the other, if there are special bodies for the purpose of registering orders, turnover figures, investment and prices so that it cannot, as a rule, be accepted without further enquiry that Article 85(1) of the EEC Treaty or Article 65(1) of the ECSC Treaty do not apply to them. A restraint of competition may occur in particular on an oligopolistic market for homogeneous products.

24—15    Joint market research and comparative studies of enterprises and economic sectors to collect information and ascertain facts and market conditions do not in themselves affect competition, in the absence of more far-reaching co-operation between the participating enterprises.

24—16    Other arrangements of this type, as for instance joint arrangements for analyses of current economic trends and for structural studies, so obviously do not affect competition that there is no need to mention them specifically.

24—17    Standardised calculation systems involving specified rates at which calculations are to be made must be regarded as recommendations that may lead to restraints of competition.

276

24—18   2.     Agreements having as their sole object:
          (a)    Co-operation in accounting matters,
          (b)    Joint provision of credit guarantees,
          (c)    Joint agencies for the collection of accounts,
          (d)    Joint agencies for providing advice on business organisation or tax matters.

24—19   In such cases, the co-operation involved covers fields that are not concerned with the supply of goods and services or the economic decisions of the enterprises taking part, so that it does not lead to any restraint of competition.

24—20   Co-operating in accounting matters is neutral from the point of view of competition as it only assists in the technical handling of the accounting work. Nor is the creation of credit guarantee associations caught by the competition rules, since it does not modify the relationship between supply and demand.

24—21   Joint collection agencies whose work is not confined to the collection of outstanding payments in accordance with the intentions and conditions of the participating enterprises, or which fix prices or exert in any other way an influence on price formation, may restrict competition. Application of uniform terms by all participating firms may constitute a concerted practice and the making of joint price comparisons may have the same result. In this connection there is no objection to use of standardised prices printed forms; such use must however not be combined with an understanding or tacit agreement on uniform prices, rebates or conditions of sale.

24—22   3.     Agreements having as their sole object:
          (a)    The joint carrying out of research and development projects,
          (b)    The joint placing of research and development contracts,
          (c)    The sharing out of research and development projects among participating enterprises.

24—23   In the field of research, too, the mere exchange of experience and results serves for information only and does not restrict competition. It therefore need not be mentioned expressly.

24—24   Agreements on the joint execution of research work or the joint development of the results of research up to the stage of industrial application do not affect the competitive position of the parties. This also applies to the allocation of fields of research and of development work if the results are available to all participating enterprises. However, if the enterprises enter into commitments which restrict their own research and development activity, or utilisation of the results of joint work, so that they do not have a free hand with regard to their own research and development outside the joint projects, this may constitute an infringement of the competition rules of the Treaties. Where no joint research work is carried out, contractual obligations or concerted practices between firms binding them to refrain from research work of their own, either completely or in certain sectors, may result in a restraint of competition. The sharing out of sectors of research without provision for mutual access to the results is to be regarded as a form of specialisation that may restrict competition.

24—25 There may also be a restraint of competition if agreements are concluded with regard to the practical exploitation of the results of research and development work carried out jointly or where the corresponding concerted practices are put into effect, particularly if the participating enterprises undertake or agree to manufacture only the products or types of product developed jointly or to share out future production among themselves.

24—26 It is of the essence of joint research that the results should be exploited by the participating enterprises in proportion to their participation. If the participation of certain enterprises is confined to a specific sector of the joint research project or to the provision of only limited financial assistance, there is no restraint of competition — so far as there has been any joint research at all — if the results of research are made available to these enterprises to an extent related to that of their participation. There may, however, be a restraint of competition if certain participating enterprises are excluded from exploitation of the results either entirely or to an extent which is inappropriate in the light of participation.

24—27 If the granting of licences to third parties is expressly or tacitly excluded, there may be a restraint of competition; but the fact that research is carried out jointly justifies imposition of an obligation not to grant licences to third parties save by common agreement or by majority decision.

24—28 The legal form taken by the joint research and development work is immaterial for the purpose of assessing the compatibility of the agreement with the rules of competition.

24—29 4.    Agreements which have as their sole object the joint use of production facilities and storage and transport equipment.

24—30 These forms of co-operation do not restrict competition, being confined to organisational and technical arrangements for the use of facilities. There may be a restraint of competition if the enterprises involved do not bear the cost of utilisation of the installation or equipment themselves or if agreements are concluded regarding joint production or the sharing out of production or the establishment or running of a joint enterprise, or if concerted practices are employed in regard thereto.

24—31 5.    Agreements having as their sole object the setting up of associations for the execution of orders in common, where the participating enterprises do not compete with each other as regards the work to be done or where, taken individually, they would not be in a position to execute the orders.

24—32 Where enterprises do not compete with each other they cannot restrict competition between them by setting up associations. This applies in particular to enterprises belonging to different industries but also to enterprises in the same industry to the extent that their contribution under the association consists only of goods or services which cannot be supplied by the other participating enterprises. It is not a question of whether the enterprises compete with each other in other sectors, but of whether in the light of the actual circumstances of a particular case there is a possibility that in the foreseeable future they may compete with each other with regard to the products or services involved. If the absence of competition between the enterprises and the maintenance of this situation are based on agreements or concerted practices, there may be a restraint of competition.

24—33 Moreover, even in the case of associations formed by enterprises which normally compete with each other, there is no restraint of competition if the participating enterprises could not in fact execute the specific order by themselves. This applies in particular if, for lack of experience, specialised knowledge, available capacity or financial resources, these enterprises, working alone, would have no prospect of success, could not finish the work by the required delivery date or could not carry the financial risk.

24—34 Nor is there a restraint of competition if it is only by the setting up of an association that the enterprises are put in a position to put forward an attractive offer. There may, however, be a restraint of competition if the enterprises undertake to deal solely within the framework of such an association.

24—35 6. Agreements having as their sole object:
   (a)   Joint selling arrangements,
   (b)   Joint after-sales and repairs service, provided the participating enterprises are not competitors with regard to the products or services covered by the agreement.

24—36 As already explained in detail under Heading 5, co-operation between enterprises cannot restrict competition if the firms do not compete with each other.

24—37 Very often joint selling by small or medium-sized enterprises — even if they are competing with each other — does not entail an appreciable restraint of competition; it is, however, impossible to establish in this Notice any general criteria or to specify what enterprises may be deemed "small or medium-sized".

24—38 There is no joint after-sales and repairs service if several manufacturers, not acting in concert with each other, arrange for an after-sales and repairs service for their products to be provided by an enterprise which is independent of them all. Nor, in such a case, is there restraint of competition if the manufacturers are competitors.

24—39 7. Agreements having as their sole object joint advertising.
   Joint advertising is designed to draw the buyer's attention to given products of an industry or to a common brand name; as such it does not restrict competition between the participating enterprises.

However, if the participating enterprises are partly or wholly prevented, by agreements or concerted practices, from advertising on their own account or if they are subjected to other restrictions, there may be a restraint of competition.

24—40   8.    Agreements having as their sole object the use of a common mark to designate a certain quality, where the mark is available to all competitors on the same conditions.

Such associations for the joint use of a quality mark do not restrict competition if other competitors, whose products objectively meet the stipulated quality requirements, can use the mark on the same conditions as the members. Nor do the obligations to accept quality control for the products bearing the mark, to issue uniform instructions for use, or to use the mark for the products meeting the quality standard constitute restraints of competition. But there may be restraint of competition if the right to use the mark is linked to obligations regarding production, marketing, price formation or other obligations of any type, as for instance when the participating enterprises are obliged to manufacture or sell only products of guaranteed quality.

# I. Commission Regulation No.1133/68.

## AMENDING COMMISSION REGULATION NO 27 OF 3 MAY 1962

25—01    THE COMMISSION OF THE EUROPEAN COMMUNITIES,

HAVING REGARD to the Treaty establishing the European Economic Community, and in particular Article 85 thereof;

HAVING REGARD to Council Regulation No 17 of 6 February 1962, and in particular Article 24 thereof;

WHEREAS under Article 24 of Regulation No 17 the Commission has power to adopt implementing provisions concerning the form, content and other details of applications pursuant to Articles 2 and 3 and of notifications pursuant of Articles 4 and 5.

WHEREAS Regulation No 27 adopted by the Commission pursuant to Article 24 of Regulation No 17 lays down, in particular, in Article 4(1) and (2) thereof that Form A must be used for applications for negative clearance under Article 2 of Regulation No 17 and Form B for notifications under Articles 4 or 5 of Regulation No 17, with a view to exemption pursuant to Article 85(3) of the Treaty;

WHEREAS it is advisable, in view of the general preference of undertakings to have the two alternatives open to them, to provide for the use of a single form for applications for negative clearance and for notification in order to simplify the procedure for all parties to an agreement and for the competent departments;

WHEREAS negative clearance and exemption pursuant to Article 85(3) of the Treaty have different consequences and whereas the single form must leave it open to undertakings to apply either for negative clearance or for a declaration of non-applicability;

HAS ADOPTED THIS REGULATION:

25—02    *Sole Article*

Article 4 of Regulation 27 shall be amended to read as follows:
"Content of applications and notifications

1. Applications under Article 2 of Regulation No 17 relating to the applicability of Article 85(1) of the Treaty and notifications under Article 4 or Article 5(2) of Regulation No 17 shall be submitted on Form A/B as shown in the Annex to this Regulation.

2. Applications and notifications shall contain the information asked for in Form A/B.

3. Several participating undertakings may submit an application or notification on a single form.

4. Applications under Article 2 of Regulation No 17 relating to the applicability of Article 86 of the Treaty shall contain a full statement of the facts, specifying, in particular, the practice concerned and the position of the undertaking or undertakings within the common market or a substantial part thereof in regard to products or services to which the practice relates."

25—03 This Regulation shall be binding in its entirety and directly applicable in all Member States.

> *Done at Brussels, 26 July 1968.*
> For the Commission
> The President
> JEAN REY

# FORM A/B

25—04 This form and the supporting documents should be forwarded in seven copies together with proof in duplicate of the representative's authority to act.

If the space opposite each question is insufficient, please use extra pages, specifying to which item on the form they relate.

25—05 TO THE COMMISSION OF THE EUROPEAN COMMUNITIES
Directorate General for Competition
170, rue de la Loi, Brussels 4
A. Application for negative clearance pursuant to Article 2 of Council Regulation No 17 of 6 February 1962 relating to implementation of Article 85(1) of the Treaty
B. Notification of an agreement, decision or concerted practice under Articles 4 and 5 of Council Regulation No 17 of 6 February 1962.

25—06 I. Information regarding parties
1. Name, forenames and address of
person submitting the application or
notification. If such person is acting as
representative, state also the name and
address of the undertaking or association
of undertakings represented and the
name, forenames and address of the proprietors or partners or, in the case of legal
persons, of their legal representatives.

Proof of representative's authority to act must be supplied.

If the application or notification is submitted by a number of persons or on behalf of a number of undertakings, the information must be given in respect of each person or undertaking.

2. Name and address of the undertakings which are parties to the agreement, decision or concerted practice and name, forenames and address of the proprietors or partners or, in the case of legal persons, of their legal representatives (unless this information has been given under I(1)).

If the undertakings which are parties to the agreement are not all associated in submitting the application or notification, state what steps have been taken to inform the other undertakings.

This information is not necessary in respect of standard contracts (see Section II 1(b) below).

3. If a firm or joint agency has been formed in pursuance of the agreement, state the name and address of such firm or agency and the names, forenames and addresses of its legal or other representatives.

4. If a firm or joint agency is responsible for operating the agreement, state the name and address of such firm or agency and the names, forenames and addresses of its legal or other representatives.

Attach a copy of the statutes.

5. In the case of a decision of an association of undertakings, state the name and address of the association and the names, forenames and addresses of its legal representatives.

Attach a copy of the statutes.

6. If the undertakings are established or have their seat outside the territory of the common market (Article 227(1) and (2) of the Treaty), state the name and address of a representative or branch

283

established in the territory of the
common market.

25—07 II. Information regarding contents of agreement, decision or concerted
practice:

1. If the contents were reduced to
writing, attach a copy of the full text
unless (a), (b) or (c) below provides
otherwise.

    (a) Is there only an outline agree-
ment or outline decision?
If so, attach also copy of the full
text of the individual agreements
and implementing provisions.

    (b) Is there a standard contract, i.e.
a contract which the under-
taking submitting the
notification regularly concludes
with particular persons or groups
of persons (e.g., a contract
restricting the freedom of action
of one of the contracting parties
in respect of resale prices or
terms of business for goods
supplied by the other contracting party)?
If so, only the text of the
standard contract need be
attached.

    (c) If there is a licensing agreement
of the type covered by Article
4(2)(2b) of Regulation No 17, it
is not necessary to submit those
clauses of the contract which
only describe a technical manufacturing process and have no
connection with the restriction
of competition; in such cases,
however, an indication of the
parts omitted from the text
must be given.

2. If the contents were not, or were only
partially, reduced to writing, state the
contents in the space opposite.

3. In all cases give the following
additional information:

    (a) Date of agreement, decision or

concerted practice.

(b) Date when it came into force
and, where applicable, proposed
period of validity.

(c) Subject: exact description of the
goods or services involved.

(d) Aims of the agreement, decision
or concerted practice.

(e) Terms of adherence, termination
or withdrawal.

(f) Sanctions which may be taken
against participating undertakings (penalty clause,
expulsion, withholding of
supplies, etc.).

25—08   III. Means of achieving the aims of the agreement, decision or concerted
practice:

1. State whether and how far the agreement, decision or concerted practice
relates to:

— adherence to certain buying or
selling prices, discounts or other
trading conditions

— restriction or control of production, technical development
or investment

— sharing of markets or sources of
supply

— restrictions on freedom to
purchase from, or resell to, third
parties (exclusive contracts)

— application of different terms
for supply of equivalent goods
or services.

2. Is the agreement, decision or concerted practice concerned with supply of
goods or services

(a) within one Member State only?

(b) between a Member State and
third States?

(c) between Member States?

25—09   IV. If you consider Article 85(1) to be inapplicable and are notifying
the agreement, decision or concerted practice as a precaution only:

(a) Please attach a statement of the
relevant facts and reasons as to
why you consider Article 85(1)

to be inapplicable, e.g., that the
agreement, decision or
concerted practice
1.   does not have the object or
     effect of preventing, res-
     tricting or distorting
     competition; or
2.   is not one which may affect
     trade between Member
     States.
(b)  Are you asking for a negative
     clearance pursuant to Article 2
     of Regulation No 17?

25—10  V. Are you notifying the agreement, decision or concerted practice, even if only as a precaution, in order to obtain a declaration of inapplicability under Article 85(3)?

If so, explain to what extent
1. the agreement, decision or concerted
practice contributes towards
—  improving production or distribution, or
—  promoting technical or
   economic progress;
2. a proper share of the benefits arising
from such improvement or progress
accrues to the consumers;
3. the agreement, decision or concerted
practice is essential for realising the aims
set out under 1 above; and
4. the agreement, decision or concerted
practice does not eliminate competition
in respect of a substantial part of the
goods concerned.

25—11  VI. State whether you intend to produce further supporting arguments and, if so, on which points.

The undersigned declare that the information given above and in the ................................ annexes attached hereto is correct. They are aware of the provisions of Article 15(1)(a) of Regulation No. 17.

........................(date)....................

Signatures:

..............................................          ..................................................

..............................................          ..................................................

*Appendix I*

25—12  EUROPEAN COMMUNITIES
              COMMISSION

Brussels, (date)..............
170, rue de la Loi

Directorate General
for Competition

To

## Acknowledgement of receipt

(This form will be returned to the address inserted above if completed in a single copy by the person lodging it).

Your application for negative clearance dated.........................................

Your notification dated..................................................................................

concerning:
(a) Parties:

1  ...................................................................................................

2  ...................................................................................... and others
(There is no need to name the other undertakings party to the arrangement)

(b) Subject:.........................................................................................

........................................................................................................

........................................................................................................

(brief description of the restriction on competition)

was received on.................................................................................

and registered under No IV.............................................................

*Please quote the above number in all correspondence.*

# J. Commission Notice,
# Concerning Minor Agreements.*

## I

26—01  The Commission considers, as it has already indicated on different occasions, that it is important to promote co-operation between undertakings insofar as it is economically desirable and does not raise any objections in respect of the policy of competition; it desires, in particular, to facilitate co-operation between small and medium-sized undertakings. It was with this in mind that it published the "Announcement on agreements, decisions and concerted practices relating to co-operation between undertakings" — hereinafter referred to as "agreements" — an announcement listing a series of agreements which, by their nature, do not restrict competition. With the present announcement, the Commission pursues its effort to define the field of application of Article 85 paragraph 1 of the Treaty establishing the European Economic Community with the aim of promoting co-operation between small and medium-sized undertakings.

26—02  The Commission considers that the prohibition on agreements set down in Article 85 paragraph 1 of the Treaty of the European Economic Community does not cover those agreements which do not affect to a significant degree competition and trade between Member States. Only those agreements are prohibited which have an appreciable effect on market conditions, in other words, which appreciably modify the market position of non-participating undertakings and of consumers, that is, their outlets and sources of supply.

26—03  In the present announcement the Commission attaches a sufficiently concrete meaning to the term "appreciable" for undertakings to be able to decide for themselves whether agreements reached with other undertakings do not fall within the scope of Article 85 paragraph 1 on account of their minor importance. The quantitative definition of "appreciable" given by the Commission, does not however have an absolute value: it is quite possible that, in particular cases, agreements

* Published 27th May 1970.

288

reached by undertakings which exceed the limits indicated below only affect competition and trade between Member States to an insignificant degree and consequently do not fall within the scope of Article 85 paragraph 1.

26—04 This announcement should eliminate the need to obtain negative clearance in the sense of Article 2 of Regulation No 17 for the agreements envisaged. Nor should it any longer be necessary to seek to clarify the legal position by individual decisions of the Commission; there is therefore no need to notify such agreements for that purpose. However, when there is doubt in a particular case whether an agreement affects competition and trade between Member States to an appreciable degree, undertakings may request a negative clearance or may notify the agreement.

26—05 This announcement does not prejudice the interpretation of the Court of Justice of the European Communities.

## II

26—06 The Commission considers that agreements between production or distribution undertakings are not covered by the prohibition of Article 85 paragraph 1 of the Treaty establishing the European Economic Community:

— when the products involved in the agreement represent, in the part of the Common Market where the agreement is effective, not more than 5% of the volume of business effected with identical products or products considered by consumers to be similar on account of their properties, price or use and

— when the aggregate annual turnover of the undertakings participating in the agreement does not exceed 15 million units of account or, in the case of agreements between commercial undertakings, 20 million units of account.

26—07 Furthermore, the Commission considers that the above agreements are not covered by the prohibition of Article 85 paragraph 1 if, in the course of two consecutive financial years, the market shares and the turnover thus fixed are exceeded by less than 10%.

26—08 The aggregate turnover is derived from the sum of the turnovers of the last financial year comprising all products and services, achieved by:

1. Undertakings taking part in the agreement;
2. Undertakings in which the undertakings taking part in the agreement hold:

— at least 25% of the capital or working capital, whether directly or indirectly,

— or at least half the voting rights,

— or the power to appoint at least half the members of the supervisory board or board of management, or of bodies

legally representing the undertaking,
—    or the right to manage the undertaking's affairs;

3. Undertakings holding, in an undertaking which is taking part in the agreement:

—    at least 25% of the capital or working capital, whether directly or indirectly,
—    or at least half the voting rights,
—    or the power to appoint at least half the members of the supervisory board or board of management, or of bodies legally representing the undertaking,
—    or the right to manage the undertaking's affairs.

The aggregate turnover does not take into account transactions between undertakings taking part in the agreement.

# K. Council Regulation No.2821/71.

## CONCERNING THE APPLICATION OF ARTICLE 85(3) OF THE TREATY TO CATEGORIES OF AGREEMENTS, DECISIONS AND CONCERTED PRACTICES

27—01     THE COUNCIL OF THE EUROPEAN COMMUNITIES,

HAVING REGARD to the Treaty establishing the European Economic Community, and in particular Article 87 thereof;

HAVING REGARD to the proposal from the Commission;

HAVING REGARD to the Opinion of the European Parliament;

HAVING REGARD to the Opinion of the Economic and Social Committee;

WHEREAS the provisions of Article 85(1) of the Treaty may, in accordance with the provisions of paragraph 3 of that Article, be delared inapplicable to categories of agreements, decisions and concerted practices which fulfil the conditions of those provisions;

WHEREAS the procedure for application of Article 85(3) must be adopted by a regulation based on Article 87;

WHEREAS the creation of a common market requires the adaptation of undertakings to the conditions of the enlarged market and whereas the cooperation of the undertakings can be a suitable means of achieving this;

WHEREAS agreements, decisions and concerted practices on co-operation between undertakings which allow the latter to work more rationally and adapt their productivity and competitiveness to the enlarged market may, in so far as they come under the prohibition in Article 85(1), under certain conditions be exempted therefrom; whereas this measure is necessary in particular as regards agreements, decisions and concerted practices in the field of standards and types, research and development of products or of processes up to the stage of industrial application and of making use of the results as well as of specialisation;

WHEREAS it is appropriate to put the Commission in a position to declare by means of a regulation that the provisions of Article 85(1) are inapplicable to those categories of agreements, decisions and concerted practices, in order to make it easier for undertakings to cooperate in ways which are economically desirable and without adverse effect from the point of view of competition policy;

WHEREAS, the conditions should be laid down under which the Commission can exercise this power in close and constant cooperation with the competent authorities of the Member States;

WHEREAS, pursuant to Article 6 of Regulation No 17, the Commission may provide that a decision taken in accordance with Article 85(3) of the Treaty shall apply retrospectively; whereas it is advisable that the Commission should be able to make such a provision also by regulation.;

WHEREAS, pursuant to Article 7 of Regulation No 17, agreements, decisions and concerted practices may be exempted from the prohibition by a decision of the Commission, in particular if they are amended in such a way that they fulfil the conditions for application of Article 85(3); whereas it is appropriate that the Commission should, by means of a regulation, be able to grant the same benefits to those agreements, decisions and concerted practices if they are amended in such a way that they come within a category specified in an exempting regulation;

WHEREAS the possibility cannot be excluded that, in a specific case, the conditions set out in Article 85(3) may not be fulfilled; whereas it must be possible for the Commission to regulate such a case in pursuance of Regulation No. 17 by means of a decision having future effect;

HAS ADOPTED THIS REGULATION:

27–02 *Article 1*

1 Without prejudice to the application of Regulation No 17, the Commission may declare, by means of a regulation and in accordance with Article 85(3) of the Treaty, that Article 85(1) is not applicable to categories of agreements between undertakings, decisions by associations of undertakings and concerted practices which have as their object:

    (a)    the application of standards and types;

    (b)    the research and development of products or processes up to the stage of industrial application, as well as making use of the results, including provisions regarding industrial property rights and confidential technical knowledge;

    (c)    specialisation, including the agreements necessary for the achievement thereof.

2 The regulation must include a definition of the categories of agreements, decisions and concerted practices to which it applies and in particular specify:

    (a)    the restrictions and provisions which may or may not appear in the agreements, decisions and concerted practices;

(b)    the provisions which must appear in the agreements, decisions and concerted practices or the other conditions which must be fulfilled.

27—03  *Article 2*

1 A regulation made pursuant to Article 1 shall be adopted for a limited period.

2 It may be repealed or amended when there has been a change in any of the factors which were basic to its adoption; in that case a period shall be provided for the adaptation of the agreements, decisions and concerted practices coming under the previous regulation.

27—04  *Article 3*

A regulation adopted pursuant to Article 1 may provide for its application with retrospective effect to the agreements, decisions and concerted practices which, on the day of its entry into force, would have been eligible for a decision with retrospective effect in accordance with Article 6 of Regulation No 17.

27—05  *Article 4*

1 A regulation made pursuant to Article 1 may provide that the prohibition laid down in Article 85(1) of the Treaty shall not apply, for the period determined in the regulation, to the agreements, decisions and concerted practices concerned which were in existence on 13 March 1962 and which do not fulfil the conditions of Article 85(3):

—    if they are amended within six months from the entry into force of the regulation, in such a way that they fulfil the conditions which are stated in the regulation, and

—    if the amendments are notified to the Commission within the period determined in the regulation.

2 Paragraph 1 shall apply to agreements, decisions and concerted practices which were notifiable before 1 February 1963, in accordance with Article 5 of Regulation No 17, only if they were notified before that date.

3 Benefits arising from provisions made pursuant to paragraph 1 cannot be invoked in legal proceedings which have been commenced before the date of entry into force of a regulation adopted in pursuance of Article 1; neither can they be invoked as grounds for damages against third parties.

27—06  *Article 5*

When the Commission proposes to adopt a regulation it shall publish the draft thereof to enable all interested parties and organisations to let it be informed of their comments within a period, which may not be less than one month, to be fixed by the Commission.

27—07  *Article 6*

1 The Commission shall consult the Advisory Committee on Restrictive Practices and Monopolies:

   (a)    before publishing a draft regulation;
   (b)    before adopting a regulation.

2 Paragraphs 5 and 6 of Article 10 of Regulation No 17 on consultation with the Advisory Committee shall apply by analogy, except that joint meetings with the Commission will take place at the earliest one month after dispatch of the notice convening them.

27—08  *Article 7*

If the Commission ascertains, on its own initiative or at the request of a Member State or of natural or legal persons who show a legitimate interest, that in a specific case agreements, decisions or concerted practices covered by a regulation made pursuant to Article 1 have nevertheless certain effects which are incompatible with the conditions specified in Article 85(3) of the Treaty, it may, in withdrawing the benefit of application of that regulation, take a decision in accordance with Articles 6 and 8 of Regulation No 17 without the notification referred to in Article 4(1) of Regulation No 17 being required.

This Regulation shall be binding in its entirety and directly applicable in all Member States.

*Done at Brussels, 20 December 1971.*

For the Council
The President
M PEDINI

# L. Council Regulation No.2822/71.

## AMPLIFYING THE PROVISIONS OF REGULATION NO 17 ON IMPLEMENTING ARTICLES 85 AND 86 OF THE TREATY

28–01    THE COUNCIL OF THE EUROPEAN COMMUNITIES,

HAVING REGARD to the Treaty establishing the European Economic Community, and in particular Article 87 thereof;

HAVING REGARD to the proposal from the Commission;

HAVING REGARD to the Opinion of the European Parliament;

HAVING REGARD to the Opinion of the Economic and Social Committee;

WHEREAS Article 4(2) of Regulation No 17 provides for an exception to the notification laid down in Article 4(1) in respect of a number of agreements, decisions and concerted practices;

WHEREAS the creation of a common market requires the adaptation of undertakings to the conditions of the enlarged market and whereas the cooperation of the undertakings can be a suitable means of achieving this; whereas it is in particular advisable to encourage cooperation in the field of research and development and the conclusion of agreements on specialisation which do not affect competition;

WHEREAS such cooperation is facilitated when the agreements, decisions and concerted practices in question no longer have to be notified;

WHEREAS, in establishing exemption from notification, account should be taken on the one hand of the concern of undertakings to have their cooperation made easier and on the other the necessity for effective supervision;

WHEREAS in general, the dangers inherent in agreements, decisions and concerted practices in which the only restriction on competition relates to joint research and development, are not such as to make notification necessary;

WHEREAS agreements on specialisation are capable of contributing to improvement in the production and distribution of products; whereas generally there is no reason to fear that competition might be affected provided that the participating undertakings do not exceed a certain size and that their share of the market does not exceed a limit fixed in regard to the specialised products; whereas agreements of this kind may, as a general rule, be exempted from the prohibition imposed by Article 85(1) of the Treaty, pursuant to paragraph 3;

WHEREAS therefore Article 4(2) of Regulation No 17 should be amplified and agreements, decisions and concerted practices regarding joint research and development, in so far as they restrict competition, together with certain agreements on specialisation should be exempted from compulsory notification;

HAS ADOPTED THIS REGULATION:

28—02 *Sole Article*

Article 4(2) of Regulation No 17 shall be expanded as follows:

"2 Paragraph 1 shall not apply to agreements, decisions and concerted practices where:

1 . . . . . . (unchanged)

2 . . . . . . (unchanged)

3 they have as their sole object:

(a) . . . . . . (unchanged)

(b) joint research and development;

(c) specialisation in the manufacture of products, including agreements necessary for the achievement thereof;

— where the products which are the object of specialisation do not, in a substantial part of the common market, represent more than 15% of the volume of business done in identical products or those considered by the consumers to be similar by reason of their characteristics, price and use, and

— where the total annual turnover of the participating undertakings does not exceed 200 million units of account.

These agreements, decisions and concerted practices may be notified to the Commission."

This Regulation shall be binding in its entirety and directly applicable in all Member States.

*Done at Brussels, 20 December 1971.*

For the Council
The President
M PEDINI

# M. Aide Memoire *

29—01 The United Kingdom Government have noted, in the Journal Officiel of the European Communities dated 7.viii.69 the publication of a decision of the Commission of 24 July, 1969 (No. IV/26267), concerning proceedings pursuant to Article 85 of the Treaty establishing the European Economic Community in the matter of dyestuffs. Article 1 of this decision declares that "the concerted practices of fixing the rate of price increases and the conditions of application of these increases in the dyestuffs sector ... constitute violations of the provisions of Article 85 of the EEC Treaty". Article 2 of the decision inflicts or purports to inflict certain fines upon the commercial undertakings who are alleged to have participated in these concerted practices. Among the undertakings specified in Articles 1 and 2 of the decision are Imperial Chemical Industries, Limited (hereinafter referred to as "I.C.I."), which is a company incorporated and carrying on business in the United Kingdom. Article 4 of the decision declares that "the present decision is directed to the undertakings mentioned in Article 1"; it then goes on to state that as far as I.C.I. and certain Swiss undertakings are concerned, "[the decision] may likewise be notified to them at the seat of one of their subsidiaries established in the Common Market".

29—02 The United Kingdom Government neither wish nor intend to take issue with the Commission about the merits of this particular case. They accept that it is for the undertakings to whom the decision is directed to pursue whatever remedies are available to them under the EEC Treaty if they desire for their part to challenge the legality or correctness of this measure taken by the Commission. It is in any event their understanding that certain of the undertakings to whom decision is directed have already indicated their intention to institute proceedings before the European Court of Justice challenging the

* Submitted by the United Kingdom Government to the E.E.C. Commission.

decision on various grounds.

29—03 The concern of the United Kingdom Government in this matter is rather directed towards the more fundamental point concerning the reach and extent of the jurisdiction exercisable by the Commission *vis-à-vis* undertakings which are neither incorporated in the territory of a Member State of the European Economic Community nor carrying on business nor resident therein.

29—04 The Commission will be aware that certain claims to exercise extra-territorial jurisdiction in anti-trust proceedings have given rise to serious and continuing disputes between Western European Governments (including the Governments of some EEC Member States) and the United States Government, inasmuch as these claims have been based on grounds which the Western European Governments consider to be unsupported by public international law.

29—05 In particular, the United Kingdom Government have for their part consistently objected to the assumption of extra-territorial jurisdiction in anti-trust matters by the courts or authorities of a foreign State when that jurisdiction is based upon what is termed the "effects doctrine" — that is to say, the doctrine that territorial jurisdiction over conduct which has occurred wholly outside the territory of the State claiming jurisdiction may be justified because of the resulting economic "effects" of such conduct within the territory of that State. This doctrine becomes more open to objection when, on the basis of the alleged "effects" within the State claiming jurisdiction of the conduct of foreign corporations abroad (that is to say, conduct pursued outside the territory of that State), such corporations are actually made subject to penal sanctions.

29—06 The United Kingdom Government are of the view that certain of the "considerations" advanced in the decision of the Commission of 24 July, 1969, conflict with the principles of public international law concerning the basis upon which personal and substantive jurisdiction may be exercised over foreign corporations in anti-trust matters. A summary statement of these principles, as seen by the United Kingdom Government, is annexed to this Aide Mémoire for ease of reference.

29—07 In particular, it will be noted that the method by which the decision of the Commission was purportedly notified to I.C.I. (Article 4 of the decision) ignores the clear legal distinction between a parent company and its subsidiaries and the separate legal personalities of the latter. The United Kingdom Government consider that this attempted "notification" of a parent company through its subsidiary is designed to support a doctrine of substantive jurisdiction which is itself open to objection as going beyond the limits imposed by the accepted principles of international law.

29—08 So far as substantive jurisdiction is concerned, the United Kingdom Government are of the view that the decision of the Commission incorporates an interpretation of the relevant provisions of the EEC

Treaty which is not justified by the accepted principles of international law governing the exercise of extra-territorial jurisdiction over foreigners in respect of acts committed abroad.

29—09 The United Kingdom Government deem it necessary to bring these considerations to the attention of the Commission lest there be any misunderstanding as to their position in the matter.

## STATEMENT OF PRINCIPLES ACCORDING TO WHICH, IN THE VIEW OF THE UNITED KINGDOM GOVERNMENT, JURISDICTION MAY BE EXERCISED OVER FOREIGN CORPORATIONS IN ANTI-TRUST MATTERS

### The basis on which personal jurisdiction may be exercised over foreign corporations

29—10 1. Personal jurisdiction should be assumed only if the foreign company "carries on business" or "resides" within the territorial jurisdiction.

2. A foreign company may be considered to "carry on business" within the jurisdiction by an agent only if the agent has legal power to enter into contracts on behalf of the principal.

3. A foreign parent company may not be considered to "carry on business" within the jurisdiction by a subsidiary company, unless it can be shown that the subsidiary is the agent for the parent in the sense of carrying on the parent's business within the jurisdiction.

4. The separate legal personalities of a parent company and its subsidiary should be respected. Such concepts as "enterprise entity" and "reciprocating partnership" when applied for the purpose of asserting personal jurisdiction over a foreign parent company by reason of the presence within the jurisdiction of a subsidiary (and a foreign subsidiary by reason of the presence of its parent company) are contrary to sound legal principle in that they disregard the distinction of personality between parent and subsidiary.

5. The normal rules governing the exercise of personal jurisdiction should not be extended in such a manner as to extend beyond proper limits the exercise of substantive jurisdiction in respect of the activities of foreigners abroad. Nor can the assertion of extended personal jurisdiction be justified on the basis that it is necessary for the enforcement of legislation which in itself exceeds the proper limits of substantive jurisdiction.

6. There is no justification for applying a looser test to methods of personal service in anti-trust matters than is permissible in relation to other matters.

### The basis on which substantive jurisdiction may be exercised in anti-trust matters

29—11 1. On general principles, substantive jurisdiction in anti-trust matters should only be taken on the basis of either

    (a)    the territorial principle, or

    (b)    the nationality principle.

There is nothing in the nature of anti-trust proceedings which justifies a wider application of these principles than is generally accepted in other matters; on the contrary there is much which calls for a narrower application.

2. The territorial principle justifies proceedings against foreigners and foreign companies only in respect of conduct which consists in whole or in part of some activity by them in the territory of the State claiming jurisdiction. A state should not exercise jurisdiction against a foreigner who, or a foreign company which, has committed no act within its territory. In the case of conspiracies the assumption of jurisdiction is justified:

    (a)    if the entire conspiracy takes place within the territory of the State claiming jurisdiction; or

    (b)    if the formation of the conspiracy takes place within the territory of the State claiming jurisdiction even if things are done in pursuance of it outside its territory; or

    (c)    if the formation of the conspiracy takes place outside the territory of the State claiming jurisdiction, but the person against whom the proceedings are brought has done things within its territory in pursuance of the conspiracy.

3. The nationality principle justifies proceedings against nationals of the State claiming jurisdiction in respect of their activities abroad only provided that this does not involve interference with the legitimate affairs of other States or cause such nationals to act in a manner which is contrary to the laws of the State in which the activities in question are conducted.

# N.  Draft Council Regulation*

## CONCERNING LIMITATION OF ACTIONS IN CASES OF PROSECUTION AND EXECUTION OF JUDGEMENT IN THE FIELDS OF TRANSPORT LAW AND COMPETITION LAW OF THE EUROPEAN ECONOMIC COMMUNITY

### Draft Regulation

30—01  The Council of the European Communities, in the light of the Treaty instituting the European Economic Community (especially Articles 75, 79 and 87), of the Commission's draft, of the opinions of the European Parliament and of the Economic and Social Committee, hereby promulgates the following Regulation.

30—02  *PREAMBLE*

Whereas,

1. The provisions of the EEC transport law and competition law confer on the Commission the power to impose fines (sanctions) and penalties upon undertakings and associations of undertakings which violate the orders of the Commission relating to the supply of information or inspections or prohibitions of discrimination, cartels or abuse of dominant positions. But these provisions do not lay down any periods of limitation.

2. It seems necessary, in order to provide legal certainty, to introduce the principle of limitation of actions and to govern its application. Rules to that effect, to be complete, should apply both to the power to impose fines (sanctions) and to the power to execute the decisions by

* Submitted by the E.C. Commission to the Council on 23 December 1971 (COM (71) 1514 final). Published in European Parliament, Sessional Papers 1971—72, Doc. 245/71 (21 February 1972).

which fines (sanctions) or penalties are imposed. Such a set of rules should fix the periods of limitation, the date from which the period of limitations runs and the measures whereby the period of limitation is interrupted or suspended.

3. In that respect account should be taken both of the interests of undertakings and associations of undertakings and the requirements of the administrative practice of the Commission.

4. As regards the power of the Commission to impose fines the periods of limitation should be fixed in relation to the nature of the infringement. The provisions governing the power of the Commission to impose fines (sanctions) lay down that the infringements of the orders of the Commission on the supply of information or inspections are less serious than violations of the prohibition of discrimination, cartels and abuse of dominant position. It is therefore justifiable to introduce the same distinction in the fixing of the limitation periods. In such circumstances it is expedient to lay down a limitation period of three years for violations of the orders of the Commission on the supply of information or inspections and of five years for all other infringements covered by the present regulation.

5. As regards prosecutions, a prescription period cannot be given to the undertakings and associations of undertakings concerned while they are violating the provisions of the EEC transport law and competition law. Therefore it should be laid down that the limitation period runs only as from the day on which those concerned have put an end to the violation.

6. Provision should be made for the possibility of interrupting the limitation period for prosecutions. The effects of the limitation period apply only in the case of inaction of the appropriate authority with regard to the violation within the period laid down. Undertakings and associations of undertakings should no longer benefit from the limitation period when such authority is, in accordance with the provisions in force, making formal inquiries [*procède à l'instruction*] or bringing proceedings for the infringement. It should therefore be provided that the limitation period be interrupted by any measure taken by the Commission or by a Member State at the request of the Commission and which is aimed at proving such infringement. It should also be provided that such measures taken against an undertaking or association of undertakings concerned interrupt the limitation period with regard to all undertakings and associations of undertakings participating in the infringement.

7. The decisions whereby the Commission imposes on undertakings or associations of undertakings fines (sanctions) or penalties are, in accordance with Article 192 of the Treaty instituting the European Economic Community, authority for their own execution [*forment titre exécutoire*]. It seems appropriate to subject the power of the Commission to execute such decisions to a limitation period of three

years as from the day on which the decision acquired binding force.

8. An interruption of the limitation period should, however, also be provided for in the case of execution. The limitation period does not run when the act upon which execution is to be levied is altered or a request to that effect is rejected. Nor may the undertakings or associations of undertakings which are subject to a pecuniary obligation benefit from limitation when the appropriate authority is engaging in distraint proceedings in accordance with the procedural provisions in force. It should therefore be provided that the limitation period is interrupted by a decision of the Commission altering the original amount of the fine (sanction) or penalty or rejecting a request to do so as well as by any measure taken by a Member State at the request of the Commission and aimed at the forcible recovery of the fine (sanction) or penalty.

9. Finally, the limitation period should also be suspended when an arrangement for payment is granted.

BE IT THEREFORE ENACTED AS FOLLOWS:

30—03 ### ARTICLE 1

*Limitations as regards prosecutions*

1. The power of the Commission to impose fines (sanctions) for infringement of the provisions of the transport law or the competition law of the European Economic Community is subject to a period of limitation. The limitation period is

  —  three years in the case of infringement of the provisions relating to requests for information or to the carrying out of inspections,

  —  five years in the case of all other infringements covered by the present regulation.

2. The limitation period runs from the day on which the infringement was brought to an end.

30—04 ### ARTICLE 2

*Interruption of the limitation period as regards prosecutions*

1. The limitation period is interrupted by any measure taken by the Commission or by a Member State at the request of the Commission and aimed at proving the infringement.

Measures interrupting the limitation period include:

  (a)  the despatch of a request for information by the Commission or by the appropriate authorities of a Member State at the request of the Commission, as well as the notification of a decision of the Commission requiring the information requested;

  (b)  the despatch or the production of an inspection warrant in writing by the Commission or by the appropriate authorities of a Member State at the request of the

Commission, as well as the notification of a decision of the Commission ordering inspection;

(c)    the communication in writing of the commencement of proceedings by the Commission;

(d)    the communication in writing of the plaints alleged by the Commission.

2. The measures referred to in paragraph 1 and taken in relation to an undertaking or association of undertakings concerned interrupt the limitation period with regard to all the undertakings or associations of undertakings participating in the infringement.

3. The limitation period begins again from each interruption.

30–05   *ARTICLE 3*
*Limitation as regards execution*
1. The power of the Commission to execute its decisions imposing fines (sanctions) or penalties for infringement of the provisions of the transport law or the competition law of the European Economic Community is subject to a period of limitation. The limitation period is three years. The limitation period runs from the day on which the Commission's decision acquires binding force.

2. The limitation period is interrupted:

(a)    by notification of a decision of the Commission altering the original amount of the fine (sanction) or penalty or rejecting a request to do so;

(b)    by any measure taken by a Member State at the request of the Commission and aimed at the forcible recovery of the fine (sanction) or penalty.

The limitation period begins again from each interruption.

3. The limitation period is suspended for as long as an arrangement for payment is granted.

30–06   *ARTICLE 4*
*Entry into force*
The present regulation shall enter into force on......................................

The present regulation shall be binding in its entirety and directly applicable in all Member States.

# O.  Draft Commission Regulation

## CONCERNING THE APPLICATION OF ARTICLE 85.3 OF THE TREATY TO CATEGORIES OF SPECIALISATION AGREEMENTS

31–01   THE COMMISSION OF THE EUROPEAN COMMUNITIES,

HAVING REGARD to the Treaty establishing the European Economic Community, and in particular Articles 87 and 155 thereof;

HAVING REGARD to Regulation 2821/71 of the 20th December, 1971, concerning the application of Article 85.3 of the Treaty to categories of agreements, decisions, and concerted practices;

HAVING REGARD to the Opinion delivered by the Advisory Committee on Restrictive Practices and Monopolies in accordance with Article 6 of Regulation 2821/71;

WHEREAS by virtue of Regulation 2821/71 the Commission is empowered to apply by regulation Article 85.3 to certain categories of agreements, decisions, and concerted practices relating to specialisation, including agreements necessary to its realisation, which come within Article 85.1;

WHEREAS since the adoption of such a regulation would not conflict with the application of Regulation 17, the right of undertakings to request the Commission, on an individual basis, for a declaration under Article 85.3 of the Treaty would not be affected;

WHEREAS specialisation agreements relating to production can come within the prohibition in Article 85.1;

WHEREAS specialisation agreements relating to production contribute in general to the improvement of production of products, in that the undertakings can concentrate their activities on the manufacture of certain products, can thus work in a more rational way and can offer their products at more favourable prices; whereas it may be expected that, by the operation of effective competition, consumers will share equitably in the resulting benefits;

305

WHEREAS this Regulation must determine the restrictions on competition which can appear in a specialisation agreement; whereas the expected restrictions on competition are in general indispensable to procuring the intended advantages for the undertakings and for consumers; whereas the parties may be left to decide which are the terms they will include in their agreements;

WHEREAS in order to ensure that competition is not eliminated for a substantial part of the products in question, this Regulation applies only if the size of the share of the market held by the participating undertakings in a substantial part of the Common Market and the size of the undertakings themselves do not exceed specified limits;

WHEREAS it is appropriate to grant the benefit of this Regulation to specialisation agreements made before the Regulation comes into force but which have been relieved of the obligation to notify by the amendment to Article 4.2(3)(c) of Regulation 17, to the extent that they comply with the conditions laid down in this Regulation;

HAS ADOPTED THIS REGULATION.

31–02 *ARTICLE 1*

Pursuant to Article 85.3 of the Treaty and subject to the provisions of this Regulation, it is hereby declared that until the 31st December, 1977, Article 85.1 of the Treaty shall not apply to agreements by which, with the object of specialisation and for the duration of the agreement, undertakings mutually undertake not to make themselves or have made by other undertakings certain products but to leave their partners to make those products or to entrust the production of them to other undertakings.

31–03 *ARTICLE 2*

Apart from the obligation specified in Article *1*, no other restrictions of competition can be imposed upon the parties except:

(a) an obligation not to make without the consent of the other parties any specialisation agreements with other undertakings concerning identical products or products considered by consumers to be similar by reason of their properties, price, or end use;

(b) an obligation to deliver the specialisation products to the other parties and to comply in this respect with minimum quantities;

(c) an obligation to draw supplies of the specialisation products exclusively from the other parties unless supplies are available elsewhere on more favourable terms;

(d) an obligation to ensure the maintenance of minimum stocks of the specialisation products and of spare parts for them;

(e) an obligation to ensure after-sales service and guarantee service for the specialisation products.

31—04 *ARTICLE 3*

1. Article *1* of this Regulation applies only
    (a)   where the specialisation products do not exceed 10% of the turnover in a substantial part of the Common Market in identical products or products considered by consumers to be similar by reason of their properties, price, or end use; and
    (b)   where the total turnover realised by the participating undertakings in any financial year does not exceed 150 million units of account.

2. For the purpose of paragraph 1, the unit of account is that adopted in drawing up the Budget of the Community by virtue of Articles 207 and 209 of the Treaty.

3. Article *1* of this Regulation will still apply even if during two consecutive financial years the market share and turnover specified in paragraph 1 are exceeded by less than 10%.

31—05 *ARTICLE 4*

The total turnover for the purposes of Article *3* is the sum of the turnovers achieved during the last financial year, including all products and services, by:

1. undertakings party to the agreement,
2. undertakings in which undertakings party to the agreement hold:
    at least 25% of the capital or of the working capital, either directly or indirectly,
    or at least half of the voting rights,
    or the power to appoint at least half of the members of the supervisory board or board of management, or of bodies legally representing the undertaking,
    or the right to manage the affairs of the undertaking,
3. undertakings which hold in an undertaking party to the agreement:
    at least 25% of the capital or working capital, either directly or indirectly,
    or at least half of the voting rights,
    or the power to appoint at least half of the members of the supervisory board or board of management, or of bodies legally representing the undertaking,
    or the right to manage the affairs of the undertaking.

The turnover does not include transactions between undertakings party to the agreement.

31—06 *ARTICLE 5*

The Commission will investigate whether Article 7 of Regulation 2821/71 applies in any particular case, especially where there are grounds for believing that the rationalisation will not give substantial results or that there will be prejudicial effects for consumers.

31—07  **ARTICLE 6**

The prohibition in Article 85.1 of the Treaty will not apply for the period from 18th January, 1972, to . . . . . . . . . . . . . . * or to the date of notification, in the case of agreements within Article *1* of this Regulation made between the 18th January, 1972, and the . . . . . . . . . . . . . . * but relieved from the obligation to notify by virtue of Regulation 2822/71 provided that they conform to the conditions specified in this Regulation or have been amended before the . . . . . . . . . . . . . * in such a way that they then conform with those conditions.

31—08  **ARTICLE 7**

Articles *1* to *6* of this Regulation apply by analogy to decisions of associations of undertakings and to concerted practices.

31—09  **ARTICLE 8**

This Regulation comes into force on . . . . . . . . . . . . *

* Date of entry into force.

# Index

(The numbers refer to paragraphs.)

Abuse of dominant position — see dominant
  position, abuse of —
Abuse principle    1—36, 5—01, 5—43
"Accession, by virtue
  of —"    4—34, 4—35 — 4—40, 6—38
Accession, Treaty of — see Treaty of
  Accession.
A.C.E.C.    3—61, 12—07
Advisory Committee on Restrictive Practices
  and Monopolies    4—03, 4—13, 4—89,
    4—98, 5—67
"Agreement"    3—04, 3—05, 3—13, 3—45
"Agreement", oral    3—04, 3—14
Alliance Machine Outils    3—31, 10—11
Aluminum Company of America    1—10
American Can Company    1—10
American Tobacco Company    1—09
Aniline Dyes Cartel    3—05, 3—11, 3—12,
    3—17, 3—18, 3—91, 4—10, 4—91
Applicant countries    4—05
"Application"    4—03
Appreciable effect    3—23 — 3—27, 3—33
— 3—37, 4—15, 4—103, 5—38, 6—23 — 6—26,
  6—30, 7—10, 8—60, 8—78, 8—82, 10—13,
    10—17
Articles of the Rome Treaty — see Rome
  Treaty
Assembly    2—05, 17—04
ASPA    7—12
Asphaltoid-Keller    4—62
Attorney General of the U.S., Report of
  National Committee    1—31, 1—37
Aziende Colori Nazionali    3—11

B.A.S.F.    3—11
Bayer    3—11
Béguelin    3—49, 6—12, 6—64, 6—65
Belgaphos    3—44, 10—08
Belgium    1—38, 2—01
Benelux    2—02, 5—21, 5—30
Berliet    3—61, 12—07
Bilger    4—53
Black Bolts and Nuts Association    1—16
Blondel    3—63
Boehringer    4—91
Brasserie de Haecht    4—105
Brewery industry    4—09, 4—61
Brinkhof    16—04
British Insulated Callenders Cables    1—29
British Oxygen Co.    1—08, 1—09, 1—10
Brooke Bond    1—22
Buderus    12—09
Burroughs    8—19 — 8—21, 8—35, 8—44,
    8—61, 8—85
Buxton    8—09
Buyers' tales    1—19, 13—11

Cable manufacturers    1—29, 3—09
Cadillon    6—25, 6—40, 6—55
Cartel    1—13 — 1—16, 1—31, 1—32
Cartoucherie Française    3—67, 11—09
Casella    3—11
CECIMO    3—69, 14—07
CEMATEX    3—70, 3—78, 4—33, 14—08
Cement Makers (Belgian)    3—35
Cement Manufacturers (British)    1—16
Ceramic Tile Manufacturers (German)    3—06

Christiani & Nielsen 6—10
Ciba 3—11, 3—91
Cimfrance 3—22, 10—07
Clima Chappée 12—09
Cobelaz 3—06, 3—22, 3—79, 10—06
Colgate-Palmolive 9—15 — 9—17
Commission of the European
Communities 2—05, 17—04
" ", liaison with
Member States 4—94 — 4—98, 5—67
" ", powers of
investigation 4—67 — 4—81, 5—60 —
5—62
" ", powers of
investigation, limits on 4—74
" ", procurement of
information 4—56 — 4—66, 5—56 —
5—59
Common Agricultural Policy 2—04
Common External Tariff 2—02, 2—06
Common Market 2—01 — 2—03
Common Transport Policy 2—04, 2—06
Competition 1—02 — 1—12
Competition, unfair 6—50, 6—59, 6—65,
7—11, 7—14
Competition Rules 2—06, 17—09, 17—15
Comptoir Français de 3—22, 3—79,
l'Azote 10—07
Concerted practices 1—22 — 1—24, 1—31 —
1—32, 3—08 — 3—14, 9—14
Conditions of sale 6—11, 6—22, 6—52,
6—55
Conflict of laws 3—88 — 3—94, 5—39 —
5—40
Conscious parallelism — see parallelism,
conscious
Consorzio 3—07
Consten 3—52, 3—71, 3—76, 6—56 —
6—63
Consumers 3—72
Continental Can 3—19, 5—04, 5—10 —
5—13, 5—16, 5—20, 5—30, 5—31, 5—33,
5—44, 5—50, 5—51, 15—14
Copyright 5—14, 8—67 — 8—79
Copyright agreements 8—77 — 8—78
" " clauses in 8—79
" existence/
exercise of 8—70 — 8—74
Costs 13—08
Council 2—05, 17—04
Countervailing power 1—16, 14—04
Courtaulds 1—06, 1—08, 1—29

Cow & Gate 1—28
Credit information 13—09

Davidson 8—22 — 8—25, 8—30, 8—31,
8—33, 8—39, 8—40, 8—42, 8—43, 8—45,
8—47, 8—85, 8—86, 8—87, 8—88
Decision (of the Commission) 4—03
Decision of association 3—06 — 3—07, 3—13
Delplanque 8—19 — 8—21, 8—61, 8—85
Denmark 1—39, 5—21
Designs — see Registered designs
Deutsche Grammophon 7—15, 8—70 —
8—74
Distribution agreements 3—86, Chapter 6
Dominant position 1—04 — 1—12, 5—07 —
5—18
Dominant position,
abuse of 1—36, 5—22 — 5—33, 8—08,
8—14, 8—57, 8—76, 15—12, 16—01
Double jeopardy 4—90, 4—91
Dunlop 1—30, 14—09
duPont de Nemours 1—07, 1—29, 5—34

Economic and Social Committee 2—05
Eddy, A.J. 1—18, 13—03
Effect, doctrine of appreciable — see
appreciable effect.
Effects principle (conflict of
laws) 3—18, 3—91, 3—92, 3—93, 3—94,
4—36, 4—40
Enterprise entity, doctrine of 3—16 — 3—19,
3—94, 5—04, 5—44, 6—09 — 6—12
Equal pay 2—04
Estoppel 8—43
Eurogypsum 9—19
European Coal and Steel Community 2—04
European Court of
Justice 2—05, 17—16 — 17—18
European Economic Community 2—01
European Social Fund 2—04
Europemballage 3—19, 5—04, 5—11,
5—30, 5—40, 5—44, 5—46, 15—14
Euratom 2—04
Exchange of information — see information
agreements
Exclusive dealing 3—73, 4—51, 6—21,
6—34, 6—63, 12—07, 12—08, 12—09
Exclusivity contracts 1—10
Exemption (see Article 85.3)
Exemption, "bloc" 3—84 — 3—87, 6—33 —
6—41, 8—16, 8—59, 8—77, 8—82, 9—09,
11—05, 12—05
Exemption, individual 3—79 — 3—83, 6—42

– 6–44, 11–07, 12–07, 12–08, 12–09,
    12–10, 14–07, 14–08, 15–10
Exemption, individual – revocation/
  amendment                 3–83
"Existing" agreements, etc.     4–27, 4–30,
    4–31 – 4–40, 4–54, 4–85, 6–38
Expediency principle            1–37

Fabrique Nationale     3–61, 3–67, 8–85,
    9–18, 11–09, 13–16
Fighting companies, secret         1–09
Fines     3–11, 4–12, 4–13, 4–18, 4–28,
    4–42, 4–68, 4–70, 4–82, 4–83 – 4–93,
    5–64 – 5–66, 18–16
Fines, parallel         4–90, 4–91
Flat glass           1–06, 1–07
Form A/B   4–18, 4–25, 6–45, Appendix I
France       1–38, 2–01, 2–02, 5–21
Freedom of movement         2–03

Galbraith, Professor J.K.         1–16
Geha           8–19 – 8–21
Geigy           3–11, 3–91
GEMA    4–60, 5–12, 5–13, 5–16, 5–20,
    5–26, 5–29, 5–36, 5–48, 5–50,
    5–51, 5–57, 16–01
Gentlemens' agreements     3–05, 3–30
Germany    1–38, 2–01, 2–02, 5–21
Glaxo              1–28
Grosfillex             6–28
Groupement d'intérêt economique    3–07
Grundig     3–52, 3–17, 3–76, 6–56 –
    6–63, 8–53

Hearings (by the Commission)     4–81,
    4–82, 5–63
Heidsieck             8–09
Henkel     4–44, 9–15 – 9–17
Hoechst             3–11
Holland     1–38, 2–01, 2–02
Höss             6–40

I.C.I.     3–11, 3–17, 3–18, 3–91, 3–94
Imports, parallel – see parallel imports
Independent trader     6–13, 6–19,
    Appendix J
Information agreements     1–17 – 1–21,
    1–22, 1–23, Chapter 13
Infringements of Article 85.1   4–07 – 4–13
Institutions (of the Community)     2–05
Insulin             1–16
Insurance           13–17
Integration, forward/

backward       15–15, 15–20
Intellectual property rights     3–87, 4–51,
    Chapter 8
Inter-Member trade   3–20 – 3–27, 5–35 –
    5–38, 6–20 – 6–22
Interessengemeinschaft     3–06, 3–07
International Cable Development
  Corporation             3–09
Ireland           1–39, 5–21
Italy      1–38, 2–01, 2–02, 5–21

Jallatte              3–64
Jaz              12–08
Jehle              4–53
Joint advertising          14–03
Joint production     10–02 – 10–03
Joint purchasing     10–15 – 10–17
Joint research agreements     Chapter 9
Joint selling        10–04 – 10–14

Know-how     4–51, 8–80 – 8–89
Know-how, agreements
  relating to            8–82
Know-how, agreements,
  clauses in        8–83 – 8–89
Know-how, rights, existence /
  exercise of           8–81
Kodak     6–11, 6–22, 6–52, 6–55

Labour relations – joint negotiation  14–04
Langen         3–73, 6–44
Lansil             1–06
Limitation of action   4–99 – 4–102, 5–68,
    15–23
London Metal Exchange     13–02
Loss leader           7–03
Loyalty rebates         3–06
Loyalty bonus          5–26
Luxembourg     1–38, 2–01, 2–02
Lyons             1–22

MAN     3–74, 3–82, 11–09, 12–10
Margarine            4–09
Market, meaning    1–05, 5–15 – 5–17
Market, insulation   6–05, 6–48 – 6–53,
    8–06
Market research     9–05, 13–12
Market transparency       13–03
Mergers   5–28, 5–30 – 5–33. Chapter 15
Mergers, horizontal    15–16 – 15–18
Mergers, vertical     15–19 – 15–20
Mergers, conglomerate   15–21 – 15–22
Metal Box             1–06

Minolta Cameras     7—14
Minor agreements     3—26, 4—15, 6—30,
    10—07, 11—06, 12—03, 13—15
    see also "Notice Concerning Minor
    Agreements" and "appreciable effect".
Monopoly     1—04 — 1—12
Monopsony     1—04

Negative clearance (Article 85)     4—14
    — 4—22
Negative clearance,
    "bloc"     4—15
Negative clearance,
    individual     4—16 — 4—22
Negative clearance, (Article 86)     5—53
"New" agreements, etc     4—41 — 4—44,
    4—54, 4—85
Nicholas Frères     3—33, 8—60
North British Rubber     1—30
Notices (issued by the Commission)
    "Co-operation between Enterprises"
      3—32, 4—15, 4—103, 8—62, 9—05
    — 9—07, 10—01, 10—02, 10—09, 10—13,
      10—15, 13—07, 13—12 — 13—14,
      14—02 — 14—03, Appendix H
    "Minor Agreements"     3—26, 3—37,
      4—14, 4—15, 4—103, 6—26, 6—30,
      7—10, 8—17, 8—60, 8—78, 8—82,
      10—13, 11—06, 12—03, 13—15,
      Appendix J
    "Patent Licence Agreements"     4—15,
      8—18, 8—30, 8—34, 8—36, 8—37,
      8—39, 8—41, 8—42, 8—46,
      Appendix D
    "Sole Agency Contracts"     4—15, 6—13
      — 6—19, Appendix C
Notification     4—03, 4—23 — 4—49
Notified agreements,
    status of     4—26 — 4—29
Norway     1—39

Off-list prices     1—19, 13—11
Oligopoly     1—25 — 1—30
Oligopsony     1—25
Omega Brandt     3—04, 6—43
"Omo"     8—55
"Open price" policy     1—18, 1—21, 13—03
"Opposabilité aux tiers"     6—05, 6—50

Parallel imports     3—50, 3—76, 6—05, 6—54
    — 6—65, 8—08, 8—13, 8—55 — 8—56, 8—75
Parallelism, conscious     1—27, 1—28, 1—29,
      1—31, 1—32, 3—14, 5—05

Parallelism, unconscious     1—28, 1—29
Parfums Marcel Rochas     6—46
Paris Treaty     2—04
Parke, Davis     5—14, 5—27, 8—12
Patents     1—12, 4—51, 5—14, 8—11 — 8—47,
      9—12 — 9—14, 9—16
Patents rights agreements     8—15 — 8—28
Patents rights agreements
    clauses     8—29 — 8—47
Patents rights, existence /
    exercise of     8—12 — 8—14
Penalties     4—11, 4—68, 4—70, 4—82, 4—83
      — 4—93, 18—17

Perfect competition     1—17, 13—01
Performing rights     8—67 — 8—79
Performing rights agreements     8—77 — 8—78
Performing rights agreements
    clauses     8—79
Performing rights, existence /
    exercise of     8—70 — 8—76
Performing rights societies     5—12, 5—26,
      5—29, 5—36, 5—48, 5—57
"Persil"     8—55
Peter-Uhren     12—08
Pilkingtons     1—06
Pirelli     14—09
Polydor     8—70 — 8—74
Portelange     4—26
Price equalization     10—06, 10—08
Price leadership     1—29, 1—30, 1—32
Prices, information as to     13—11, 13—13,
      13—18
Private suit     3—55 — 3—57, 4—29, 4—32,
      4—43 — 4—44, 4—54, 5—42, 16—05
Privilege, professional     4—65, 4—75 — 4—80,
      5—58, 5—61
Privity of Contract     7—05
Proctor & Gamble     1—26
Procurement of information (by the Commis-
    sion) — see Commission
Profit pooling     3—44
Prohibition principle     1—35, 5—01, 5—43

Quinine Cartel     3—05, 4—13, 4—91, 4—100

Rationalization     14—06 — 14—08
Raymond     8—26 — 8—28, 8—30,
      8—31, 8—40, 8—42, 8—43, 8—45, 8—65
Reciprocal supply     3—73, 6—34, 14—09
Recommendations     1—24, 3—08, 3—13
Refusal to supply     5—24, 16—01
Registered designs     4—51, 8—65 — 8—66

Regulation 17/62    Chapter 4, 5—01, 5—44
                 — 5—67, Appendix B
Art. 1                 4—04, 14—09
Art. 2            4—14, 4—16, 4—81
Art. 3            4—95, 5—46, 5—67
Art. 3.1             4—08, 4—13
Art. 3.2                4—10
Art. 3.3             4—12, 5—48
Art. 4.2      4—51, 4—52, 4—53, 4—54,
                      6—32, 6—34
Art. 4.2(1)    4—51, 4—52, 4—53, 7—10,
    8—16, 8—59, 8—77, 8—82, 12—03,
                 13—15, 15—10
Art. 4.2(2)(a)        4—51, 7—10
Art. 4.2(2)(b)    4—51, 8—16, 8—59,
                   8—77, 8—82
Art. 4.2(3)(a)       4—51, 11—04
Art. 4.2(3)(b)    4—51, 9—04, 9—08,
                       15—10
Art. 4.2(3)(c)      4—51, 15—10
Art. 5         4—31, 6—31, 6—34
Art. 6.              4—47, 4—54
Art. 7.1    4—32, 4—33, 4—34, 4—39,
                  4—44, 11—07
Art. 7.2                     4—54
Art. 8      4—46, 4—47, 4—49, 5—06
Art. 9.1             4—24, 5—46
Art. 9.3             4—07, 4—16
Art. 10    4—21, 4—45, 4—46, 5—46,
                       5—54
Art. 10.1    4—10, 4—19, 4—94, 5—54
Art. 10.3       4—13, 4—49, 5—49
Art. 11  4—09, 4—11, 4—20, 4—45, 4—56
  — 4—66, 4—68, 4—96, 4—98, 5—47, 5—56
             — 5—59, 5—64, 5—67
Art. 11.1—4              4—58
Art. 11.5       4—59, 4—92, 5—65
Art. 11.6                 4—71
Art. 12    4—09, 4—72, 5—47, 5—64
Art. 13    4—09, 4—11, 4—20, 5—47,
             5—54, 5—60, 5—64
Art. 14    4—09, 4—11, 4—20, 4—67,
  4—68, 4—73, 4—97, 4—100, 5—47, 5—54,
           5—60, 5—64, 5—67
Art. 14.1—2              4—69
Art. 14.3    4—69, 4—70, 4—92, 5—65
Art. 15    4—89 — 4—91, 4—98, 4—101,
                       5—64
Art. 15.1    4—18, 4—25, 4—68, 4—70
Art. 15.2           4—13, 5—52
Art. 15.3                 4—89
Art. 15.5           4—28, 4—42
Art. 16    4—92, 4—98, 4—101, 5—65

Art. 16.1                    4—70
Art. 16.2                    4—93
Art. 19     4—13, 4—21, 4—46, 4—81,
                   5—49, 5—54
Art. 20    4—66, 4—73, 5—59, 5—62
Art. 21    4—22, 4—48, 4—49, 5—54
Art. 25  4—34, 4—35, 4—38, 4—39, 4—71
Regulation 19/65  3—85, 6—33, 8—16, 8—59,
           8—77, 8—82, Appendix F
Regulation 67/67    3—86, 6—33 — 6—41,
        6—43, 6—65, 8—38, Appendix G
Regulation 99/63  4—82, 4—89, Appendix E
Regulation 1133/68         4—18, 5—54,
                     Appendix I
Regulation 2821/71    3—85, 5—06, 8—47,
  8—89, 9—09, 11—05, 12—05, 15—10,
                   Appendix K
Regulation 2822/71   3—26, 3—27, 3—37,
     5—19, 9—08, 12—04, Appendix L
Relief from the obligation
to notify         4—50 — 4—54, 6—32
Reproduction rights      8—67 — 8—79
Reproduction rights
agreements            8—77 — 8—78
Reproduction rights agreements,
clauses in                  8—79
Reproduction rights, existence /
exercise of           8—70 — 8—76
Reproduction rights, exhaustion
of rights                  8—71
Requirements contracts    1—10, 16—03
Resale price maintenance   3—42, Chapter 7
Research and development  4—51, Chapter 9
Restraint upon competition  1—13 — 1—33,
      3—28 — 3—37, 6—27 — 6—30, 8—08
Rieckermann                3—34, 6—29
Rome Treaty     2—01, 2—02, 2—04,
                    Appendix A
Art. 1              2—01, 17—01
Art. 2              2—01, 17—02
Art. 3         2—02, 2—06, 17—03
Art. 4              2—05, 17—04
Art. 5                  17—05
Art. 30            2—02, 17—06
Art. 34            2—02, 17—07
Art. 36       2—02, 8—07, 17—08
Art. 48                  2—03
Art. 52                  2—03
Art. 67                  2—03
Art. 85    2—06, Chapter 3, 15—08 —
                       15—10
Art. 85.1   3—02 — 3—44, 8—12, 17—09
Art. 85.1(a)                  3—39

Art. 85.1(b)                          3—40
Art. 85.1(c)                          4—41
Art. 85.1(d)                          3—42
Art. 85.1(e)                          3—43
Art. 85.2            3—45 — 3—57, 17—09
Art. 85.3            3—58 — 3—87, 17—09
Art. 86           2—06, 3—43, 5—01 — 5—42,
       15—11 — 15—23, Chapter 16, 17—10
Art. 87              2—06, 4—01, 17—11
Art. 88                   2—06, 17—12
Art. 89              2—06, 4—07, 17—13
Art. 90                   2—06, 17—14
Art. 92                        17—15
Art. 173                 5—51, 17—16
Art. 177                       17—17
Art. 184                       17—18
Art. 191                 3—17, 17—19
Art. 222                       17—20

SAFCO                          10—10
Sandoz                    3—11, 3—91
SAVIEM                    3- 82, 12—10
Schmalbach-Lubeca-Werke      5—04, 5—11,
   5—13, 5—16, 5—20, 5—30, 5—37, 15—14
Secrecy, professional   4—66, 4—73, 5—62
Secrets, business     4—13, 4—22, 4—82
Sector investigations       4—09, 5—47
Services              1—33, 3—60, 3—62
Severability            3—50 — 3—52
S.I.A.E.                        5—57
Signers — non-signers, see resale price
maintenance.
Sirena                   5—27, 8—54
Smith Corona Marchant           4—26
SOCEMAS                 3—23, 10—17
Social Policy                  2—04
Société des Matieres Colorantes   3—11
Solus site system        1—11, 1—28
Sopelem          3—73, 6—44, 10—14
SPAR                          10—16
Specialization agreements     3—27, 4—51,
                   5—06, Chapter 12
Standard form agreements   4—27, 6—45 —
                               6—46
Standardization agreements      4—51,
                           Chapter 11
Standardization of costs        13—08
Study No.1 "La Reparation des Consé-
   quences Dommageables d'une Violation
   des Articles 85 et 86 du Traité Instituant
   la C.E.E."                   3—56
Study No.3 "Le Problème de la Concentra-
   tion dans le Marché Commun"     5—07,

                           5—28, 15—07
Substantial part of the
   Common Market         5—19 — 5—21
Sulexco                        1—16
Supexie                        10—07
Sylvania                       1—29

Tag Manufacturers        1—19, 13—03
Technique Minière         3—50, 6—06
Termination of infringements
   Art. 85.1            4—07 — 4—13
   Art. 86             5—46 — 5—52
Territorial principle (conflict
   of laws)    3—18, 3—90, 3—94, 4—39
Thomassen    5—20, 5—30, 5—31, 5—37,
                  5—44, 5—46, 15—14
Trade Associations    1—14, 1—24, 3—06
Trade between Member States — see inter-
   Member trade
Trade marks   4—51, 5—14, 8—48 — 8—66
Trade marks agreements    8—58 — 8—60
Trade marks agreements,
   clauses in                  8—61
Trade marks, certification
   marks           8—50, 8—62 — 8—64
Trade marks, exhaustion
   of rights                   8—09
Trade marks, quality
   marks           8—50, 8—62 — 8—64
Trade marks, registered
   user                        8—49
Trade mark rights, existence /
   exercise of         8—53 — 8—57
Trade representative     6—13 — 6—19,
                           Appendix J
Transocean Marine Paint
   Association   3—65, 8—63, 11—07
Treaty of Accession            4—05
Trufood                        1—28
Turnover       13—10, 13—13, 13—18
Tyre manufacturers             1—23

Ulm                            6—06
Undertaking   3—15 — 3—19, 5—03 — 5—06,
                               6—08
Unfair competition — see competition
Unilever              1—26, 8—55
Union de Remorquage            16—03
Unit of account                4—93
United Kingdom        1—39, 5—21
United Kingdom Government, Aide
   Mémoire        3—17, 3—93, 4—39,
                          Appendix M

## Index

United Shoe Machinery
  Corporation                          1—07, 1—10

Van Katwijk                           3—30, 3—77
Vereeniging van Cementhandelaren      3—80
Vervaecke                                    6—24
Vitapointe                                   3—33
Vitapro                                      3—33
Void                                  3—53 — 3—54
Völk                                         6—24

V.V.V.F.                             8—64, 11—08

Wage negotiations                    14—04
Wild                                 10—12
Wilkin                               4—105

"Yoga"                               3—48

Z.P.U.                               4—60